T0301558

.

How Can HR Drive Growth?

NEW HORIZONS IN MANAGEMENT

Series Editor: Cary L. Cooper, CBE, *Distinguished Professor of Organizational Psychology and Health, Lancaster University, UK*

This important series makes a significant contribution to the development of management thought. This field has expanded dramatically in recent years and the series provides an invaluable forum for the publication of high quality work in management science, human resource management, organizational behaviour, marketing, management information systems, operations management, business ethics, strategic management and international management.

The main emphasis of the series is on the development and application of new original ideas. International in its approach, it will include some of the best theoretical and empirical work from both well-established researchers and the new generation of scholars.

Titles in the series include:

How Can HR Drive Growth?

Edited by

George Saridakis

*Professor of Small Business and Entrepreneurship,
Small Business Research Centre, Kingston University, UK*

Cary L. Cooper CBE

*Distinguished Professor of Organizational Psychology and
Health, Lancaster University, UK*

NEW HORIZONS IN MANAGEMENT

Edward Elgar

Cheltenham, UK • Northampton, MA, USA

Published by
Edward Elgar Publishing Limited
The Lypiatts
15 Lansdown Road
Cheltenham
Glos GL50 2JA
UK

Edward Elgar Publishing, Inc.
William Pratt House
9 Dewey Court
Northampton
Massachusetts 01060
USA

A catalogue record for this book
is available from the British Library

Library of Congress Control Number: 2013930507

This book is available electronically in the ElgarOnline.com
Business Subject Collection, E-ISBN 978 1 78100 226 1

ISBN 978 1 78100 225 4

Typeset by Servis Filmsetting Ltd, Stockport, Cheshire
Printed and bound in Great Britain by T.J. International Ltd, Padstow

Contents

Figures and tables

FIGURES

TABLES

About the editors

GEORGE SARIDAKIS

George Saridakis is Professor of Small Business and Entrepreneurship at Kingston University. He is also Associate Fellow of the Centre for Small & Medium-Sized Enterprises at Warwick Business School, Honorary Fellow of the Sir Arthur Lewis Institute of Social and Economic Studies at the University of the West Indies and Fellow of the Higher Education Academy. He received his PhD in Economics from the Institute for Social and Economic Research (ISER) at the University of Essex in 2006. His research interests encompass the economics of small firms and entrepreneurship, and also cover empirical work in the field of the economics of crime. He has published in prestigious journals including the British Journal of Management, Human Resource Management, British Journal of Industrial Relations, International Small Business Journal and Journal of Applied Statistics.

CARY L. COOPER

Cary L. Cooper is the Distinguished Professor of Organizational Psychology and Health at Lancaster University Management School, Lancaster University. He is Chair of the Academy of Social Sciences, which is comprised of 47 learned societies in the social sciences (Royal Geographical Society, British Psychological Society, British Academy of Management, Royal Statistical Society, etc.), representing over 87,000 social scientists. Professor Cooper is the Founding President of the British Academy of Management, President of RELATE, Immediate Past President of the British Association of Counselling and Psychotherapy and President of the Institute of Welfare. He has a number of honorary doctorates from universities (e.g. Sheffield, Aston), is an Honorary Fellow of the Royal College of Physicians and a Fellow of the Academy of Management (US), and serves on the Global Agenda Council on Wellbeing and Mental Health of the World Economic Forum. He was awarded the CBE in 2001 for services to occupational health.

Contributors

James Bloodgood is Professor at the Department of Management, Kansas State University.

Hai-Ming Chen is a Professor, Department of Management Sciences, Tamkang University.

Kevin Daniels is Professor of Organizational Behaviour, Norwich Business School, University of East Anglia.

John Field is Professor of Lifelong Learning at the School of Education, University of Stirling.

Nigel Haworth is Professor of Human Resource Development at the University of Auckland Business School.

James C. Hayton is Professor of HRM and Entrepreneurship in the Entrepreneurship and Innovation Group, Warwick Business School, The University of Warwick, and the UK Enterprise Research Centre.

Jeffrey S. Hornsby is the Henry Block/Missouri Endowed Chair of Entrepreneurship and Innovation and Associate Director of the Regnier Institute for Entrepreneurship and Innovation, University of Missouri-Kansas City.

Yen-Lin Huang, Audit Department, Deloitte and Touche.

Stewart Johnstone is a Lecturer in Human Resource Management at Newcastle University Business School, Newcastle University.

John Kitching is a Reader in Small Business and Entrepreneurship at Small Business Research Centre, Kingston Business School, Kingston University.

Yanqing Lai is a PhD candidate, Small Business Research Centre, Kingston Business School, Kingston University.

Jonathan Lavelle is a Lecturer at the Department of Personnel and Employment Relations, Kemmy Business School, University of Limerick.

Ku-Jun Lin is an Associate Professor, Department of Accounting, Tamkang University.

Susan Marlow is Professor of Entrepreneurship at Nottingham Business School, University of Nottingham.

Anthony McDonnell is a Senior Lecturer in the School of Management, University of South Australia.

Chidiebere Ogbonnaya is a PhD candidate, Norwich Business School, University of East Anglia.

Christine Sahadeo is a Senior Lecturer at University of the West Indies.

Hugh Scullion is Professor of International Management at the Department of Management, National University of Ireland, Galway.

Sandra Sookram is a Fellow at the Sir Arthur Lewis Institute of Social and Economic Studies, The University of the West Indies.

Olga Tregaskis is Professor of International Human Resource Management, Norwich Business School, University of East Anglia.

Marc van Veldhoven is Professor of Work, Health and Well-being at the Department of Human Resource Studies, Tilburg University.

Adrian Wilkinson is Director of the Centre for Work, Organisation and Wellbeing and Professor of Employment Relations, Griffith University.

Jonathan Winterton is Professor of Employment and Director of International Development at Toulouse Business School.

1. Editorial introduction

George Saridakis and Cary Cooper

In a dynamic working and economic environment characterized by globalization, deregulation of markets and financial engineering, increasing product-market competition, sectoral shifts, free trade in goods and services, labour mobility and free movement of capital, the role of human resources (HR) in leading and delivering sustainable national and regional growth and improving individuals' well-being is becoming increasingly important. Governments, decision-makers and public and private firms of different sizes and management ownership are called to respond by putting skills, knowledge and capabilities into action and to learn by innovating and adapting to economic, technological, social and environmental challenges, and to external forces and downturns. Through HR there could be enhanced role empowerment and employee relations, entrepreneurial ability and job creation, strengthened competitive advantage, promotion of equal opportunities in employment and production of better matches between jobs and workers, encouragement of rural development and investment, the upgrade of infrastructure and networking, the ensuring of social, cultural and professional integration of minorities, and the support of strategies and policies on safety, health and behaviour (see, for example, Lado and Wilson, 1994; Ichniowski et al., 1997; Guest, 2002; Handel, 2003; Barling et al., 2003; Chadwick et al., 2004; Gardner et al. 2005; Hayton, 2005; Saridakis et al., 2008; Chadwick and Dabu, 2009; Storey et al., 2010).

The ten up-to-date research studies that are presented in this volume provide new insights into the HR academic literature and provide clear lessons to learn from, along with crafts, strategies, approaches and processes in which HR could be used by both practitioners and policy makers to raise a workforce's knowledge, leadership skills, involvement, safety and well-being and enhance performance within small and large, single-site and multi-site firms. Furthermore, this volume may provide useful insights as to how the public and private sectors could potentially learn from each other, an issue that is relatively timely since many public sectors across Europe experienced major restructuring to address the debt crisis. To accomplish this aim, the studies included in this volume draw upon economics, psychology and human resource management theories and empirical evidence providing for the first time an interdisciplinary perspective to experts and students in the specific fields, and a more complete view to practitioners and those involved in policy making and HR issues.

In this respect, after the editorial introduction in Chapter 1, Anthony McDonnell, Hugh Scullion and Jonathan Lavelle in Chapter 2 provide a critical overview on "Managing human resources in international organizations" focusing particularly on global staffing, global talent management and managing industrial relations in the multinational firm. John Kitching and Susan Marlow in Chapter 3, "HR practice and small firm growth: balancing informality and formality", examine HR policy and practice in small firms and consider whether such practices enable, or constrain, business growth. In Chapter 4, "Promoting innovation and entrepreneurship through HR practices", James C. Hayton, Jeffrey S. Hornsby and James Bloodgood examine the role of HR on corporate entrepreneurship and incorporate environmental factors and entrepreneurial orientation. Jonathan Winterton and Nigel Haworth in Chapter 5, "Government policy and human resource development" examine the role of government policies in promoting training and development to achieve sustainable growth.

John Field in Chapter 6, "Investing in labour force and skills development" presents a comprehensive review of the literature and policies on learning and skills development and how these generate growth. Christine Sahadeo and Sandra Sookram in Chapter 7 examine "Mentorship, leadership and human resource development in Trinidad and Tobago" through a detailed survey study and highlight the importance of a mentorship program on firm performance. In Chapter 8 Stewart Johnstone and Adrian Wilkinson examine issues on "Employee voice, partnership and performance" and stress the importance of a mix of human, resource, and management-focused dimensions to achieve desirable performance outcomes. In Chapter 9, "Employee attitudes, HR practices and organizational performance: what's the evidence?", Yanqing Lai and George Saridakis review the theoretical and empirical literature on the relationship among employee attitudes, HR practices and organizational performance. Hai-Ming Chen, Ku-Jun Lin and Yen-Lin Huang in Chapter 10, "Creating and sustaining economic growth through HR", focus on behaviour perspective and attitudes of employees to examine organizational outcomes. The volume concludes with Chidiebere Ogbonnaya, Kevin Daniels, Olga Tregaskis and Marc Van Veldhoven, who in Chapter 11, "Using HPWP [high-performance work practices] to drive towards growth: the impact of occupational health and safety leadership", provide a comprehensive overview on links among HPWP, OHS and organizational growth.

This volume will be of interest to academics, research students, policy makers, the business world and other stakeholders who wish to gain better understanding of how HR can drive growth and prosperity at both the micro and macro levels.

REFERENCES

Barling, J., Iverson, R. and Kelloway, K. (2003). High-quality work, job satisfaction, and occupational injuries. *Journal of Applied Psychology*, 88 (2), 276–283.

Chadwick, C. and Dabu, A. (2009). Human resources, human resource management, and the competitive advantage of firms: towards a more comprehensive model of causal linkages. *Organization Science*, 20 (1), 253–272.

Chadwick, C., Hunter, I. and Walston, S. (2004). Effects of downsizing practice on the performance of hospitals. *Strategic Management Journal*, 25 (5), 405–420.

Gardner, T.M., Wright, P.M. and Moynihan, L.M. (2005). The impact of motivation, empowerment, and skill-enhancing practices on aggregate voluntary turnover: the mediating effect of collective affective commitment. *Personnel Psychology*, 64, 315–350.

Guest, D. (2002). Human resource management, corporate performance and employee wellbeing: building the worker into HRM. *Journal of Industrial Relations*, 44 (3), 335–358.

Handel, M.J. (2003). Skills mismatch in the labor market. *Annual Review of Sociology*, 29, 135–165.

Hayton, J.C. (2005). Promoting corporate entrepreneurship through human resource management practices: a review of empirical research. *Human Resource Management Review*, 15, 21–41.

Ichniowski, C., K. Shaw and G. Prennushi (1997). The effects of human resource management practices on productivity: a study of steel finishing lines. *American Economic Review*, 87, 291–313.

Lado, A.A. and Wilson, M.C. (1994). Human resource systems and sustained competitive advantage: a competency-based perspective. *Academy of Management Review*, 19 (4), 699–727.

Saridakis, G., Sen-Gupta, S., Edwards, P. and Storey, D.J. (2008). The impact of enterprise size on employment tribunal incidence and outcomes: evidence from Britain. *British Journal of Industrial Relations*, 46 (3), 469–499.

Storey, D.J., Saridakis, G., Sen-Gupta, S., Edwards, P.K. and Blackburn, R.A. (2010). Linking HR formality with employee job quality: the role of firm and workplace size. *Human Resource Management*, 49 (2), 305–329.

2. Managing human resources in international organizations

Anthony McDonnell, Hugh Scullion and Jonathan Lavelle

1. INTRODUCTION

The topic of international human resource management (IHRM) has gained importance in the field of international business and become a key issue for senior managers in multinational enterprises (MNEs). The issues and challenges facing organizations operating across national borders has a long history, and the importance of physically relocating managers to foreign locations where business operations are based has been recognized for centuries (Moore and Lewis, 1999: 66–7). The role of parent country national expatriates dominated the research agenda of IHRM for much of the latter part of the 20th century, which reflected the ethnocentric view of multinational management adopted by many companies and researchers, particularly from North America (Scullion and Brewster, 2001). In recent years, scholarship from a more critical European perspective has emerged which is less ethnocentric in nature.

For many years IHRM was one of the least studied areas of international business (Brewster and Scullion, 1997; McDonnell et al., 2011a) but the theoretical and empirical foundations of IHRM alongside their application in practice have developed significantly since the 1980s when the field was very much in its infancy. A comprehensive review of the field argued that "as an area of research, IHRM is vibrant and diverse and has grown even more so in the last decade" (Lazarova, 2006: 43). This can in no small part be ascribed to globalization and the increasing consensus that the effective management of a firm's human resources can bring competitive advantage. As a result, "IHRM is a highly dynamic and constantly evolving field, with new themes emerging that transcend traditional approaches" (Björkman and Stahl, 2006: 6).

Recent research identifies a range of influences on the development of IHRM including the changing spatial landscape of international business.

We highlight three key factors here (see Evans et al., 2011 for a full discussion). The first is the rapid emergence of the emerging markets (Dicken, 2011) which presents unique challenges for western MNEs including the difficulty of recruiting and retaining managerial talent with the skills to operate in these environments (Li and Scullion, 2010). This has led to the emergence of global talent management as a key management concern and an area of academic research interest. Second, in terms of social trends, the changing nature of careers is also a key factor impacting on managing HR on a global scale (Thomas et al., 2005). Research suggests a shift in how employees view their careers, with increasing emphasis placed on career mobility and decreasing commitment to specific organizations (DeFillipi and Arthur, 1996). Also, there is a growth of self-initiated international assignments (Suutari and Brewster, 2000). Both of these trends impact significantly on IHRM policy and practice (Scullion et al., 2007). Third, increasing global terrorism challenges senior MNE managers to adequately assess the risks of assignments in volatile countries for managers and their families. This threat has also led to a re-evaluation of options with regard to staffing arrangements in some high risk countries (Collings et al., 2007). However, despite continued uncertainties prevailing in the current international climate, MNEs need to continue to encourage staff to work abroad to gain better understanding of global markets and to develop the skills to work effectively across cultures (Meyskins et al., 2009).

IHRM is far more complex and challenging than HRM in the domestic context (Lazarova, 2006). Researchers point to the considerable demands which internationalization places on a company's HR function and highlight the need for the HR strategy to be integrated with the organization's corporate strategy (Scullion and Starkey, 2000). One key theme in IHRM is standardization versus localization in the transfer of IR/HR policies and practices, which focuses on the extent to which the MNE can implement globally standard policies and practices vis-à-vis the extent to which they must be adapted to account for local norms and traditions (Björkman and Xiucheng, 2002; Evans et al., 2011). The area of employee relations is particularly important in this context because it represents an area that is likely to have the largest amount of local idiosyncrasies.

In this chapter we review three areas of IHRM which are critical to MNEs effectively managing their global operations, namely, global staffing, global talent management and managing industrial relations in the multinational firm. Our objective is to provide the reader with a critical and more nuanced understanding of these three areas of IHRM.

2.   GLOBAL STAFFING

In this section we explore the issue of global staffing, which refers to the critical issues faced by MNEs in staffing their headquarters (HQ) and subsidiary operations (Scullion and Collings, 2007). Global staffing represents one of the primary HR practices used by MNEs to control and coordinate their spatially dispersed global operations (Scullion, 1994). We now discuss MNEs' common global staffing approaches, and then consider the reasons behind why MNEs use expatriates, before finally examining the emerging trends in global staffing.

Staffing Foreign Subsidiaries

Perlmutter's (1969) seminal paper introduced a classification of MNEs which differentiated firms based on their attitude toward the geographic sourcing of their management teams. Ethnocentric organizations are those in which all key positions both in the HQ and in subsidiary operations are filled by parent country nationals (PCNs) or citizens of the country where the HQ is located. Polycentric organizations refer to foreign subsidiaries that have a large degree of autonomy and that are primarily staffed by host country nationals (HCNs). Geocentric organizations are those in which positions at both HQ and subsidiary level are filled with the "best person for the job" regardless of nationality. Regiocentric organizations represent those structured on a regional basis, in which international transfers are generally restricted within regions (Heenan and Perlmutter, 1979). This research helps us understand staffing in foreign subsidiaries, but it is primarily focused on top management team (TMT) positions at HQ and subsidiary locations (Harzing, 1999) and it represents a number of ideal types of organization. It is unlikely that many MNEs will exactly fit any of the ideal types and in practice most are likely to operate with elements of more than one type. For example, Harzing (2001b) suggested that less than 10 per cent of the companies in her study had a uniform staffing policy (i.e. only HCNs or PCNs).

Reasons Why MNEs Use Expatriates and Their Applicability in Practice

A key theme in debates on global staffing concerns the reasons why MNEs use expatriates to staff their foreign operations. Edström and Galbraith's classic study (1977) identified three main motives for utilizing international transfers: position-filling, individual development and organizational development. In the first case, expatriates are employed to fill key technical and managerial roles where qualified local country nationals are not available, particularly in developing countries. In the second, assignments are used mainly for individual development purposes and primarily aimed at developing the global competence of the individual manager, and in the third case assignments are used to build organizational competence at the organizational level and to promote the transfer of knowledge within the MNE network.

More recently there has been an increasing awareness of the role of expatriates in controlling foreign subsidiaries. Harzing's (2001a) study made a key contribution to the debate and identified three control roles of expatriates. Firstly, expatriate managers can act as "bears" in that they become the main focal point of control over the subsidiary in contrast to centralized control systems. Secondly, expatriates can perform as "bumble bees" used to control subsidiaries through socialization and the development of informal networks. Finally, expatriates can act as "spiders" seeking to achieve control through the weaving of informal communication networks within the MNE. Harzing's study goes beyond the question of why MNEs use expatriates and examines the applicability of the different roles of expatriate assignees in different circumstances, which is a significant contribution of the study. Her findings suggest that while expatriates tend to perform their roles as bears regardless of the situation, their roles as spiders and bumble bees tend to be more context specific. For example, the bumble bee role appeared more important in newly established subsidiaries while the spider roles were more significant in well established subsidiaries. Significantly, the level of localization of subsidiary operations and lower levels of international integration were positively related to the likelihood of expatriates performing the bumble bee and spider roles.

Pucik (1992) developed Edström and Galbraith's typology in terms of theory, and his analysis differentiates between demand-driven and learning-driven motives for expatriation. Assignments for the purposes of position filling or control are generally classified into the former category while assignments for the purposes of individual or organization development fit the latter. Drawing on Pucik's earlier work, Evans et al. (2011) have developed a framework for classifying the duration and purposes of international assignments and suggest that managerial development reasons for the assignment will foster expatriate personnel change and role innovation. Traditionally, expatriate assignments were predominately demand driven and were usually used where there was a lack of suitably qualified HCNs. Learning-driven assignments focus primarily on learning rather than teaching and become more common as subsidiaries develop local managerial and technical capability (Tungli and Peiperl, 2009). In contrast, in learning-driven assignments there is a growing emphasis on developing a global mindset in MNE managers, reflecting the greater potential for career development from these assignments (Kraimer et al., 2009).

Emerging Issues in Global Staffing

Inpatriation
An increasingly important theme in the global staffing literature over the last decade is the practice of developing HCNs and TCNs through developmental transfers to the corporate HQ, called inpatriation (Collings et al., 2010). Research emphasizes the key role which such inpatriate employees can play in staffing the HQ operation (Harvey et al., 1999a; Collings et al., 2010). The key drivers of the recruitment of inpatriate managers include a desire to create a global competency and a diversity of strategic perspectives among the top management team (Harvey and Buckley, 1997); the growing need to provide career opportunities for high potential employees in host countries (Collings et al., 2010); and a more strategic approach to management development in the global environment (Harvey et al., 1999a), particularly in the emerging markets (Scullion and Collings, 2011). However, the successful integration of inpatriates into the HQ team provides considerable challenges for the MNE (Reiche, 2006, 2007). The process is complex and inpatriates have to adjust to a different external cultural environment. They may also be new to the organization and will have to adjust to the organizational culture (Harvey et al., 1999b). Some researchers have called for greater attention to be paid to inpatriation in order to better understand the specific needs of this group and in particular they call for more empirical research on the processes of knowledge transfer in the context of inpatriate assignments in the emerging markets (Collings et al., 2010; Reiche and Harzing 2011).

Alternative international assignments
The main focus of research on international assignments over the last 20 years has been on the traditional long-term assignment which usually involves the relocation of the expatriate and their family to a different environment for a period of between one and five years. The changing context of global staffing has resulted in organizations re-evaluating their staffing options. Recent research suggests the emergence of newer, short-term, more flexible non-traditional forms of international assignments which are increasingly being used as alternatives to the traditional long-term expatriate assignment (Collings et al., 2007; Welch et al., 2007). There has been significant growth in alternative forms of international assignments, such as short-term assignments, frequent flyer assignments, and

commuter and rotational assignments, and practitioner evidence suggests this trend will continue (Brookfield GMAC, 2010). While some research has highlighted the limited degree of HR support for those on alternative assignments (Mayerhofer et al., 2004), there is a dearth of research on both employee experiences in undertaking alternative assignments and the career implications of the alternative international assignments (cf. Demel and Mayrhofer, 2010). The impact of alternative forms of international assignment on the family and employees' work-life balance remains an important area for further study but early work suggests potentially negative consequences.

It is argued that alternative forms of international assignments provide more flexibility to MNEs in terms of global staffing, in contrast to the more inflexible contractual arrangements associated with traditional expatriate assignments (Collings et al., 2007). The emergence of this "portfolio approach" to international assignments poses considerable challenges for the HR function of the multinational firm and further research is required to help us understand how staff on alternative assignments manage the multiple demands of their lifestyle and whether companies are developing adequate family friendly staffing arrangements (Mayerhofer et al., 2004).

Summary

We urge organizations to strategically consider their global staffing approaches more carefully and in particular to consider the potential negatives of alternative staffing approaches. While they may bring flexibility they are not without limitations from both an organizational and an individual perspective. Researchers should continue to engage with this critical area of IHRM where an increased focus on alternative international assignments would be especially welcome.

3. TALENT MANAGEMENT IN MULTINATIONAL ENTERPRISES

This section focuses on talent management, which is increasingly viewed as an area of both great importance and concern by senior organizational management. More particularly, we review the emergence of talent management, the identification of pivotal positions and potential, and the role of the HR function in effective talent management.

The Emergence of Talent Management

Now, a couple of decades on from HR practitioners discussing the growing talent war (Chambers et al., 1998), it is evident that talent management has very much become part of the mainstream management and academic research lexicons. The drivers behind the increased focus on talent management include globalization, worsening global demographic trends, and employee shortages to address the increasing need for higher levels of competencies, coupled with a groundswell of agreement that effective talent management can make a significant contribution to achieving competitive advantage (Boudreau, 2005; Pfeffer, 1998; Tarique and Schuler, 2010). Arguably, the surge of interest stemmed from the increasing difficulties organizations in the US faced in satisfying their skills needs (Chambers et al., 1998) but since then the context of talent management has become a more global issue (e.g. Beechler and Woodward, 2009; Collings et al., 2011b; McDonnell et al., 2010; McDonnell et al., 2012).

MNEs face unique opportunities and challenges with respect to talent management due to their ability to resource talent from across their global operations. The MNE context has led to the development of *global* talent management, as opposed to talent management, defined by Tarique and Schuler (2010: 124) as:

> systematically utilizing IHRM activities (complementary HRM policies and practices) to attract, develop and retain individuals with high levels of human capital (e.g., competency, personality, motivation) consistent with the strategic directions of the multinational enterprise in a dynamic, highly competitive, and global environment.

Despite the global financial crisis (GFC) and the uncertainty this has brought for organizations, it appears that organizations are facing increased competition for talent worldwide. There is much evidence to suggest that the attraction, development and retention of talent, particularly international managers, remains a key challenge to MNEs (Cohn et al., 2005) and that significant numbers and types of organizations worldwide, including MNEs, are grappling with talent shortages. Although MNEs possess the opportunity to maximize the strategic advantage of a global workforce through a diverse talent pool incorporating different nationalities, the greatest challenges, notwithstanding shortages in the external labour market, are effectively identifying their talent and ensuring that they are positioned in the pivotal organizational positions. It is clear that the "availability of talent per se is of little strategic value if it is not identified, nurtured and used effectively" (Mellahi and Collings, 2010: 5).

Identifying Pivotal Positions and Potential: Towards Effective Global Talent Management

There appears to be an increasing view that the first element of effectively managing talent should be to define what talent means in the context of an organization's pivotal positions (Collings and Mellahi, 2009). Consequently, it goes beyond the idea of just identifying organizational "stars". This line of thought calls for organizations to identify pivotal positions and differentially distribute resources according to their strategic value (Boudreau and Ramstad, 2007). Specifically, there is the need to be able to differentiate between roles where once a particular performance threshold is achieved significantly improved value or impact is unlikely to result from higher performance, versus those positions where once performance goes beyond the expected threshold there will continue to be an increased strategic contribution, i.e. pivotal positions (Boudreau and Ramstad, 2007). This means that pivotal positions may incorporate more than just senior managerial roles which have tended to receive the greatest focus (McDonnell et al., 2011b; McDonnell, 2011).

Once the pivotal positions are filled, it is imperative the right employees fill them and that there is essentially a supply chain in situ where there are individuals who can move into such roles when they become available (Cappelli, 2008). This raises a number of challenges for all organizations, such as do you make or buy talent? What competencies, traits, skills, knowledge are essential to be effective in a pivotal position? In the case of the MNE, you then have the increasing challenge of having talent located around the world and there are different cultures at play. The tests and tools used in the HQ for assessing high performance and potential may not be as effective in these host contexts. The MNE needs to be cognisant of such issues and that some people are likely to be more easily recognized as talent compared to others (Makela et al., 2010).

Makela et al. (2010) explored the factors that increased the likelihood of individuals being labelled as talent in a major MNE. They found that organizational decision-makers take greater credence in appraisals from subsidiaries which are culturally and institutionally close, and individuals from these operations are more likely to be incorporated into corporate talent pools. Further, there was evidence of homophily, that is, individuals were more likely to be included in the corporate talent pool where the decision-maker saw similarities to him/herself in the candidate. This then causes the potential limitation of attempting to identify and build clones. Further, it was found that the higher a candidate was in terms of their position in the central organizational network, the more likely they were to be included in the talent pool.

While this finding provides further support for scholarship that has long pointed out the role of social networks in obtaining jobs and promotions, it also raises the issue that MNEs may be missing out on potential talent because some staff are likely to be less visible than other individuals. These issues are particularly relevant for organizational decision-makers that strongly believe in the value of effective global talent management. The biases highlighted by Makela et al. (2010) are not necessarily surprising as such issues have previously been discussed in recruitment and selection scholarship but it requires decision-makers to have greater cognisance of them if they truly wish to consider the full breadth of their potential global talent pool (McDonnell, 2011). If MNEs are unable to do so then it diminishes the argued advantage they possess over domestic firms in being able to draw on a globally diverse workforce (Earley and Gibson, 2002). Through greater diversity in their talent pool it can be argued that MNEs are likely to be more successful in taking local contexts into account, gaining new skills and knowledge, as well as improving, what seems to be one of the most critical attributes of successful business, innovation (Mellahi and Collings, 2010).

Research suggests that future decades will see the Asian economies of China and India as the main drivers of business growth (Dicken, 2011) and thus the issues highlighted above are likely to become even more important. For instance, are Western MNEs well placed to effectively attract and retain talented staff in these markets? The recent PwC report (2011) from global chief executive officers indicated 90 per cent of survey respondents stated their Asian operations would continue to grow. In spite of China being the most populated country in the world, there has been much commentary suggesting talent shortages are going to be the greatest impediment to the country's continued development and economic success (Ma and Trigo, 2008; Zhu et al., 2005).

The Role of the HR Function in Global Talent Management

As a result of concerns over availability of talent and the increasing consensus on the ability of talent to achieve competitive advantage it is evident that effective global talent management is going to be a strategic challenge for MNEs with the corporate HR function needing to play a major role. Scullion and Starkey's (2000) seminal work on the corporate HR function of MNEs noted there were different functions depending on the approach to international strategy and whether the company was more centralized/globalized or decentralized. The corporate HR function in centralized MNEs tends to have a wider range of activities than decentralized MNEs but a common role across the function in centralized and decentralized MNEs was with respect to managing top talent across the company (Farndale et al., 2010).

Farndale et al. (2010) propose four principal roles of corporate HR in effective global talent management. First, there is the "champions of processes" role which focuses on building top management team commitment, the provision of coaching for managers, integrating HR information systems and monitoring the effectiveness of subsidiaries calibrating and balancing their talent. Second, there is the "guardian of culture" role which centres on the HR function's role in implementing global values and ensuring a strong culture of effective talent management is in place across the worldwide subsidiary network. Third, "network leadership" refers to the importance of networking across borders both inside and outside of the company and the critical role HR should be playing in developing social capital. Finally, HR needs to manage "internal receptivity". Here, the HR function plays a proactive role in the career management of their globally mobile employees which requires a more flexible approach than in the past due to increasing use of alternative international assignments. These employees should stem from the different MNE operations and not just be concentrated with parent country nationals. These roles hold many complementarities (see Farndale et al. 2010 for discussion) in facilitating greater effectiveness in managing global talent. In line with the argument proposed by Caplan (2011), talent management must be more than just some systems and processes, and must actually encompass a talent mindset across the entire organization, permeating all levels from the individual up and top down. The aforementioned corporate HR roles consider this in that while there is much discussion of systems and practices, so too is there consideration of the importance of talent management being enshrined in the organizational culture.

Talent management is not just about systems and processes but what you do with these and how you implement them so that you achieve a talent mindset across the organization. A talent mindset means that line managers will recognize their responsibility to manage talent effectively, just as they are expected to manage other resources. Directors or chief executives will review talent as critically as they review the organization's finances. Individuals will actively seek to develop or update their own talents (Caplan, 2011: 7).

The approach taken to global talent management, and the role of corporate HR, needs to be considered within the context of the stage of the internationalization process the organization is in (Scullion and Starkey, 2000). Thus, it is important that HR practitioners move beyond the idea of there being best practice talent management and instead focus on their own organizational context. For example, a highly globalized firm is likely to require significantly more control over global mobility of their high potentials than a more decentralized MNE adopting a strongly multi-domestic approach. MNEs face an array of key decisions about how to effectively leverage and manage their global talent. These decisions need to encompass the internationalization stage as already mentioned, in addition to keeping future directions and requirements firmly in mind. Guthridge et al. (2008) identified several obstacles to effective talent management. These include senior management spending insufficient time on talent management, organizational structures inhibiting collaboration, failure to overcome silo mentalities (Farndale et al., 2010), failures in learning and knowledge diffusion, inadequate involvement of the line manager in career development for their reports, and limited interest and ownership in talent management by staff. This final barrier may stem from failing to adequately involve them in formulating the strategy and system.

Talent Management Post-GFC

Following the GFC and the sharp increase in unemployment across much of the developed world, there is a fear that the agenda will move from the "war for talent" to a "war on talent". This would appear to be an ill-advised approach to take where MNEs pay less attention to engaging, developing and retaining their best talent. Beechler and Woodward (2009), in the context of the GFC, argued that talent management would continue to be a critical organizational agenda item for some time to come. Additionally, these challenging trading conditions provide opportunities to recruit talent that other firms have discarded, place greater attention on the effectiveness of systems and practices, and develop more innovative rewards that go beyond solely financially based ones. MNEs with a globally diverse talent pool are arguably going to be better placed in taking advantage of the opportunities that will arrive post-GFC.

4.   INDUSTRIAL RELATIONS IN MNES

Collings (2008), in a review of MNEs and industrial relations (IR), notes that whilst IHRM has received widespread attention in the literature, comparatively, IR issues within MNEs have not received anywhere near the same attention (notable exceptions include Bomers and Peterson, 1977; Cooke, 2003; Almond et al., 2005; Ferner et al., 2005; Lavelle et al., 2010; Marginson et al., 2010). Despite this, Collings (2008: 176) postulates that ". . . [international industrial relations] has the potential to provide insights into aspects of the management of employees in MNEs which are often neglected in the mainstream IHRM literature, including trade union recognition and avoidance, collective bargaining and the like". This section addresses issues in relation to managing IR in MNEs.

Industrial Relations and MNEs: The Challenges

MNEs operate across a number of different countries and in doing so, operate within different types of IR systems. IR systems develop from different historical, political, economic and social experiences (Briscoe et al., 2012) and as a result, IR systems are markedly different across countries – see "comparative IR" as a field of study. Thus MNEs face considerable IR challenges when establishing operations in countries outside of their country of origin. These challenges include issues in relation to trade unions, collective bargaining, employer associations, industrial action, and other operational aspects of IR (cf. Hollinshead, 2010; Grimshaw et al., 2011; Briscoe et al., 2012).

The first issue is in relation to trade unions. A key issue for MNEs is the legal arrangements in relation to trade unions – essentially will they have to recognize a trade union? In some countries, like Ireland, trade union recognition is voluntary, whereas in other countries, such as the UK and the USA, MNEs may be required to recognize a trade union if certain conditions are met, e.g. a certain percentage of workers wish to be represented by one. Even where trade union recognition is voluntary, there may still exist strong institutional and cultural pressures for a MNE to recognize a trade union. A follow up issue is the number of unions that a MNE may have to engage with. For example, will the MNE have to recognize more than one trade union or can it simply engage with just one?

Related to this issue is the ease with which MNEs can avoid engaging with trade unions. In less regulated IR environments this task may be quite easy and straightforward, but in more regulated environments, the task is likely to be more problematic, albeit not unachievable. Another issue for MNEs is the power and influence that trade unions enjoy in a location. Often, measures such as trade union membership and density across countries (cf. Visser, 2006) are used as indicators of union influence, e.g. the higher the density rate, the greater the union influence. However, simply focusing on density levels can be unreliable and misleading as the relationship between density rates and trade union power and influence is not as clear cut as described. For example, in France the trade union density rate is 8 per cent, yet trade unions enjoy strong political and industrial influence (e.g. collective bargaining coverage is circa 95 per cent). The types of trade unions such as craft, white collar or general trade unions are also of interest to MNEs. Furthermore, some trade unions may also have strong religious and political affiliations and this can impact on their activities. Finally the level that trade unions operate at – establishment, industrial, regional and national – is of interest to MNEs.

The area of collective bargaining is another important IR issue to consider. A key factor is whether the MNE will have to engage in collective bargaining and, if so, who with – trade unions and/or government, and how – through an employer association or the MNE itself. The level at which collective bargaining takes place – single establishment, multi-establishment, industrial, regional or national – will also interest MNEs. The types of issues that are included in the collective agreements are important as some may be the subject of collective bargaining in some countries but covered by legislation in others. The legal status of such agreements is hugely important. In some countries, collective agreements are legally binding on parties, whereas in other countries, these agreements tend to be binding in honour only. The coverage of collective agreements is also of interest to MNEs. Whilst the collective agreement will normally cover parties involved in the process, in some countries the terms of the agreement may be extended to include companies outside of the process. For example, in France, it is common for agreements to be extended to cover all employees in a particular sector. Even where there are no formal mechanisms for extending collective agreements, they may still be influential. For example in Ireland, between 1987 and 2009, collective bargaining occurred at the national level and largely covered the public sector and unionized companies, but the significance of the collective agreement (the national wage agreement) meant that non-unionized companies often mirrored the terms of the agreement, if not bettered them.

In some countries, employer associations can play a significant role in IR (e.g. Germany), whereas in other countries (e.g. the USA) they have little or no role to play. So the significance of employer associations within an IR system is of importance. A key question to raise is, are MNEs legally obliged to join an employer association or can they avoid doing so? Additionally, is joining an employer association something to be encouraged and what benefits can membership offer?

Another key aspect of IR that raises key questions for MNEs is in relation to industrial action. For example, what are the common forms of industrial action? Under what circumstances can workers take industrial action? What is the level and trajectory of strike activity in the host IR system? Operational issues are also crucial within the sphere of IR. There will be variations across countries on the status of employee representative bodies. For example in Germany, works councils are a key distinctive feature of the German IR system and play a significant role within the workplace. MNEs will have to be cognisant of whether there are any issues around compliance with the provision of information and consultation, or specific rights and protections for employee representatives.

From this brief review it is evident that the IR challenges MNEs face in different contexts are many. Given this diversity in host country IR systems, it is unsurprising that IR considerations may have an influence on the locational decisions of MNEs. Since IR systems and practices differ between countries, MNEs may engage in "regime shopping" as they seek to invest in countries that offer the most favourable context (Traxler and Woitech, 2000). In a review of the impact of IR systems on the locational decisions of MNEs, Cooke (2006) notes that the evidence would appear to illustrate that, everything else being equal, MNEs invest less in countries with higher union penetration rates and where collective bargaining is more centralized (Cooke, 1997, 2001; Cooke and Noble, 1998). Whilst it is often difficult to fully ascertain the influence of IR on MNEs' locational decisions (cf. Collings, 2008), it nonetheless draws attention to the importance of the host country IR system and the challenges that MNEs face in managing IR.

Managing IR in MNEs

Having outlined the challenges facing MNEs in relation to IR, we now consider the IR practices of MNEs within host countries. MNEs are faced with the dual pressures of internal consistency (standardized practices across the MNE operations) and local isomorphic pressures (pressure to adapt practices consistent with the prevailing institutional and cultural environment). A key question in IR in MNEs is whether they seek to transfer IR practices across their operations or whether they adapt to the prevailing IR practices in the host country. In dealing with this dilemma, Cooke (2006) suggests that MNEs undertake a cost benefit analysis in relation to the transfer of their IR practices. MNEs that believe that they enjoy IR ownership advantages in their home country must decide on whether they will transfer these IR practices across the MNE. On the benefit side, MNEs must determine if their approach to managing IR is superior to other approaches and benefits can be accrued from adapting a standardized approach to the management of IR across the MNE. On the cost side, the host country IR environment must be considered along with the capacity and receptivity of local staff to change. Costs associated with achieving the necessary buy-in to implement practices must also be considered. MNEs will only transfer IR where the perceived benefits outweigh the perceived costs (Cooke, 2006). In reviewing the empirical research on this question, Cooke (2006) suggests that the transfer of IR practices within MNEs varies from near full transfer of preferred IR practices at one end to little or no transfer of practices at the other end.

Within this debate, the issue of trade union recognition and avoidance within MNEs has received particular attention in the general IR literature (Edwards and Ferner, 2002; Almond et al., 2005). Some scholars argue that foreign-owned MNEs are no different in terms of recognizing trade unions in the host environments (Stopford and Turner, 1985; Purcell et al., 1987). Others suggest that foreign-owned MNEs are less likely to recognize unions in these environments (cf. Guest and Hoque, 1996). The issue of trade union recognition and avoidance within foreign-owned MNEs has received considerable attention in the Irish literature (Kelly and Brannick, 1985; Turner et al., 1997a, 1997b; Geary and Roche, 2001; Gunnigle et al., 2005; Collings et al., 2008). Indeed Edwards and Rees (2011) suggest that Ireland represents the best illustration of where this particular debate has been pursued. In the most comprehensive empirical research undertaken on employment practices in MNEs operating in Ireland, Lavelle et al. (2009) support the view that a new orthodoxy is emerging in Irish IR whereby foreign-owned MNEs are implementing home country practices that are at odds with the more traditional pattern of IR existing in the Irish IR context.

By transferring IR practices, MNEs may act as a source of innovation within host countries. For example, Ferner and Quintanilla (2002: 245) postulate that foreign-owned MNEs "act as agents of change by introducing innovations into their subsidiaries and thence into the host business system". Indeed MNEs have been described as the "foremost 'innovators'– for good and ill – within national business systems" (Ferner and Varul, 2000: 115). Following this theme, Collings et al. (2011a) differentiate between adaptive and disruptive innovation – seeing innovation not as a value-laden concept but something which can have both positive and negative consequences. Adaptive innovation is where the MNE respects the established traditions and institutions of the host country and looks to build on such traditions. Disruptive innovation on the other hand refers to MNEs who introduce practices that are at odds with the established traditions and institutions of the host environment. Thus MNEs, through innovations at subsidiary level, may impact the host country IR system.

Again we can point to Ireland as an example of where MNEs have shaped the host country IR environment. Such MNE influence in Ireland is evidenced in areas including employment legislation, employee representation and workplace information and consultation. Trade unions in Ireland have long called for the introduction of statutory trade union recognition legislation, but such calls have been rejected, largely on the back of opposition from MNEs, outlining the potential detrimental effect such legislation would have on MNEs investing or remaining in Ireland. Even where legislation has been introduced, MNEs have influenced such legislative changes. One example is the implementation of the European Union Information and Consultation Directive, where the MNE sector was quite vocal in their views in relation to the introduction of legislation covering information and consultation rights. The implementation of the Directive in Ireland was described as "minimalist" with "the 'voice' of large US multinationals in Ireland, the American Chamber of Commerce, [leaving] its mark on [the Directive]" (Industrial Relations News, 2005: 2). Donaghey (2004) in his work looking at social partnership pointed to a strong influence of MNEs, particular US MNEs, in the process, whereby US MNEs were able to resist any institutional changes around the introduction of works council arrangements similar to those existing in Germany. Collings et al. (2008) explored the impact of MNEs on the Irish IR system and concluded that there was some evidence of change in the Irish IR system – change they indirectly trace to the influence of the US MNE sector in Ireland.

5.   CONCLUSION

It is without question that business is increasingly international in operation which has seen the continued rise of the MNE. This has brought IHRM to the attention of organizational leaders because effectively managing people across country borders is a complex, challenging and important area if an organization is to successfully compete internationally. In this chapter, we reviewed three critical areas of IHRM that MNEs need to pay particular attention to when managing their global operations. First, we noted that the nature of global staffing is becoming increasing complex and challenging as the landscape of global business continues to evolve. Due to this, MNEs need to reassess international assignments as conventionally understood and be more strategic in their use of them (Scullion and Collings, 2007; Bonache et al., 2010).

Second, we focused on one of the fastest growing areas of interest amongst management practitioners and consultants – talent management. Globalization and changing demographics in the developed world are key drivers of talent management (Tarique and Schuler, 2010), which has emerged as one of the foremost concerns of organizational leaders across the world. MNEs face particularly significant challenges, in addition to opportunities, due to being able to source talent from across their network of operations. Two of the foremost issues in effective talent management in MNEs are being able to identify pivotal positions and high potentials, and ensuring the HR function's role is in keeping with the international strategy of the organization.

The final section of the chapter provided an overview of the many issues and challenges that MNEs face in the management of industrial relations. Specifically, we highlighted the challenges faced from operating in different countries with respect to the role of trade unions and employer associations, the nature of collective bargaining, industrial activity, and operational level aspects. MNEs are faced with the competing pressures of standardizing practice across their operations versus adapting to be consistent with the prevailing cultural and institutional environment. We discussed whether MNEs seek to transfer IR practices across borders to bring standardization and the challenges and opportunities doing so brings, in addition to the possible consequences of the IR system in host countries.

REFERENCES

Almond, P., Edwards, T., Colling, T., Ferner, A., Gunnigle, P., Muller-Camen, M., Quintanilla, J. and Waechter, H. (2005). Unravelling home and host country effects: an investigation of the HR policies of an American multinational in four European countries. *Industrial Relations*, 44: 276–306.

Beechler, S. and Woodward, C. (2009). The global war for talent. *Journal of International Management*, 15: 273–285.

Björkman, I. and Stahl, G. (2006). International human resource management research: an introduction to the field. In G. Stahl and I. Björkman (eds.), *Handbook of Research in International Human Resource Management*, Cheltenham, UK and Northampton, MA, USA: Edward Elgar.

Björkman, I. and Xiucheng, F. (2002). Human resource management and the performance of Western firms in China. *International Journal of Human Resource Management*, 13: 853–864.

Bomers, G. and Peterson, R. (1977). Multinational corporations and industrial relations: the case of West Germany and the Netherlands. *British Journal of Industrial Relations*, 15: 45–62.

Bonache, J., Brewster, C., Suutari, V. and De Saa, P. (2010). Expatriation: traditional criticisms and international careers: introducing the special issue. *Thunderbird International Business Review*, 52: 263–274.

Boudreau, J.W. (2005). Talentship and the new paradigm for human resource management: from professional practices to strategic talent decision sciences. *Human Resource Planning*, 28 (2): 17–26.

Boudreau, J.W. and Ramstad, P.M. (2007). *Beyond HR: The New Science of Human Capital*. Boston, MA: Harvard Business School Press.

Brewster, C. and Scullion, H. (1997). A review and an agenda for expatriate HRM. *Human Resource Management Journal*, 7 (3): 32–41.

Briscoe, D., Schuler, R. and Tarique, I. (2012). *International Human Resource Management Policies and Practices for Multinational Enterprises*. New York: Routledge.

Brookfield GMAC (2010). *Global Relocation Trends 2010*. London: Brookfield.
Caplan, J. (2011). *The Value of Talent. Promoting Talent Management Across the Organization*. London: Kogan Page.
Cappelli, P. (2008). Talent management for the twenty first century. *Harvard Business Review*, March: 74–81.
Chambers, E.G., Foulon, M., Handfield-Jones, H. and Michaels, E. (1998). The war for talent. *McKinsey Quarterly*, 3: 44–57.
Cohn, J.M., Khurana, R. and Reeves, L. (2005). Growing talent as if your business depended on it. *Harvard Business Review*, 83 (10): 62–70.
Collings, D.G. (2008). Multinational corporations and industrial relations research: a road less travelled. *International Journal of Management Review*, 10 (2): 173–193.
Collings, D.G. and Mellahi, K. (2009). Strategic talent management: a review and research agenda. *Human Resource Management Review*, 19 (4): 304–313.
Collings, D.G., Scullion, H. and Morley, M.J. (2007). Changing patterns of global staffing in the multinational enterprise: challenges to the conventional expatriate assignment and emerging alternatives. *Journal of World Business*, 42 (2): 198–213.
Collings, D.G., Gunnigle, P. and Morley, M.J. (2008). Between Boston and Berlin: American MNEs and the shifting contours of industrial relations in Ireland. *International Journal of Human Resource Management*, 19: 242–263.
Collings, D.G., McDonnell, A., Gunnigle, P. and Lavelle, J. (2010). Swimming against the tide: outward staffing flows from multinational subsidiaries. *Human Resource Management*, 49 (4): 575–598.
Collings, D.G., Lavelle, J. and Gunnigle, P. (2011a). The role of MNEs. In A. Wilkinson and M. Barry (eds), *Handbook on Comparative Employment Relations*. Cheltenham, UK and Northampton, MA, USA: Edward Elgar.
Collings D.G., Scullion, H. and Vaiman, V. (2011b). European perspectives on talent management. *European Journal International Management*, 5: 453–462.
Cooke, W.N. (1997). The influence of industrial relations factors on U.S. foreign direct investment abroad. *Industrial and Labor Relations Review*, 50: 3–17.
Cooke, W.N. (2001). The effects of labour costs and workplace constraints on foreign direct investment among highly industrialised countries. *The International Journal of Human Resource Management*, 12: 697–716.
Cooke, W.N. (2003). *Multinational Companies and Global Human Resource Strategies*. Westport, CT: Quorum Books.
Cooke, W.N. (2006). Multinationals, globalization and industrial relations. In M.J. Morley, P. Gunnigle and D.G. Collings (eds), *Global Industrial Relations*. London: Routledge.
Cooke, W. and Noble, D. (1998). Industrial relations systems and US foreign direct investment abroad. *British Journal of Industrial Relations*, 36: 581–609.
DeFillipi, R. and Arthur, M. (1996). Boundaryless contexts and careers: a competency based perspective. In M.B. Arthur and D.M. Rousseau (eds), *The Boundaryless Career: A New Employment Principle for a New Organizational Era*. New York: Oxford University Press.
Demel, B. and Mayrhofer, W. (2010). Frequent business travelers across Europe: career aspirations and implications. *Thunderbird International Business Review*, 52: 301–311.
Dicken, P. (2011). *Global shift: Mapping the Change Contours of the World Economy*, 6th edition. London: Sage.

Donaghey, J. (2004). Social partnership and labour market governance in the Republic of Ireland. Unpublished Ph.D. thesis, School of Management and Economics: Queens University Belfast.

Earley, P.C. and Gibson, C.B. (2002). *Multinational Teams: New Perspectives.* Mahwah, NJ: Lawrence Erlbaum Associates.

Edström, A. and Galbraith, J.R. (1977). Transfer of managers as a coordination and control strategy in multinational organizations. *Administrative Science Quarterly*, 22: 248–263.

Edwards, T. and Ferner, A. (2002). The renewed "American Challenge": a review of employment practice in US multinationals. *Industrial Relations Journal*, 33 (2): 94–111.

Edwards, T. and Rees, C. (2011). *International Human Resource Management: Globalization, National Systems and Multinational Companies*, 2nd edition. London: Pearson Education.

Evans, P., Pucik, P. and Björkman, I. (2011). *The Global Challenge: Frameworks For International Human Resource Management*, 2nd edition. New York: McGraw-Hill.

Farndale, E., Scullion, H. and Sparrow, P. (2010). The role of the corporate HR function in global talent management. *Journal of World Business*, 45: 161–168.

Ferner, A. and Quintanilla, J. (2002). Between globalisation and capitalist variety: multinationals and the international diffusion of employment relations. *European Journal of Industrial Relations*, 8 (3): 243–50.

Ferner, A. and Varul, M. (2000). Vanguard subsidiaries and the diffusion of new practices: a case study of German multinationals. *British Journal of Industrial Relations*, 38: 115–140.

Ferner, A., Almond, P., Colling, T. and Edwards, T. (2005). Policies on union representation in US multinationals in the UK: between micro-politics and macro-institutions. *British Journal of Industrial Relations*, 43: 703–728.

Geary, J. and Roche, W. (2001). Multinationals and human resource practices in Ireland: a rejection of the "new conformance thesis". *The International Journal of Human Resource Management*, 12: 109–127.

Grimshaw, D., Rubery, J. and Almond, P. (2011). Multinational companies and the host country environment. In A.-W. Harzing and A. Pinnington, *International Human Resource Management*. London: Sage.

Guest, D. and Hoque, K. (1996). National ownership and human resource management in UK greenfield sites. *Human Resource Management Journal*, 6 (4), 50–74.

Gunnigle, P., Collings, D.G. and Morley, M.J. (2005). Exploring the dynamics of industrial relations in US multinationals: evidence from the Republic of Ireland. *Industrial Relations Journal*, 36 (3): 241–256.

Guthridge, M., Komm A.B. and Lawson, E. (2008). Making talent management a strategic priority. *The McKinsey Quarterly*, January: 49–59.

Harvey, M. and Buckley, M.R. (1997). Managing inpatriates: building a global core competency. *Journal of World Business*, 32: 35–52.

Harvey, M., Speier, C. and Novicevic, M.M. (1999a). The role of inpatriation in global staffing. *International Journal of Human Resource Management*, 10: 459–476.

Harvey, M., Novicevic, M. and Speier, C. (1999b). Inpatriate managers: how to increase the probability of success. *Human Resource Management Review*, 9: 51–82.

Harzing, A.W. (1999). *Managing the Multinationals: An International Study of Control Mechanisms.* Cheltenham, UK and Northampton, MA, USA: Edward Elgar.

Harzing, A.W. (2001a). An analysis of the functions of international transfer of managers in MNEs. *Employee Relations*, 23: 581–598.

Harzing, A.W. (2001b). Who's in charge? An empirical study of executive staffing practices in foreign multinationals. *Human Resource Management*, 40: 139–158.

Heenan, D.A. and Perlmutter, H.V. (1979). *Multinational Organizational Development.* Reading, MA: Addison-Wesley.

Hollinshead, G. (2010). *International and Comparative Human Resource Management.* Berkshire: McGraw-Hill Education.

Industrial Relations News (2005). US Chamber leaves indelible stamp on Employee Consultation Bill. *Industrial Relations News*, 30: 2–3.

Kelly, A. and Brannick, T. (1985). Industrial relations practices in multinational companies in Ireland. *Journal of Irish Business and Administrative Research*, 7 (1): 98–111.

Kraimer, M.L., Shaffer, M.A. and Bolino, M.C. (2009). The influence of expatriate and repatriate experiences on career advancement and repatriate retention. *Human Resource Management*, 48: 27–47.

Lavelle, J., McDonnell, A. and Gunnigle, P. (2009). *Human Resource Practices in Multinational Companies in Ireland: A Contemporary Analysis.* Dublin: The Stationery Office.

Lavelle, J., Gunnigle, P. and McDonnell, A. (2010). Patterning employee voice in multinational companies. *Human Relations*, 63: 395–418.

Lazarova, M.L. (2006). International human resource management in global perspective. In M.J. Morley, N. Heraty and D.G. Collings (eds), *International Human Resource Management and International Assignments.* Basingstoke: Palgrave Macmillan.

Li, S. and Scullion, H. (2010). Developing the local competence of expatriate managers for emerging markets: a knowledge based approach. *Journal of World Business*, 45: 190–196.

Ma, S. and Trigo, V. (2008). Winning the war for managerial talent in China. *The Chinese Economy*, 41 (3): 34–57.

Makela, K., Bjorkman, I. and Ehrnrooth, M. (2010). How do MNEs establish their talent pools? Influences on individuals' likelihood of being labelled talent. *Journal of World Business*, 45: 134–142.

Marginson, P., Edwards, P., Edwards, T., Ferner, A. and Tregaskis, O. (2010). Employee representation and consultative voice in multinational companies operating in Britain. *British Journal of Industrial Relations*, 48: 151–180.

Mayerhofer, H., Hartmann, L.C., Michelitsch-Riedl, G. and Kollinger, I. (2004). Flexpatriate assignments: a neglected issue in global staffing. *The International Journal of Human Resource Management*, 15: 1371–1389.

McDonnell, A. (2011). Still fighting the "war for talent"? Bridging the science versus practice gap. *Journal of Business and Psychology*, 26 (2): 169–173.

McDonnell, A., Lamare, R., Gunnigle, P. and Lavelle, J. (2010). Developing tomorrow's leaders – evidence of global talent management in multinational enterprises. *Journal of World Business*, 45: 150–160.

McDonnell, A., Stanton, P. and Burgess, J. (2011a). Multinational enterprises in Australia: two decades of international human resource management research reviewed. *Asia Pacific Journal of Human Resources*, 49: 9–35.

McDonnell, A., Hickey, C. and Gunnigle, P. (2011b). Global talent management: exploring talent identification in the multinational enterprise. *European Journal of International Management*, 5 (2): 174–193.

McDonnell, A., Collings, D.G. and Burgess, J. (2012). Guest editors' note: Talent management in the Asia Pacific. *Asia Pacific Journal of Human Resources*, 50: 391–398.

Mellahi, K. and Collings, D.G. (2010). The barriers to effective global talent management: the example of corporate élites in MNEs. *Journal of World Business*, 45 (2): 143–149.

Meyskins, M., Von Glinow, M.A., Wertjer, W.B. and Clarke, L. (2009). The paradox of international talent: alternative forms of international assignments. *International Journal of Human Resource Management*, 20 (6): 1439–1450.

Moore, K. and Lewis, D. (1999). *Birth of the Multinational*. Copenhagen: Copenhagen Business Press.

Perlmutter, H.V. (1969). The tortuous evolution of the multinational corporation. *Columbia Journal of World Business*, 4: 9–18.

Pfeffer J. (1998). *The Human Equation: Building Profits By Putting People First*. Boston: Harvard Business School Press.

Pucik, V. (1992). Globalization and human resource management. In V. Pucik, N.M. Tichy and C.K. Barnett (eds), *Creating and Leading the Competitive Organization*. New York: Wiley.

Purcell, J., Marginson, P., Edwards, P. and Sisson, K. (1987). The industrial relations practices of multi-plant foreign-owned firms. *Industrial Relations Journal*, 18 (2): 130–137.

PwC. (2011). *14th Annual Global CEO Survey*, www.pwc.com/ceosurvey (accessed 16 October 2011).

Reiche, B.S. (2006). The inpatriate experience in multinational corporations: an exploratory case study in Germany. *The International Journal of Human Resource Management*, 17: 1572–1590.

Reiche, B.S. (2007). The effect of international staffing practices on subsidiary staff retention in multinational corporations. *The International Journal of Human Resource Management*, 18 (4): 523–536.

Reiche, S. and Harzing, A.W. (2011). International assignments. In A.W. Harzing and A. Pinnington (eds), *International Human Resource Management.* London: Sage.

Scullion, H. (1994). Staffing policies and strategic control in British multinationals. *International Studies of Management and Organization*, 4 (3): 18–35.

Scullion, H. and Brewster, C. (2001). Managing expatriates: messages from Europe. *Journal of World Business*, 36: 346–365.

Scullion, H. and Collings, D.G. (2007). *Global Staffing*. London: Routledge.

Scullion, H. and Collings, D.G. (2011). *Global Talent Management*. London: Routledge.

Scullion, H. and Starkey, K. (2000). In search of the changing role of the corporate human resource function in the international firm. *The International Journal of Human Resource Management*, 11: 1061–1081.

Scullion, H., Collings, D.G. and Gunnigle, P. (2007). International HRM in the 21st century: emerging themes and contemporary debates. *Human Resource Management Journal*, 17 (4): 309–319.

Stopford, J.M. and Turner, L. (1985). *Britain and the Multinationals*. Chichester: Wiley.

Suutari, V. and Brewster, C. (2000). Making their own way: international experience through self-initiated foreign assignments. *Journal of World Business*, 35: 417–436.

Tarique, I. and Schuler, R.S. (2010). Global talent management: literature review, integrative framework, and suggestions for future research. *Journal of World Business*, 45: 122–133.

Thomas, D.C., Lazarova, M.B. and Inkson, K. (2005). Global careers: new phenomenon or new perspectives? *Journal of World Business*, 40: 340–347.

Traxler, F. and Woitech, B. (2000). Transnational investment and national labour market regimes: a case of "regime shopping". *European Journal of Industrial Relations*, 6 (2), 141–159.

Tungli, Z. and Peiperl, M. (2009). Expatriate practices in German, Japanese, U.K. and U.S. multinational companies: a comparative survey of changes. *Human Resource Management*, 48: 153–171.

Turner, T., D'Art, D. and Gunnigle, P. (1997a). Pluralism in retreat: a comparison of Irish and multinational manufacturing companies. *The International Journal of Human Resource Management*, 8: 825–840.

Turner, T., D'Art, D. and Gunnigle, P. (1997b). US multinationals: changing the framework of Irish industrial relations? *Industrial Relations Journal*, 28 (2): 92–102.

Visser, J. (2006). Union membership statistics in 24 countries. *Monthly Labor Review*, 129: 38–49.

Welch, D.E., Welch, L. and Worm, L. (2007). The international business traveller: a neglected but strategic human resource. *The International Journal of Human Resource Management*, 18: 173–183.

Zhu, C., Cooper, B., De Cieri, H. and Dowling, P. (2005). A problematic transition to a strategic role: human resource management in industrial enterprises in China. *The International Journal of Human Resource Management*, 16: 513–531.

3. HR practice and small firm growth: balancing informality and formality

John Kitching and Susan Marlow

1. INTRODUCTION AND AIMS

Small and medium-sized enterprises (SMEs) are major employers in the UK. In 2012, there were 1.24 million private sector employers (Department for Business, Innovation and Skills/BIS, 2012); more than 99 per cent of these being SMEs employing fewer than 250 employees.[1] Collectively, SMEs employ 10.2 million people, approximately a third of the UK workforce. Small firm HR practices inevitably shape organizational performance and the experience of work for a large number of people through their influence on recruitment, pay, work organization, skill development, employee motivation and retention, appraisal, communication, discipline and dismissal. A number of studies over the past 25 years have demonstrated that HR practices within small firms differ from larger employers, as well as exhibiting substantial diversity (see for example Goss, 1991; Moule, 1998; Ram and Edwards, 2003; Marlow et al., 2005).

Supporting small business growth has been a prominent concern for UK policy-makers for three decades. The current coalition Government has declared that the UK should be one of the best places in Europe to start, finance and grow a business (HM Treasury/BIS, 2011). Policymakers have designated small businesses as the principal engines of economic recovery and growth following the financial crisis and economic recession of 2008–09. Given this emphasis on small firms as employment creators, their socio-economic importance has certainly increased in recent years (Wright and Marlow, 2012). Whether small business owners themselves are willing and able to play the role prescribed by government is highly debateable. Very few small businesses become substantial employers (Storey, 1987, 2011). Most business owners are content simply to own their own jobs or to employ a small number of people, in order to retain managerial control (Scase and Goffee, 1980; FSB, 2012). Policy proposals encouraging small business owners to expand employment might, therefore, be in tension with most owner-manager aspirations. Accordingly, this chapter explores how HR policy and practice is enacted in small firms and considers to what extent such practices enable, or constrain, business growth. We begin by defining the scope of the chapter before turning to theory and evidence concerning small firm HR practices and employment relations, and consider the implications for growth.

Different definitions of the small firm, qualitative and quantitative, exist. In 1971, the influential Bolton Committee report referred to independent ownership and a small market share; the Companies Act of 1985 combined turnover and employment criteria, with the EU having the most comprehensive criteria of turnover, employment, assets and independence. In the UK, governments rely on the somewhat simplistic measure of numbers employed (Department for Business, Innovation and Skills/ BIS, 2012):

- small firm = 0–49 employees
- medium firm = 50–249 employees
- large firm = 250 or more employees

An alternative, qualitative definition would focus upon the importance of the social relations of production, team working, the role of the family, finding idiosyncratic responses to business problems and the problems of juggling finance. Thus, the first problem we encounter in this debate is outlining the field. Drawing these definitions together, our focus in this chapter is on firms independently owned by an identifiable owner, a small management team, employing fewer than 50 people, with limited resources, and operating informal management systems and practices. For some time, small businesses have been recognized as very different in their approach to management, markets and business outlook from larger enterprises; it is no longer presumed that such enterprises are merely embryonic corporates (Carter and Jones-Evans, 2012). Despite these similarities, the sector is recognized as profoundly heterogeneous. A significant challenge in analysing small firm behaviour, therefore, is identifying common themes and trends. So, any conclusions drawn regarding small employer HR policy and practice must always be qualified with the same caution applied to larger firms. Consequently, our overview is necessarily 'broad brush' and cannot capture all of this enormous diversity.

2.　HR PRACTICES AS GENERATORS OF BUSINESS GROWTH

Considerable attention has been afforded to the role and influence of HR practices on employee and organizational performance (Tansky and Heneman, 2006; Marlow et al., 2005). Employers vary in their HR practices, in how far employment practices constitute an internally coherent, integrated package and in how far such practices are aligned with business objectives. The concept of the 'high performance work system' (HPWS) has been introduced to refer to combinations of HR practices intended to generate high levels of employee capability and commitment that enable enterprises to achieve sustainable competitive advantage (e.g. Evans and Davis, 2005; Combs et al., 2006; Guthrie et al., 2009). HPWS typically incorporate particular formal practices related to recruitment, reward and career progression, work organization and employee autonomy, training and communication.

Most HPWS research has centred on large companies, where formalization is axiomatic. Studies of small firms show that the adoption of 'full' HPWS is low, due to limited awareness of HPWS practices and the control and cost implications of implementation, and, consequently, small employers typically adopt a more narrowly focused set of practices (Way, 2002; Sels et al., 2006; Drummond and Stone, 2007; Kroon et al., 2012). The question arises whether small employers must adopt formal HPWS-type approaches in order to generate high levels of employee skills and commitment – or whether alternative, distinctive approaches might be equally successful in small business environments. Small businesses are typically highly labour intensive and, combined with the liabilities of size, this suggests small employers must pay particular attention to selecting, developing, motivating and retaining employees; failure to perform these tasks adequately might lead to poor performance and closure. Limited resources and market power make it difficult for small employers to offer similar financial incentives to larger companies. Such questions raise issues surrounding labour quality: are small employers able to attract suitably skilled workers in sufficient numbers? In the following sections, we consider these issues by investigating theory and evidence on small firm HR processes and practices.

3.　LOOKING FOR HR IN SMALL FIRMS

Exploring HR practices in small firms raises the pointed question whether there is a degree of contradiction in this quest or, as Taylor (2005) suggests, an activity analogous to 'hunting the snark'.[2] Whilst the detailed configuration and impact of HRM as policy and practice upon contemporary organizations is subject to debate and some controversy (see Chapter 1), the theoretical application of the construct is largely taken as a given. Thus, there is broad agreement that HRM is a blanket term referring to the management of labour within the firm but in addition, there is a suggestion of a strategic and diverse range of policies delivered by a recognized cadre of professional accredited managers (Guest, 2011). As such, the underpinning rationale for the HR function is to add value to the organization through exploiting and enhancing employee effort when mapping labour management approaches onto organizational strategy and culture (Marlow, 2006). Thus, there is a normative assumption within current theorizing that HRM, as an approach to labour management, is both beneficial and desirable to order, manage and extract value from the labour process (Legge, 2005). So, as a generic model, HR strategies cover all aspects of the employment process with contextualized practices extending from recruitment and selection through to exit interviewing. However, we are aware that in practice, the employment relationship is a subjective, 'messy' process even within larger firms where HR professionals oversee policy and practice (Edwards, 2006). Moreover, this particular normative image of the role of HRM in the contemporary workplace does not accord well with what we know of the prevailing management model within most small firms. Indeed, the evidence suggests employer preference for informal policies and practices; reluctance by owner-managers to delegate labour management responsibilities to dedicated HR professionals; employee resistance to formality; and reactive strategic management (Marlow et al., 2005; Storey et al., 2010).

Despite tension between the formality of the normative HR model, drawn from large firms, and the informality of the small firm model, the employment relationship in small firms must still be managed. Small employers, like their larger counterparts, must create and maintain a set of working practices and relations through which employees' capacity to work is transformed into the production of goods and services as market commodities. Small firm owners must strive to generate employee commitment to their business objectives. However, the policies and practices enacted to achieve this order may not necessarily 'look' like more formal understandings of normative HRM. In the small firm, HR practices are likely to exhibit a distinctive texture. Research has suggested a number of key features of small firm HR practice and relations that, despite other important differences in workforce characteristics and business context, appear to be widespread: the inter-penetration of the public and private,

social and spatial proximity, the influence of informal practices and relations, and familial relations and ideologies (Ram and Holliday, 1993;
Moule, 1998; Ram, 1994, 2001).

4. HR APPROACHES IN SMALL FIRMS

The Bolton Committee (1971) suggested that firm size was a critical influence shaping approaches to labour management and the employment
relationship. The team environment of the small workplace in conjunc-
tion with the proximity of owner-managers and employees was deemed
to create a 'small is beautiful' culture of harmony and accord. Formal
regulatory practices such as those associated with trade unions, professional personnel practices and bureaucratic management were deemed to
be disruptive of this cultural ambience. However, this harmony thesis was
subject to criticism (Goss, 1991; Ram, 1994). In their marginal position as
market price takers, rather than price makers, small firm owners arguably
possess limited autonomy regarding labour management. Consequently,
employment relationships are marked by a so-called 'bleak house' scenario (Guest and Conway, 1997; Harney and Dundon, 2006) whereby
owner-managers adopt exploitative labour management approaches to
extract maximum value from employees. Within this context, a professionally informed formal HR role would be inappropriate unless enacted
as an overtly exploitative set of practices. However, firm owners forced to
use such exploitative tactics would have few resources to afford a formal,
costly HR function. Such approaches treat market conditions as determining employment relations with little space for owner-manager or employee
agency.

  This notion of market determinism has been repeatedly challenged by
analyses suggesting market forces are mediated through the internal social
relations of production leading to a negotiated employment relationship
(Ram, 1994; Moule, 1998; Ram et al., 2001; Ram and Edwards, 2003;
Edwards and Ram, 2006; Storey et al., 2010). Gilman et al. (2002: 54) sum-
marize this succinctly: 'the whip of the market is likely to be mediated by
employee skill, scarcity value and the extent to which there are fraternal or
familial relationships within a firm'. As Ram and Edwards (2003) argue,
this process of negotiated consent arises largely from the social proximity
of owners and employees in combination with market forces which generates contextualized employment relationships defined by informality. The
notion of informality comprising particularistic/individualistic management of employees and the absence of professional HR managers, policies and practices is the underpinning construct informing contemporary

analyses of HR practices in small firms (Ram, 1994; Gilman et al., 2002; Marlow et al., 2010).

5. THE PREVALENCE OF INFORMALITY

Understanding the personal dimension of employer-employee relations in small businesses is crucial. In small firms, capital is personified in the shape of the owner-manager who, in many cases, works alongside, or close to, employees or interacts frequently with employees personally. Owner-manager capital is at risk and, consequently, they often find it difficult to delegate responsibility to others and/or seek to retain control even where tasks and responsibilities are formally delegated (Marlow, 2002; Wapshott, 2012). Many small employers do not adopt formal HR rules governing work procedures and practices relating to health and safety, discipline and dismissal, or equal opportunities (van Wanrooy et al., 2013; Storey et al., 2010). Instead, working practices and relations are governed by informal rules, unwritten customs and tacit understandings, arising from employer-employee interaction at the workplace. Recruitment, pay-setting, learning and training provision, communications, grievance-handling and even disciplinary and dismissal matters are often dealt with informally (Kitching, 1994, 2007, 2008; Benmore and Palmer, 1996; Carroll et al., 1999; Ram, 1999; Cassell et al., 2002; Ram and Edwards, 2010), although this permits wide variety in substantive employment terms, practices and relations. Although some aspects of employment practice are more likely to be governed by formal rules than others – perhaps pay and working time – employer preferences for informality, the absence of institutional influences such as trade unions, and employee preference for, or accommodation to, informal practices reduces the pressure towards procedural formalization. Even where formal policies and rules are in place, they may not be adhered to in practice (Moore and Read, 2006). Informality permits employers to respond flexibly, promptly and inexpensively to particular HR challenges free from the institutional constraints of formal procedure.

Employment regulation is an enduring, though variable influence on HR practice in small enterprises. Regulatory interventions often seek to formalize employer practices; such interventions presuppose a willingness and capacity to adapt existing HR practices in ways promoted by policy-makers. In the absence of formal HR policy and practice, or professional HR managers, combined with employee ignorance of their rights, employer ignorance and disinterest often prevail (Marlow, 2002; Ram and Edwards, 2003; Harney and Dundon, 2006). Studies demonstrate variable employer awareness of individual employment rights (Blackburn and

Hart, 2002) and diverse modes of adaptation to employment regulations (Edwards et al., 2003). Employment regulation does not generate uniform impacts on small employers. Even straightforward measures such as the National Minimum Wage have been found to stimulate a wide range of employer responses (e.g. Arrowsmith et al., 2003; Ram et al., 2003; Grimshaw and Carroll, 2006).

6. THE CONSEQUENCES AND CONTRADICTIONS OF INFORMALITY

Employer preferences for informal HR practices suggest a unitarist perspective (Moore and Read, 2006), namely, that employers and employees share common objectives, as determined by owner prerogative. Informality encourages both parties to define their relations in personal terms, diverting attention away from the market exchange and authority relations that structure their relationship. Social and spatial proximity give rise to material and ideological pressures that encourage employees to define their interests in ways that overlap with those of employers. Proximity enables employers to manipulate personal ties to inculcate a sense of obligation on the part of employees in order to encourage them to intensify their efforts (Marlow et al., 2010: Wapshott, 2012), but may also encourage employee perceptions that their livelihoods materially depend on their own personal contribution towards firm performance. Employers often draw upon familial ideologies to elicit employee effort, although such notions can encourage resistance and conflict where employees draw upon these to construct positive 'us' and negative 'them' identities in relation to family owner-managers and employees working alongside them (Ainsworth and Wolfram Cox, 2003). Employee cooperation is grounded in their experience of the likely consequences to employers of reducing their personal work effort.

Storey et al. (2010), however, suggest that informality can be an appropriate and effective response within particular organizational contexts. Evidence suggests that relationships between small employers and employees are a source of satisfaction for both parties. Employers and employees might seek, and acquire, economic, social and psychological rewards from their personal and particular relations. Proximity can be drawn upon to engender employee commitment, enable swift decision-making, facilitate mutual problem-solving and so add to competitive advantage (Tsai et al., 2007). Employers often prefer informal arrangements in order to retain personal, particular relationships with individual employees that might stimulate employee identification with, or at least an instrumental pragmatic accommodation to, employer objectives, rendering the task of managing HR easier. Successful employer attempts to develop such ties produce close personal bonds based on direct communication, personal trust, normative obligation and mutual reciprocity (Marlow, 2002). Employer recognition of the individual's contribution may be valued by employees in contrast to being treated impersonally as one member of a collective, particularly because individual employee performance is both more critical to business survival, and more visible to employers, in small enterprises (Storey et al., 2010). But even in less successful situations, employer HR practices might generate a pragmatic employee loyalty that produces sufficient employee effort (Tsai et al., 2007). Moore and Read (2006) argue that social relations in small businesses inhibit the articulation of employee grievances; proximity to working employers means framing grievances is a 'high risk' strategy likely to incur employer displeasure. Informal HR practices and relations might enable employers to mask the power imbalance inherent in the relationship and secure higher levels of employee commitment at lower cost; in short, they may be able to displace the contradictions inherent in the employment relationship onto employees. Invoking formal procedures to achieve HR goals is likely to be perceived by employers as introducing an unnecessary impersonal, bureaucratic element into a personal relationship which might place at risk the trust, loyalty and reciprocity that supports business survival and growth.

Data from small business employees suggests a similar picture (van Wanrooy et al. 2013). Informal HR practices can be a source of satisfaction for employees too if they feel able to take advantage of personal ties with employers to obtain pay and non-pay benefits beyond those formally specified and receive greater recognition for good work performance. Workplace Employment Relations Survey data suggests that measures of employee self-reported job quality are higher in single-site SME workplaces than in multi-site workplaces, and higher in multi-site workplaces owned by SMEs than in multi-site workplaces owned by larger organizations (van Wanrooy et al. 2013). Storey et al. (2010) found that differences in self-reported job quality, measured by employee perceptions of 22 aspects of job quality, are partly explicable by the formality of HR practices. Formality increases with workplace size and is associated with lower levels of self-reported job quality. As the authors pithily argue, in large firms, fairness means treating everyone the same: in small firms, it means treating everyone differently - which may explain higher degrees of employee satisfaction!

But, informality cannot guarantee employee commitment in small business contexts any more than formality can guarantee it in larger organizations. The existence of informal HR practices carries no necessary implications for the benefits, or costs, that accompany them or for employer or employee commitment to them. Employer attempts to create personal, particular relations with employees do not always succeed. Such interpersonal relations do not negate the structured antagonism underlying employment relationships; they provide the context within which such contradictions are played out (Edwards and Ram, 2006). Informal arrangements can merely cloak managerial autocracy (Holliday, 1995), or inequitable employer treatment, under a thin veneer of 'personal' – and, therefore, supposedly, satisfying – relationships. Where employees perceive they are being treated unfairly in relation to others with regard to rewards or work obligations, for instance, this will likely generate employee resentment, resistance or exit (Wapshott, 2012). The individual and particularistic character of informal HR practices renders employee perceptions of employer favouritism or unfair treatment more likely. The benefits of informality for employers are not unlimited.

The contradictory consequences of informality are evident in employer attempts to discipline employees for perceived poor performance. Employers may be reluctant to discipline staff because it lays bare the 'structured antagonism' at the heart of the employment relationship while at the same time threatening the close, personal ties employers often try to cultivate with staff, preferring a degree of 'indulgence' regarding employee timekeeping and non-pay benefits, anticipating reciprocation when employees are required to increase effort levels in order to meet deadlines, for example (Scott et al., 1989; Ram et al., 2001). Marlow (2002) reported that small employers often do not deal effectively with employee problems until issues become critical. Decisions to discipline employees are often taken without due regard to formal procedure (where one exists) or to principles of natural justice (where one does not), occasionally leading to dismissal, thereby risking litigation. Small employers are over-represented in employment tribunal applications and cases (Saridakis et al., 2008), although the likelihood of employer loss remains very low (Ewing and Hendy, 2012).

7. SMALL FIRM PSYCHOLOGICAL CONTRACTS

A literature is developing on psychological contracts between small business employers and employees (e.g. Nadin and Cassell, 2007; Atkinson, 2008; Martin et al., 2008; Nadin and Williams, 2012). Psychological contract theory focuses on the nature and extent of mutual expectations within the small business setting, the nature of breaches or violations of expectations, and responses to violations. Other studies that do not use the concept of the psychological contract explicitly also show how employer and employee expectations of their conduct shape HR practices and relations, even if subject to negotiation and contestation (Bacon and Hoque, 2005). Organization size might be expected to influence the content of psychological contracts given the distinctive character of employer-employee relationships in small business contexts, giving rise to relational, rather than transactional, contracts in which the parties' obligations are more open-ended and diffuse, entailing elements of moral or emotional commitment, as well as a pragmatic, instrumental compliance (Atkinson, 2008).

Employer expectations of employee conduct incorporate contractual terms but, given the 'silences' of employment contracts, inevitably extend beyond formal, written terms to cover issues that are difficult, if not impossible, to specify contractually as well as broader issues such as theft (Nadin and Williams, 2012). Employers report employee obligations such as flexibility, loyalty and commitment and a willingness to take responsibility and show initiative (Nadin and Cassell, 2007). Such informal understandings constitute a large part of the content of psychological contracts, yet are often fluid and ambiguous – because of their informality. Such contracts shape behaviour although changes in the external environment, notably product and labour market conditions, pose a persistent challenge to customary workplace practices and the expectations that influence, and are influenced by, them (Ram et al., 2001). Employer and employee expectations evolve over time as relationships develop (Nadin and Cassell, 2007). Business growth generates changes in psychological contracts as individual roles change and newcomers with novel ideas are recruited, potentially unsettling workplace understandings, practices and relationships (Martin et al., 2008).

Employer perceptions of employee violations of the psychological contract are often felt intensely and are a source of conflict (Nadin and Cassell, 2007). Employers and employees may define their obligations in divergent terms but proximity might aggravate responses to perceived violation by the other party. Perceptions of poor performance or unfair treatment might be perceived as personal slights rather than as arising from the structured antagonism underlying the employment relationship. This creates a serious dilemma for small employers as they grow: to formalize practices, in order to clarify the obligations and expectations of the two parties but risk depersonalizing the relationship and reducing the satisfactions that derive from informality; or to continue with the informal, personal approach and live with the (occasional) violations of the psychological contract that inevitably occur.

8. UNDERSTANDING SMALL FIRM HR IN ITS WIDER CONTEXT

Small employers operate in a wider economic and political context that structures their employment relationships (Edwards et al., 2006). Product and labour market conditions, all underpinned by a regulatory framework, shape but do not determine employer and employee activities. Contrasting views exist regarding the impact of market influences on small firms; some emphasize their vulnerability to external market shocks (e.g. Storey 2011) and how this determines employer autocracy; others report a variety of small firm experiences of competitive pressures (Forth et al. 2006). While small employers experience market pressures in diverse ways, reflecting their resource bases, market positions and growth intentions, we suggest that small businesses are particularly susceptible to external cost and demand shocks, and the influence of powerful external actors (Bacon and Hoque, 2005), that would impact on employer-employee relations.

Market and regulatory pressures do not impose a single logic on employer and employee behaviour, in part because the parties interpret those pressures variably, and partly because the environment generates contradictory signals, encouraging divergent responses. Studies have shown how a workplace 'negotiation of order' emerges from employer-employee interaction over the terms of the pay-effort bargain in response to perceptions of external environmental pressures and alternative opportunities. In the context of relatively enduring relationships, neither party has an interest in exploiting temporary advantages deriving from changes in external conditions in such a way that might jeopardize long-term relations (e.g. Ram, 1994; Li and Edwards, 2008; Ram and Edwards, 2010).

9. IS HR INFORMALITY AN IMPEDIMENT TO GROWTH?

Small business HR practices combine both informal and formal elements; this balance shifts as firms grow. Formalization is driven by both internal organizational dynamics and external pressures and incentives (Kotey and Slade, 2005; Forth et al., 2006; Marlow et al., 2010; Wapshott, 2012). Here we examine whether the informal working practices and employment relations typically found in small firms might facilitate, or impede, business growth. Does informality grant employers sufficient flexibility to adapt HR practices as firms grow – or does it constrain growth; indeed, does a preference for informality deter employers from seeking growth at all?

Some argue that a critical advantage of small firms arises from their size advantage which facilitates rapid flexible adaptation to shifting market demands (Storey and Greene, 2010). Firm size, flexibility and informality enmesh to generate a particular context where employee effort can be directed to meet production demands. Once greater complexity and formality ensue such that the personalized relationship with the owner-manager diminishes, employee affiliation can become diluted (Martin et al., 2008; Marlow et al., 2010). This generates a paradox that the very context which supported firm growth initially must be reconstructed to enable future expansion. Thus, managing this transition is critical. Care must be taken, however, not to construct a simplistic dichotomy between informality/formality and small/large firms respectively (Marlow et al., 2005). Informality in small firms is a matter of degree and not kind (Ram et al., 2001). The distinction between small and large organizations lies in the manner in which formal policy and procedure surround and order the employment relationship. Employment relations in the largest organizations operate through both formal policies and informal interactions or negotiation (Edwards, 2006). Managers must navigate a path between rationality and intuition, formality and informality, professional norms and personal preference or idiosyncrasy. Within small firms the absence of professional knowledge or practice and the context of social and spatial proximity create a fertile environment for the persistence and dominance of informal employment relations.

Employer motivations for HR formalization arise largely from firm growth; as organizations become larger and more complex it is increasingly difficult for owners to control all managerial functions, and so they must delegate authority to others (Storey and Greene, 2010). Axiomatically, such delegation will diminish opportunity for idiosyncratic owner/manager interference. Importing professional HR policy and practice can generate a variety of consequences for employers, managers and employees (Gilman and Edwards, 2008; Wapshott, 2012). Whilst clearly a more formal systematic approach to the employment relationship will facilitate more efficient and effective people management, recognizing the need for organizational fairness and equality (Cox, 2005), it will disrupt existing custom and practice. Workplace norms and associated networks and practices are threatened, potentially stimulating evasion and resistance. Marlow et al. (2010) explored how growing firms managed the introduction of formal HR processes; surprisingly, the greatest resistance arose from incumbent managers as their power and prerogative to engage in intuitive localized labour management was eroded by the adoption of formal HR processes. Indeed, different subterfuges emerged as, for example, when encouraging preferred job candidates to apply for formally advertised vacancies and then prioritizing their applications (Marlow et al., 2010).

It is conceivable that anticipation of increasing formalization might deter growth where this loosens personal ties with employees and jeopardizes the maintenance of managerial control (Martin et al., 2008). Instituting formal procedures requires a substantial input either from the managerial team or from external support providers; this is likely to be costly in terms of time, money or disruption to existing practice, with potential adverse reactions from employees. Depersonalizing relationships with employees will bureaucratize employee relations and may paradoxically damage firm performance as the personal nature of the social relations of production are eroded (Verreynne et al., 2011). So, within all firms informal and formal labour management approaches coexist, suggesting employers must strive to create a workable balance between the informal and the formal in HR practice. There are no panaceas: employers might experience internal and external pressures to adapt practices, as regulations, market conditions and employee expectations change.

To illustrate the arguments above, we outline two short vignettes of growing firms, drawing on interview data from owners, managers and employees, who attempted to incorporate formal HR policies and practices to facilitate improved performance. One firm, RadCo, successfully managed this transition and continues upon a growth trajectory; the second, HaulageCo, struggled with the transition, failed to manage growth and maintain performance and subsequently went into bankruptcy.

10. SUMMARY AND CONCLUSIONS

Small firms are, numerically, the dominant employers in the UK. Like their larger counterparts, small employers must implement a set of HR practices intended to attract, retain and motivate employees to produce goods and services, with a view to achieving profitable sale. The extant literature demonstrates that HR practices and employment relations in small firms typically differ from those in larger organizations. Small employers characteristically operate informal practices in order to construct personal and particular relationships with employees. The proximity of the owner/management team and employees in the absence of a professional HR manager leads to fluid and flexible approaches to labour management. Such informal practices, and the personal and particular relations they give rise to, are often a source of high levels of satisfaction among employers and employees.

But informal HR practice generates tensions and contradictions.

BOX 3.1   RADCO, MANUFACTURER OF
            RADIATOR COVERS, 150 EMPLOYEES

The firm is fifteen years old; the CE is the original founder; the management team has grown substantially with the emergence of discrete managerial functions. The current (and first) HR manager, Gill, originally PA to the owner, was offered the opportunity to take on the HR role when the firm reached 100 employees three years ago. She accepted this role and completed her CIPD professional accreditation. Working with an assistant, she manages all HR policy and practice and works closely with the management team to develop employment strategies to manage growth. This transition was successful as the CE agreed to delegate the HR function to Gill to support growth and enhance performance; the firm paid for her to gain CIPD professional accreditation. Gill protected her role by taking full control of HR and reminding the CE of her role; 'he did try to interfere in the beginning but I reminded him firmly that it was my job and he had to let go'. The CE supported Gill by ensuring that other managers, previously undertaking HR line management tasks, relinquished these roles and did not undermine Gill's authority; she was also included in all senior management meetings to plan future growth; the role and importance of the HR function was emphasized and embedded. As Gill summarized the process,

> it was very difficult at first. The others [managers] did not want to give up their special relationships with their team members [employees] and they in turn, always ran back to their favourite manager when something went wrong – it was very cliquey. I had to stand my ground and always had support of [CE] who backed me up 100 per cent. Now, everyone knows I do the HR and that's just the way it is.

Particularistic management might generate employee perceptions of unfair treatment and discrimination; indeed, small firms are over-represented at employment tribunals for unfair dismissal (Forth et al., 2006). Moreover, reliance upon informal HR practices suggests a lack of strategic insight and sophistication in harnessing employee effort to enhance production and lay foundations for firm growth. So, whilst informality may enhance

---

BOX 3.2   HAULAGECO, HGV HAULAGE SERVICES, 135 EMPLOYEES AT TIME OF CLOSURE

HaulageCo was a family owned firm, founded in 1995. The management team consisted largely of family members with more professional, specialist managers employed as the firm grew. The HR function was offered to the owner's PA, Karen, who was already undertaking most HR tasks; she was not encouraged to undertake professional accreditation. The greatest problem for Karen was the failure of the owner and management team to fully delegate the HR function to her. Her attempts to formalize HR processes could not be effectively actioned because management and employees circumvented or ignored them. The owner compounded the problem by continuing to micro manage individual employees, often awarding financial bonuses and changing job specifications without consulting Karen. Consequently, there was very high labour turnover, managerial salaries reflected family affiliations, there was an absence of strategic growth plans, very little formal managerial or employee training and high levels of dissatisfaction. As Karen summarized just prior to closure, 'it is very difficult; Kevin [owner] makes snap decisions which was fine when there were 20 people but now, it doesn't work. People don't know where they are and just leave, they all earn different rates and it is still a very family run place so it is still, "if your face fits". It is too chaotic'. Whilst clearly the family dynamic was influential, the difficulty of ordering the employment relationship to indicate consistency, fairness and transparency through formal policies and practices was highly problematic.

---

employees' sense of job satisfaction, it might also be highly damaging to the firm's future prospects. Yet, rapid business growth is a rare phenomenon. Very few small business owner-managers pursue growth; most prefer to remain small. Employer preferences for personal, particularistic relations and the employee commitment, loyalty and trust presumed to flow from them might further discourage growth. In addition, managerial and financial resource constraints, and competitive product market conditions, restrict growth potential. Among growing enterprises, tensions might arise as employers seek to formalize HR practice in order to manage employees more effectively and fairly. Accordingly, attempting to match formal HR models, such as HPWS, to smaller firms is unlikely to stimulate or support business growth unless they specifically fit the operating context of the firm. Rather, if growth does occur it is likely to be uneven and contested (Storey, 2011) with nascent HR policies and practices emerging to support this amorphous and uncertain process; the success and reach of such policies are likely to depend upon the degree of support offered by owner/management teams.

So, most small firms prefer to maintain an informal and idiosyncratic employment relationship which is untroubled by professional HR policy and practice initiatives. Indeed, there is some suggestion that this promotes high degrees of job satisfaction amongst employees (Storey et al., 2010). Where growth does occur, owners and managers will have to manage the tensions arising from shifting the balance between informal and formal labour management. The emergent HR function is likely to lag behind rather than stimulate growth such that effectively managing labour in growing firms will be an uncertain combination of serendipity and skill.

NOTES

1. Employers comprise a quarter of the UK business stock. The remaining three quarters, 3.6 million businesses, are owned by people working alone, or with partners, but employing no-one else.
2. The snark is a mythical creature created by Lewis Carroll which was the object of much speculation and effort to capture it; however, this would never occur as it was, indeed, a myth.

REFERENCES

Ainsworth, S. and Wolfram Cox, J.S. (2003) 'Families divided: culture and control in small family business', *Organization Studies*, 24 (9), 1463–1485.

Arrowsmith, J., Gilman, M., Edwards, P. and Ram, M. (2003) 'The impact of the national minimum wage in small firms', *British Journal of Industrial Relations*, 41 (3), 435–456.

Atkinson, C. (2008) 'An exploration of small firm psychological contracts', *Work, Employment and Society*, 22 (3), 447–465.

Bacon, N. and Hoque, K. (2005) 'HRM in the SME sector: valuable employees and coercive networks', *International Journal of Human Resource Management*, 16 (11), 1976–1999.

BBC (2013), 'Economy tracker: GDP', online at http://www.bbc.co.uk/news/10613201.

Benmore, G. and Palmer, A. (1996) 'Human resource management in small firms: keeping it strictly informal', *Journal of Small Business and Enterprise Development*, 3 (2), 109–118.

Blackburn, R. and Hart, M. (2002) 'Small firms' awareness and knowledge of individual employment rights' DTI, online at http://www.bis.gov.uk/files/file13207.pdf.

Bolton Committee (1971) *Report of the Committee of Enquiry on Small Firms*, Cmnd 4811, London: HMSO.

Carroll, M., Marchington, M., Earnshaw, J. and Taylor, S. (1999) 'Recruitment in small firms: processes, methods and problems', *Employee Relations*, 21 (3), 236–50.

Carter, S. and Jones-Evans, D. (2012) *Enterprise and Small Business*, London: Prentice Hall.

Cassell, C., Nadin, S., Gray, M. and Clegg, C. (2002) 'Exploring human resource management practices in small and medium sized enterprises', *Personnel Review*, 31 (6), 671–692.

Combs, J., Liu, Y., Hall, A., and Ketchen, D. (2006) 'How much do high-performance work practices matter? A meta analysis of their effects on organizational performance', *Personnel Psychology*, 59, 501.

Cox, A. (2005) 'Procedural justice in small firms', in S. Marlow, D. Patton and M. Ram (eds), *Managing Labour in Small Firms*, London: Routledge, pp. 213–225.

Department for Business, Innovation and Skills (BIS) (2012) *Business Population Estimates for the UK and the Regions, 2012*, online at https://www.gov.uk/government/organisations/department-for-business-innovation-skills/series/business-population-estimates.

Drummond, I. and Stone, I. (2007) 'Exploring the potential of high performance work systems in SMEs', *Employee Relations*, 29 (2), 192–207.

Edwards, P. (ed.) (2006) *Industrial Relations: Theory and Practice*, Oxford: Blackwell Press.

Edwards, P. and Ram, M. (2006) 'Surviving on the margins of the economy: working relations in small low wage firms', *Journal of Management Studies*, 43 (4), 895–916.

Edwards, P., Ram, M. and Black, J. (2003) *The Impact of Employment Legislation on Small Firms: a Case Study Analysis*, DTI Employment Relations Research Series No. 20, London.

Edwards, P., Ram, M., Sengupta, S. and Tsai, C.-J. (2006) 'The structuring of working relationships in small firms: towards a formal framework', *Organization*, 13 (5), 701–724.

Evans, W. and Davis, W. (2005) 'High-performance work systems and organizational performance: the mediating role of internal social structure', *Journal of Management*, 31, 758–775.

Ewing, K. and Hendy, J. (2012) 'Unfair dismissal law changes – unfair?', *Industrial Law Journal*, 41 (1), 115–121.

Federation of Small Businesses (FSB) (2012) *FSB Voice of Small Business Index: Quarter 1, 2012*, online at http://www.fsb.org.uk/policy/assets/q1%20vosb%20index.pdf.

Gilman, M. and Edwards, P. (2008) 'Testing the framework of the organisation of small firms: fast-growth, high-tech SMEs', *International Small Business Journal*, 26 (5), 531–558.

Gilman, M., Edwards, P., Ram, M. and Arrowsmith, J. (2002) 'Pay determination in small firms in the UK: the case of the response to the national minimum wage, *Industrial Relations Journal*, 33 (1), 52–67.

Goss, D. (1991) *Small Business and Society*, London: Routledge.

Grimshaw, D. and Carroll, M. (2006) 'Adjusting the national minimum wage: constraints and incentives to change in six low-paying sectors', *Industrial Relations Journal*, 37 (1), 22–47.

Guest, D. (2011) 'Human resource management and performance: still searching for some answers', *Human Resource Management Journal*, 21 (1), 3–13.

Guest, D. and Conway, N. (1997) *Employee Motivation and the Psychological Contract*, London: Institute of Personnel and Development.

Guthrie, J., Flood, P., Liu, W. and MacCurtain, S. (2009) 'High performance work systems in Ireland: human resource and organizational outcomes', *International Journal of Human Resource Management*, 20 (1), 112–125.

Harney, B. and Dundon, T. (2006) 'An emergent theory of HRM: a theoretical and empirical exploration of determinants of HRM among Irish SMEs', *Advances in Industrial and Labor Relations*, 15, 109–159.

HM Treasury/BIS (2011) *The Plan for Growth*, online at http://cdn.hm-treasury. gov.uk/2011budget_growth.pdf.

Holliday, R. (1995) *Investigating Small Firms: Nice Work?*, London: Routledge.

Kitching, J. (1994) 'Employers' workforce construction policies in the small service sector enterprise', in J. Atkinson and D. Storey (eds), *Employment, the Small Firm and the Labour Market*, London: Routledge.

Kitching, J. (2007) 'Regulating employment relations through workplace learning: a study of small employers', *Human Resource Management Journal*, 17 (1), 42–57.

Kitching, J. (2008) 'Rethinking UK small employers' skills policies and the role of workplace learning', *International Journal of Training and Development*, 12 (2), 100–120.

Kotey, B., and Slade, P. (2005) 'Formal human resource management practices in small growing firms', *Journal of Small Business Management*, 43, 16–40.

Kroon, B., Van De Voorde, K. and Timmers, J. (2012) 'High performance work practices in small firms: a resource-poverty and strategic decision-making perspective', *Small Business Economics*, published online 15 March 2012.

Legge, K. (2005) *HRM Rhetoric and Realities,* London: Routledge.

Li, M. and Edwards, P. (2008) 'Work and pay in small Chinese clothing firms: a constrained negotiated order', *Industrial Relations Journal*, 39 (4), 296–313.

Marlow, S. (2002) 'Regulating labour management in small firms', *Human Resource Management Journal*, 12, 5–25.

Marlow, S. (2006) 'HRM in small firms: fact or fiction?', *Human Resource Management Review*, 16 (4), 466–476.

Marlow, S., Patton, D. and Ram, M. (2005) (eds) *Managing Labour in Small Firms*, London: Routledge.

Marlow, S., Thompson, A. and Taylor, S. (2010) 'Informality and formality in medium sized companies: contestation and synchronisation', *British Journal of Management,* 20 (4), 313–326.

Martin, L., Janjuha-Jivraj, S., Carey, C. and Reddy, S. (2008) 'Formalising relationships? Time, change and the psychological contract in team entrepreneurial companies', in R. Barrett and S. Mayson (eds) (2008a) *International Handbook of Entrepreneurship and HRM*, Cheltenham, UK and Northampton, MA, USA: Edward Elgar.

Moore, S. and Read, I. (2006) 'Collective organisation in small- and medium-sized enterprises – an application of mobilisation theory', *Human Resource Management Journal*, 16 (4), 357–375.

Moule, C. (1998) 'The regulation of work in small firms: a view from the inside', *Work, Employment and Society*, 12 (4), 635–653.

Nadin, S. and Cassell, C. (2007) 'New deal for old? Exploring the psychological contract in a small firm environment, *International Small Business Journal*, 25 (4), 417–443.

Nadin, S. and Williams, C. (2012) 'Psychological contract violation beyond an employees' perspective: the perspective of employers', *Employee Relations*, 34 (2), 110–125.

Ram, M. (1994) *Managing to Survive*, London: Routledge.

Ram, M. (1999) 'Managing autonomy: employment relations in small professional services firms', *International Small Business Journal*, 17 (2), 13–30.

Ram, M. (2001) 'Family dynamics in a small consultancy firm: a case study', *Human Relations*, 54 (4), 395–418.

Ram, M. and Edwards, P. (2003) 'Praising Caesar not burying him: what we know about employment relations in small firms', *Work, Employment and Society*, 17, 719–30.

Ram, M. and Edwards, P. (2010) 'Industrial relations in small firms', in T. Colling and M. Terry (eds), *Industrial Relations: Theory and Practice (3rd edn)*, Chichester: John Wiley & Sons.

Ram, M. and Holliday, R. (1993) 'Relative merits: family culture and kinship in small firms', *Sociology*, 27 (4), 629–648.

Ram, M., Edwards, P., Gilman, M. and Arrowsmith, J. (2001) 'The dynamics of informality, employment regulations in small firms and the effects of regulatory change', *Work, Employment and Society*, 15, 845–61.

Ram, M., Gilman, M., Arrowsmith, J. and Edwards, P., (2003) 'Once more into the sunset? Asian clothing firms after the national minimum wage', *Environment and Planning C: Government and Policy*, 21 (1), 71–88.

Saridakis, G., Sen-Gupta, S. Edwards, P. and Storey, D. (2008) 'The impact of enterprise size on employment tribunal incidence and outcomes: evidence from Britain', *British Journal of Industrial Relations*, 46 (3), 469–499.

Scase, R. and Goffee, R. (1980) *The Real World of the Small Business Owner*, London: Croom Helm.

Scott, M., Roberts, I., Holroyd, G. and Sawbridge, D. (1989) *Management and Industrial Relations in Small Firms*, Dept of Employment, Research Paper No. 70, London.

Sels, L., De Winne, S., Maes, J., Delmotte, J., Faems, D. and Forrier, A. (2006) 'Unravelling the HRM–performance link: value-creating and cost-increasing effects of small business HRM', *Journal of Management Studies*, 43 (2), 319–342.

Storey, D. (1987) *The Performance of Small Firms*, London: Croom Helm.

Storey, D. (2011) 'Optimism and chance: the elephants in the entrepreneurship room', *International Small Business Journal*, 29 (4), 303–321.

Storey, D. and Greene, F. (2010) *Small Business and Entrepreneurship*, London: Prentice Hall.

Storey, D., Saridakis, G., Sen-Gupta, S., Edwards, P. and Blackburn, R. (2010) 'Linking HR formality with employee job quality: the role of firm and workplace size', *Human Resource Management*, 49 (2), 305–329.

Tansky, J. and Heneman, J. (2006) *Human Resource Strategies for the High Growth Entrepreneurial Firm,* Greenwich CT: Information Age Publishing.

Taylor, S. (2005) 'HRM in small firms: hunting the snark?', in S. Marlow, D. Patton and M. Ram (2005) (eds) *Managing Labour in Small Firms*, London: Routledge, pp. 212–226.

Tsai, C.-J., Sengupta, S. and Edwards, P. (2007) 'When and why is small beautiful? The experience of work in the small firm', *Human Relations*, 60, 1779–1808.

van Wanrooy, B., Bewley, H., Bryson, A., Forth, J., Freeth, S., Stokes, L. and Wood, S. (2013) 'The 2011 workplace employment relations study: first findings, online', https://www.gov.uk/government/uploads/system/uploads/attachment_data/file/175479/13-535-the-2011-workplace-employment-relations-study-first-findings1.pdf.

Verreynne, M.-L., Parker, P. and Wilson, M. (2011) 'Employment systems in small firms: a multilevel analysis', *International Small Business Journal*, published online 29 July.

Wapshott, R. (2012) 'The unspoken side of mutual adjustment: understanding intersubjective negotiation in small professional service firms', *International Small Business Journal*, 31 (forthcoming).

Way, S. (2002) 'High performance work systems and intermediate indicators of firm performance within the US small business sector', *Journal of Management*, 26 (6), 765–785.

Wright, M. and Marlow, S. (2012) 'Entrepreneurial activity in the venture creation and development process', *International Small Business Journal*, 30 (2), 107–115.

4. Promoting innovation and entrepreneurship through HR practices

James C. Hayton, Jeffrey S. Hornsby and James Bloodgood

1. INTRODUCTION

Entrepreneurship is not limited to the domain of individuals and startups, but is highly relevant to organizations seeking to adapt to complex and turbulent competitive environments. A significant proportion of innovations emerge from within existing organizations, despite the fact that established organizations may suffer from a number of innate disabilities when it comes to promoting entrepreneurial behavior. Established organizations naturally tend to be more bureaucratic, routinized, compelled to serve existing customer needs, blind to new technological developments, and hindered by their own cost structures (e.g. Christensen, 1997). On the other hand, established organizations possess significant resource advantages over new startups; they have capabilities for production, marketing and distribution of their products or services, and possess legitimacy in their strategic fields and among stakeholders, particularly potential customers and suppliers. It has long been noted that organizations differ in their capacity for behaving entrepreneurially (Miller, 1983). These differences have also been related to measures of organizational performance (e.g. Rauch et al., 2009; Zahra, 1996).

Besides an established association with various performance metrics such as sales growth and financial success, entrepreneurship within organizations represents a significant outcome in its own right. Corporate entrepreneurship reflects a capacity for adaptive, and often proactive transformation, which aids adjustment to ever changing technological, economic and competitive landscapes. A focus solely on bottom line performance has long been understood as a form of myopia that has dysfunctional consequences for long-term survival (Levinthal and March, 1993). Organizations preparing for the long haul must seek to build capabilities

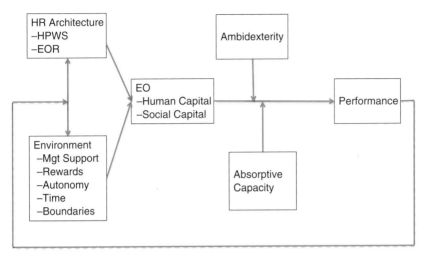

Figure 4.1   An integrative model of the HR and CE process

for constant learning, renewal and recombination of resources as new opportunities arise (and existing markets fade or become commoditized). A question of interest for as many years is what are the correlates of an entrepreneurial orientation (EO; e.g. Miller, 1983) and how do human resource management (HRM) practices and related aspects of the organizational environment support or inhibit entrepreneurial behavior in established organizations (e.g. Hayton, 2005; Hornsby et al., 2002; Hornsby et al., 2009; Hornsby et al., 2012; Kuratko et al., 1990).

In this chapter, we examine some of the main strands within the literature that have connected HRM with corporate entrepreneurship. We organize our review around a conceptual framework shown in Figure 4.1. This framework articulates a mediating relationship between investments in human resource architectures, related environmental factors, and EO. This reflects a typical framing of the role of HRM acting upon organizational performance through the mediating constructs of human and social capital (e.g. Collins and Clark, 2003). Our attention is primarily focused on two important categories of factors that have been found to be associated with entrepreneurship in an organizational setting: human resource architectures, and organizational environmental factors such as culture, structure, resource availability and leadership. We focus on these sets of variables as prior research examining organizational antecedents has consistently identified these as major antecedents to corporate entrepreneurship (Hayton, 2005; Hayton and Kelley, 2006; Hornsby et al., 1993; Hornsby et al., 1999; Hornsby et al., 2002).

In addition to reviewing ways in which HRM and environmental variables impact the creation of an innovative and entrepreneurial workforce, we also acknowledge two important moderators of the relationship between EO and ultimate organizational performance. We address the components of this framework over the following pages. Having presented the model, we then conclude with a discussion of opportunities for future research that addresses these relationships.

2.   ENTREPRENEURIAL ORIENTATION (EO)

EO is an organizational state or quality that is defined in terms of several behavioral dimensions. Based on the pioneering work of Miller (1983), Covin and Slevin (1989) defined EO in terms of risk taking, innovativeness and proactiveness. EO is an organizational level construct, however it is significantly influenced by the behaviors of organizational members (Burgelman, 1988). As noted by Burgelman (1983), employee strategic behaviors may be either induced through organizational routines and management processes, or may be autonomous and reflect proactive and innovative contributions. Often such contributions come from middle managers (e.g. Hornsby et al., 2009; Kuratko et al., 2005). However, organizational entrepreneurship is also influenced by networks of diverse roles (Hayton and Kelley, 2006; Kelley et al., 2009), and these roles may be either concentrated or dispersed throughout an organization (e.g. Wolcott and Lippitz, 2007). Therefore, to the extent that key employees and groups are able, motivated and have the opportunity to engage in innovation, risk taking and proactive entrepreneurial behaviors, the organization as a whole is likely to possess an EO (Hayton, 2005).

EO is interesting and important because of its significant correlation with organizational performance (Rauch et al., 2009). There have been numerous studies that have examined the connection between EO and both financial and nonfinancial performance. The financial indicators examined have linked EO to growth, sales, and profit. Nonfinancial measures include the number of ideas implemented and satisfaction of the owner, organizational leaders, or employees. These studies have generally supported a positive connection between EO and firm performance, particularly financial performance. This support has been underscored by the recent meta-analysis by Rauch et al. (2009), who observed that the strength of the estimated population correlation with performance $(r = .235)$ is analogous to that of taking a sleeping pill and expecting a better night's sleep. In other words, the performance impact of EO is considered to be strong and reliable.

3.   THE HUMAN RESOURCE ARCHITECTURE

Understanding the strategic role of HRM involves attending to several closely related variables (e.g. Becker and Huselid, 2006; Lepak and Snell, 1999; Wright et al., 2001). Wright et al. (2001) refer to this broader concept as the 'people management system', which in addition to systems of HRM practices includes employment relationships and employee behaviors. Similarly, in their development of a broader concept of the investments made in the workforce, Lepak and Snell (1999) propose that human resource architectures encompass configurations of HRM practices, employment contracting modes, and the employee-organization exchange relationship (e.g. Tsui et al., 1997). The rationale for a broader conceptualization of investments in the workforce is that employees are induced to participate in and contribute to the organization not only by HRM practices, but also by their formal and informal relationships with their employers (e.g. Tsui et al., 1997; Tsui and Wang, 2002). Following Lepak and Snell (1999, 2002; also Wright et al., 2001) we focus on three dimensions of the HR architecture: HR systems, employment modes and the employee-organization exchange relationship.

HR Systems

Human resource practices that impact the human and social capital within the firm help to enhance the levels of creativity, innovation, and entrepreneurial behavior within the organization and can be categorized as part of a high performance work system (HPWS). Bohlander and Snell (2004: 690) suggest that the HPWS reflects 'a specific combination of HR practices, work structures, and processes that maximizes employee knowledge, skill, commitment and flexibility.' According to Nadler et al. (1992) HPWS are implemented via: '. . . an organizational architecture that brings together work, people, technology and information in a manner that optimizes the congruence of fit among them in order to produce high performance in terms of the effective response to customer requirements and other environmental demands and opportunities.' Nadler et al. (1997: 147–53) identified ten important principles for designing an effective HPWS, each of which centers around building a system based upon design clarity, empowerment, culture, and accountability:

1. Start the design with an outward focus on customer requirements and then work backward to develop appropriate organizational forms and work processes.
2. Design work around self-managed teams responsible for producing complete products or processes.
3. Work must be guided by clear direction, explicit goals, and a full understanding of output requirements and measures of performance.
4. Variances should be detected and controlled at the source.
5. Design the social and technical systems to be closely linked.
6. Ensure continuous flow of information to all areas of the system.
7. Enriched and shared jobs increase the motivation of individuals and enhance flexibility in assigning work and solving problems.
8. Human resource practices must complement and strengthen the empowerment of teams and individuals.
9. The management structure, culture, and processes all must embrace and support the HPWS design.
10. The organization and its work units must have the capacity to reconfigure themselves to meet changing competitive conditions.

Specifically, they argue that:

> The key to maintaining this flexible architecture is having clear design intent. If the purpose of the original design – to enhance speed, accountability, customer focus, technological innovation, flattened hierarchy, or whatever – is explicitly articulated, then there are clear boundaries for adding, deleting, or rearranging design elements. (Nadler et al., 1997)

In the case of fostering innovation and entrepreneurship, the key is to strategically foster innovative behavior by designing human resource systems that support, incentivize, and reinforce such behavior. In a review of the relationships between HRM practices and corporate entrepreneurship, Hayton (2005) identified job designs with high levels of autonomy and discretion, careful socialization and investments in team-oriented training, extensive use of cross functional teams, and performance management combined with incentives to promote risk taking behaviors by employees as major levers available to the HR function in pursuit of an entrepreneurial organization.

Recent empirical research confirms many of the propositions made in the Hayton (2005) conceptual model. For example, Beugelsdijk (2008) provides evidence of the impact of changing six human resource practices on incremental and radical innovations. In a study of 988 Dutch firms, he found that firms with decentralized organizational structures and a focus on employee empowerment, as reflected in the use of task autonomy and flexible working hours, generated more product innovations. He also found that performance-based pay and training and development were positively associated with incremental innovation, but not with radical innovation. This was also supported by Messersmith and Guthrie (2010) in a study of small US based firms, where a positive association was reported between the utilization of a high performance work system and both product and organizational innovation. Rather than treat the entire HRM system as a menu of practices, we can examine the key human resource subsystems in terms of three bundles of interrelated activities: knowledge management, compensation and incentives, and participation and communication.

Knowledge management
Knowledge management includes attracting, retaining, and developing individuals with the knowledge, skills, and abilities to meet the goals of the organization. This is the first component of creating the HPWS and includes utilizing selective staffing techniques and investing in appropriate training and development activities. A selective approach to staffing is distinguished by standardized practices, such as ability testing and structured interviews, to identify the best talent available (Huselid, 1995; Way, 2002). Selective staffing places an emphasis on both enhancing the quality of candidates and also increasing the likelihood of finding quality employees with the right profile of knowledge, skills, and abilities that will fit the firm's innovative posture. Utilizing a multi-hurdle selection process that allows for an assessment of an individual's creativity, intellect, and ability to work well with others will provide better information to decision makers and increases the firm's face validity by signaling to applicants that the organization is selective about whom it hires (Way, 2002). Greater rigor in the selection process enhances the quality of human capital that enters the organization and increases the likelihood that the firm will be able to produce new innovations.

In addition, firms willing to invest in training and development activities for their employees in job-specific, company-specific, and industry-specific areas will likely see an increase in the levels of human capital within the firm (Way, 2002). By pairing training systems with selective staffing the firm can experience enhancements to human capital endowments that will allow them to achieve higher, more productive levels of innovation (Thornhill, 2006). Employees who are able to continually refine their skill sets as necessary to exploit new market opportunities are likely to be more productive in entrepreneurial organizations. Corporate entrepreneurship is promoted by the simultaneous presence of competency in the four roles of innovating, brokering, championing, and sponsoring (Hayton and

Table 4.1   Knowledge, skills and personality characteristics associated with entrepreneurial roles

	Innovating	Brokering	Championing	Sponsoring
Knowledge				
Specialized core	X	X		
Multidisciplinary	X	X	X	X
Organizational		X	X	X
Skills				
Cognitive ability	X	X		
Creativity	X	X		
Analogic reasoning		X	X	
Influencing		X	X	
Transformational leadership			X	X
Emotional intelligence		X	X	
Networking		X		
Personality				
Conscientiousness	X	X		
Openness to experience	X	X		
Confidence		X	X	
Credibility		X	X	
Risk Tolerance			X	X
Tenacity	X	X	X	X
Passion	X	X	X	X

Source: Hayton and Kelley, 2006.

Kelley, 2006). In order to foster corporate innovative activity, employee development activities focused on engendering these competencies should be a central focus of a corporate innovation strategy. The knowledge, skills and other characteristics underlying these competencies are depicted in Table 4.1. When these are incorporated within staffing and development activities, it is expected that entrepreneurial roles are more likely to emerge in organizations (Hayton and Kelley, 2006).

It bears noting that traditional selection and employee development procedures may not always be productive when it comes to hiring and developing entrepreneurial employees. Typical procedures tend to be job-based and are built to identify individuals that adhere to policies and procedures, follow instruction, and work towards fitting into a company profile. Very little empirical research exists to help us better understand the requirements for and the impact of directly seeking creative and entrepreneurial employees. However, there is ample discussion in the applied literature on some recommendations to attract, retain and develop these types of individuals (Cascio and Aguinis, 2008; Sutton, 2001).

Compensation and incentives
The second component in creating a HPWS that promotes EO is employee compensation and incentives (Hayton, 2005). While knowledge building practices such as staffing and training help to prepare employees and organizations for making entrepreneurial contributions, effective compensation management provides positive incentive and reward for risky, innovative, and proactive behaviors (Hayton, 2003). Organizations need to find a way to link pay with performance in order to incentivize an employee to focus 'on outcomes that are beneficial to themselves and the organization as a whole' (Bolander and Snell, 2004). Entrepreneurial behavior is developed and enhanced by reward systems that account for feedback and organizational goals while also emphasizing organizational results, collaboration, and individual responsibility (Hayton, 2005; Hornsby et al., 1993).

Incentives can take many forms, with some examples being stock options and other equity plans, profit sharing plans, pay raises, bonuses for meeting performance targets and other monetary incentives. In addition, incentives can take the form of non-monetary options such as time off, flextime, autonomy and other special employee benefits. In terms of innovation and entrepreneurship, the types of incentives should vary based on the need for incremental or radical innovations. Traditional incentives including intrinsic rewards (flextime, autonomy, etc.) and extrinsic rewards (bonuses, merit increases, profit sharing, etc.) may be more suited to promoting incremental innovation. However, radical innovation may require more substantial forms of incentives that are often difficult to administer and tend to foster apprehension from top management. These incentives include organizational equity in the form of stock, stock options, or even large equity stakes in venture spin-offs. Beugelsdijk (2008) affirmed this in his study of Dutch firms and found that incremental innovations are relatively easier to motivate with traditional HR practices but the ability to motivate radical innovations is much more limited because more sophisticated reward systems are not available.

In a study of CE in Israeli defense firms, Lerner et al. (2009) confirmed the importance of building effective entrepreneurship-oriented compensation programs. The findings of their research suggest that management should not only call for compensation for entrepreneurs, but should also make sure that the system they choose is valued and acceptable to the entrepreneurs. Their results show that there is a large gap between the perception of the desired compensation incentives by corporate entrepreneurs and the ones actually practiced by the enterprise. They also found that even when more desirable compensation programs were utilized, many of the corporate entrepreneur respondents were not aware that such incentives were in place.

Participation and communication
The promotion of participation and communication of information is a third important dimension of the HPWS. An entrepreneurial firm should place a greater emphasis on designing policies and structures that enhance participation, open communication and collaboration. While knowledge management practices ensure that the workforce has the needed knowledge and skills, and rewards and incentives support and direct motivation, participation and communication ensure that employees have the opportunity to engage in entrepreneurial actions. Furthermore, providing an increased opportunity to participate in decisions is critical to creating an EO. With greater information sharing and transparent communication organizations can demonstrate managerial support and help to equip individuals at all levels of the organization. By enabling collaboration and open communication, an organizational structure can decrease the impediments to the pursuit of entrepreneurial initiatives (Hornsby et al., 1993; Hornsby et al., 1999; Hornsby et al., 2002).

Conversely, innovation and entrepreneurial behavior is limited by organizations that focus on policies that create boundaries and overly regulate individual behavior. Traditional human resource practices such as creating job descriptions, policy manuals, safety manuals, and operating standards can inhibit desired behavior (Hayton, 2003). Also, a manager's rigid enforcement of policies can also have unwanted effects on employee behavior. While some of these are necessary and important to the operation of the organization (especially those legally required), these traditional practices may also inhibit the creativity and entrepreneurial behavior desired when implementing a corporate entrepreneurship strategy.

Human resource management practices fall into two categories, traditional HR practices and discretionary HRM (Hayton, 2003). The traditional practices focus upon 'clearly defining jobs in terms of their tasks, duties, and responsibilities; carefully structuring equitable rewards for those jobs; and monitoring individual performance.' These traditional practices are incongruent with the creativity, innovation and risk taking required for innovation and entrepreneurship. Discretionary HRM practices, on the other hand, focus on the discretionary performance of employees by offering incentives and mechanisms for exchanging knowledge and encouraging organizational learning. In a study of 99 small and medium size enterprises, discretionary HR practices, specifically employee participation in decision making, empowerment, incentive pay, formal socialization, and long term variable rewards (e.g. employee stock ownership and/or profit sharing) were positively associated with innovative performance (Hayton, 2003). This positive relationship was found to be strongest in high technology industries where opportunities for entrepreneurship and innovation are greater. These discretionary HRM practices related to information sharing and employee involvement are recognized as key elements of the HPWS because they allow employees to make decisions that affect their immediate environment, which in turn affects the entire organization. Empowerment leads to higher levels of commitment and organizational citizenship, which contribute to the creation of trust and social capital within the firm and support collaboration, learning, innovation, and risk taking.

Employment Mode

Although employment security and internal promotion policies are often considered an element within the HPWS model (e.g. Delery and Shaw, 2001; Huselid, 1995) the contracting mode (full-time, part-time, short-term, long-term) is treated as a complementary component within the HR architecture framework (Lepak and Snell, 1999, 2002). This distinction is warranted on theoretical grounds, since employment mode choices are explained by transaction cost theorizing (Lepak and Snell, 1999) while HPWS are justified in terms of their capacity for creating the ability, motivation and opportunity for employees to contribute effectively (Becker and Huselid, 1998; Combs et al., 2006; Delery and Shaw, 2001). Choices with respect to HRM practices and employment mode are also independent in practice, and it is this independence that is required for differentiated architectures to exist (Lepak et al., 2003). That is, different architectures involve simultaneous variations across both HRM practices and employment modes (e.g. Lepakand Snell, 1999).

As human capital becomes increasingly specialized and firm specific, it creates a greater opportunity for strategic value creation, but information asymmetry increases contracting costs due to greater risks of moral hazard and opportunism. As a result, where human capital is highly specialized, long run employment relationships reduce transaction costs relative to relying on temporary contracts or quasi spot-market type relationships (e.g. Williamson, 1975). Long-term contractual relationships are therefore most economically efficient for strategically important jobs involving unique and valuable human capital, while short-term contractual relationships are more efficient for less strategically valuable jobs (Lepak and Snell, 1999, 2002). Thus, in addition to HRM practices, long-term employment contracts are an important consideration for impacting organizational learning, innovation and entrepreneurial actions.

Employee-Organization Exchange

The employment exchange relationship represents a third dimension that features in broader models of HR investments (Lepak and Snell, 1999; Tsui et al., 1997; Wright et al., 2001). Employment relationships may be conceived in terms of an inducements-contributions framework (e.g. March and Simon, 1958) in which organizations offer inducements to join in exchange for accepting obligations to contribute. These inducements and contributions include both economic and social exchanges (Rousseau, 1995; Tsuiand Wang, 2002). Where extensive autonomy and discretionary behaviors are needed, as is the case where entrepreneurial behaviors are desired, then high levels of mutual investments, including social exchanges, support these contributions through their influence on affective organizational commitment (e.g. Rousseau, 1995; Tsui et al., 1997). Inducements in the form of social exchanges are more effective than economic exchanges when employee obligations are complex or uncertain (Rousseau, 1995).

An architecture that incorporates not only high performance HRM, but also long-term employment contracts, and strong and relational employee-organization exchanges is expected to hold the greatest potential for the development of EO (e.g. Hayton, 2003, 2005). This is the configuration described by Lepak and Snell (2002) as 'commitment-based'. According to Lepak and Snell (1999) the HRM practices in the commitment-based architecture are consistent with those commonly observed in HPWS or commitment oriented HRM systems (e.g. Batt, 2002; Collins and Smith, 2006). Policies and practices such as extensive recruitment, careful selection, and above average investments in training and development together contribute to building a workforce with skills and knowledge that are needed to support organizational learning, innovation and entrepreneurship (Hayton and Kelley, 2006). These development oriented management practices help to attract and retain the high quality human capital and motivate in-role and extra-role performance that is supportive of EO (e.g. Chandler et al., 2000; Eisenberger et al., 1990; Hayton, 2005; Zhang and Jia, 2010; Zhang et al., 2008). Social exchange between organization and employees promote the acquisition of firm specific knowledge, and contribute to the organization's knowledge base (Tsui et al., 1997), providing an important foundation for entrepreneurial learning. This is also complemented by permanent or long-term employment contracts that reduce opportunism, and support mutual investment in the employment relationship (Tsui et al., 1997).

The foregoing suggests that examining the impact of HRM practices on organizational outcomes without consideration of the employment mode and employment relationship leads to an incomplete specification of the investment in people management systems (Huselid and Becker, 2011; Wright et al., 2001). Individual reactions to specific HR policies and practices are conditioned by the context in which they occur (e.g. Bowen and Ostroff, 2004). The influence of HRM practices will be strengthened when values signaled are consistent with the formal commitments implied by the contracting mode, and obligations created by the exchange relationship.

The influence of a commitment-based HR architecture is expected to positively affect the levels of human capital (knowledge, skills, and abilities) and social capital (interaction, helping behaviors, and relational connections) within the firm. Each of these resources has been linked to important individual, unit, and firm-level performance outcomes (Ployhart and Moliterno, 2011; Sun et al., 2007; Wright and Boswell, 2002; Youndt and Snell, 2004). This model reflects the dominant view in the strategic HRM field that the connection between HPWS and performance is channeled through a firm's human resources (Wright et al., 1994). In particular, a firm's human resources are seen as an important element in developing entrepreneurial behaviors (Wiklund and Shepherd, 2003).

4.   THE ORGANIZATIONAL ENVIRONMENT

A growing body of research suggests that not only HRM practices, but broader concerns such as resource availability, organizational culture and leadership are all important influences on entrepreneurship within organizations (e.g. Hayton, 2005; Kuratko et al., 2001; Zahra et al., 2004). The Corporate Entrepreneurial Assessment Instrument (CEAI) is one of the few research-based tools that attempt to measure an organization's cultural or environmental readiness for entrepreneurial activity. Five factors have been identified, including Top Management Support, Rewards and Reinforcement, Autonomy and Discretion, Time Availability, and Organizational Boundaries. These factors reflect such issues as strategy and leadership, slack resources, and organizational culture. The development of the survey items has been based on extensive research (eg. Hornsby et al., 2002; Hornsby et al., 2009; Hornsby et al., 2012) that has gone through numerous iterations since publication of the original instrument (Kuratko et al., 1990). The importance of macro-level variables (company type, environment, structure, and decision-making with entrepreneurship) has long been acknowledged. Miller (1983) found that firm type (simple, planning, and organic) moderated the relationship between the firm's entrepreneurial behavior and several of the other variables identified, and concluded that varying conditions within a firm are associated with an entrepreneurial strategy. Quinn (1985) identified a number of organizational antecedents for large corporations to consider when seeking innovative activity including developing the 'atmosphere' and vision for such activity and structuring the organization for innovation. Sathe (1989) suggested that individual innovation is significantly associated with supportive leadership, organizational structure, and the availability of resources. Hisrich and Peters (1986) established nine characteristics needed for an effective organizational environment for new venture creation, including management support, resources, experimentation, and multi-functional teamwork. Zahra (1991) developed and tested a model that proposed the elements of environment, corporate strategy, and organization as the antecedents to corporate entrepreneurship. He also found evidence of a relationship between these antecedents and firm financial performance. Lastly, Damanpour (1991) conducted a meta-analysis of a large number of studies on corporate innovation and identified a number of factors that consistently appear to be related to corporate innovation activities such as specialization, managerial attitude, and slack resources.

From this wide variety of factors that influence corporate entrepreneurship, we can distill the five recurring factors identified by the CEAI. The first element is management support, which relates to the willingness of senior managers to support an EO and to facilitate entrepreneurial ideas. The second factor is the use of rewards and reinforcement as already described under our review of HRM practices. The third factor is autonomy and discretion. Employees must perceive an environment that empowers them to focus on entrepreneurial projects and make decisions about process and implementation. The fourth factor is time availability and related resources. Innovative activities require that employees perceive the availability of slack resources to focus on entrepreneurial activity. Finally, the fifth element is organizational boundaries. Employees must perceive that the structure and processes in the organization do not obstruct idea implementation.

Numerous studies have been conducted to assess the reliability and validity of the CEAI. Kuratko et al. (1990) initially established the Intrapreneurship Assessment Instrument (IAI) which included Top Management Support, Autonomy/Work Discretion, and Rewards/ Reinforcement as factors related to an effective CE environment. Their results were reinforced by the findings of a study of 199 CEOs of US based corporations which examined these antecedents and the association between internal entrepreneurship and the financial performance of the firm (Zahra, 1991). Kuratko et al. (1999) expanded IAI and renamed it the CEAI. The expanded CEAI added Time Availability and Organizational Boundaries, and Hornsby et al. (1999) supported the existence of these factors in a cross-cultural study of Canadian and US firms. Hornsby et al. (2002) found additional support for the five-factor CEAI and established sound psychometric properties.

There is some limited knowledge about the role of organizational culture in promoting corporate entrepreneurship (e.g. Morris et al., 1994; Zahra et al., 2004). The limited research to date has tended to emphasize the role of individualism and collectivism, although without doubt other aspects of culture are expected to influence innovation and entrepreneurship (e.g. Chandler et al., 2000). With respect to individualism-collectivism, this is typically treated as a single continuum on which an organization may be more individualistic or more collectivistic. This dimension is relevant because on the one hand, it is the deviant behaviors of individuals willing to breach social norms, do something different, and pursue individual interests which lead to the acquisition or creation of new knowledge and ideas that present the foundation for innovation. On the other hand, for new knowledge to become embedded in products, processes or services it is essential that it be shared, combined and integrated, which requires com- munication and collaboration. Such behaviors are underpinned by more collectivistic values. As a result the case has been argued, and supportive empirical evidence produced, for a balance between collectivism and indi- vidualism. Such a balance provides sufficient individualistic values that mavericks can emerge and pursue their own interests, while still rewarding and valuing collectively oriented collaboration and sharing. Both Morris et al. (1994) and Zahra et al. (2004) provide evidence for an inverted 'U' shaped relationship between scores on a scale of individualism-collectivism and measures of entrepreneurship in organizations.

In summary, there is a growing body of evidence both for the broad contextual factors described in research on organizational environments, cultures, and leadership, and for the more specific dimensions of the human resource architecture. As described in Figure 4.1, these are inter- dependent rather than independent influences, and it is rare for studies to include all of these dimensions simultaneously. Nevertheless, the evidence is quite strong that these elements, individually and in combination, are influential upon EO and performance outcomes.

5. PERFORMANCE

Much research on the association between EO and performance has demonstrated a positive and often strong association. For example, Wiklund and Shepherd (2003) provide support for the hypothesis that through organizing knowledge-based resources to discover and exploit entrepreneurial opportunities, EO is related to multiple aspects of performance. In their study of Swedish SMEs they find a significant correlation between EO and their compound measure of performance of r=.34 (p<.01), and the effect of EO was not only direct, but also in interaction with a measure of the knowledge held by organizational members. A correlation greater than .30 is quite common within research on the performance influence of EO (Rauch et al., 2009) but it is not universal and it is not consistent over time. For example, Zahra and Covin (1995) provide evidence that it is in the most competitively hostile environments that corporate entrepreneurship pays off in terms of financial performance. Furthermore, the benefits of an entrepreneurial orientation do increase over time, reflecting the fact that it is a resource intensive strategy whose outcomes are only realized after a degree of development. In the case of Zahra and Covin's (1995) study of larger US companies across 14 industry sectors, the financial benefits were quite modest in the first few years with the strongest effects observed in the last two years (years six and seven) of the period under study.

The meta-analysis conducted by Rauch et al. (2009) provides the best evidence for the degree to which EO is associated with financial performance. They assembled 51 studies involving 53 independent samples that addressed the EO-performance relationship. Using Hunter and Schmidt's (1990) meta-analytic procedures to correct for measurement and sampling errors, Rauch et al. report an estimated population correlation of .242, which is considered to be moderately large (Cohen, 1977). For all performance measures (perceived nonfinancial performance, perceived financial performance, archival measures of financial performance, growth, and profitability), the corrected estimated population correlation ranged between .21 and .26, indicating a consistent relationship regardless of the ultimate metric.

However, Figure 4.1 also indicates that this relationship is not without important contingencies. Two that have emerged consistently in research over the last decade are absorptive capacity and ambidexterity. These two variables are expected to moderate the association between EO and organizational performance, measured in terms of market or financial outcomes. We now describe these relationships in more detail.

Absorptive Capacity

When organizational environments are characterized by uncertainty and change, teasing out cause and effect relationships, such as those between behaviors and outcomes, becomes increasingly difficult (Murray, 1984; Teese and Pisano, 1994). In such environments, it becomes even more important for organizations to understand how augmenting their existing processes with additional capabilities can help them become more successful (Zahra et al., 2009). In addition, ongoing knowledge acquisition and utilization becomes even more critical (Bottazzi et al., 2001; Chandler and Lyon, 2009).

The knowledge-based view of the firm suggests that knowledge resources are essential for facilitating an organization's performance (Grant, 1996). Knowledge of internal capabilities enables managers to more effectively align resources with initiatives (Kor and Mahoney, 2005). The ability to access heterogeneous knowledge bases and the differential use of similar knowledge bases can assist an organization in achieving its goals and gaining advantage over its rivals. In particular, when different but related innovations undergo R&D efforts, complementarities can be created that enhance the development of each innovation (Cohen and Malerba, 2001). Moreover, to the extent that much of the knowledge created during this process is tacit or intangible, this knowledge becomes increasingly important as organizations grow (Langlois and Robertson, 1996; Sanders and Boivie, 2004). Thus, an organization's ability to understand and utilize knowledge is instrumental in its efforts to develop in competitive environments.

Central to an organization's ability to comprehend and use knowledge is absorptive capacity. Absorptive capacity is the ability to 'recognize the value of new, external information, assimilate it, and apply it to commercial ends' (Cohen and Levinthal, 1990: 128). This ability is important for carrying out innovation. Consistent with this portrayal, Zahra and George (2002: 186) defined absorptive capacity as 'a set of organizational routines and processes by which firms acquire, assimilate, transform, and exploit knowledge to produce a dynamic organizational capability.' Zahra and George (2002) further separated absorptive capacity into potential and realized forms. Potential absorptive capacity focuses on the acquisition and assimilation of knowledge, while realized absorptive capacity focuses on the transformation and exploitation of knowledge. Together, these two forms of absorptive capacity provide an organization with the ability to use knowledge to innovate.

In particular, absorptive capacity influences the organization's ability to make the most of existing knowledge stocks and flows (Dierickx and Cool, 1989). This knowledge can flow from a variety of sources including customers (von Hippel, 1988), geographic locations, alliances, and research and development activities (DeCarolis and Deeds, 1999). Knowledge resources can be very valuable (Grant, 1996; Kogut and Zander, 1992), but those related to innovation can be difficult to manage effectively because of information asymmetry throughout the organization (He and Wang, 2009). The knowledge and the ability to utilize it are not spread uniformly around the organization so there may be some inefficiency if it is not broadly disseminated (Lenox and King, 2004). Thus, absorptive capacity enables an organization to effectively utilize knowledge to enhance organizational performance.

A widely used indicator of absorptive capacity is investment in R&D (e.g. Zahra and Hayton, 2008). Such investments create a stock of knowledge that can facilitate the identification of relevant new knowledge and technology underpinning innovation and entrepreneurship (Cohen and Levinthal, 1990). Without these investments in knowledge stocks, which are needed to support both recognition and the assimilation of new knowledge, the workforce's ability and the organization's opportunity for entrepreneurial action will be undermined. Absorptive capacity therefore serves as a constraint on organizations' capacity for generating value from EO. While an HR architecture and the organizational environment might promote an innovative, risk seeking and proactive workforce, without sufficient capacity to identify, acquire, and assimilate new knowledge within the organization, there will not be sufficient 'raw materials' for innovation and entrepreneurship to take place.

Ambidexterity

Organizations vary in the extent to which they focus on creating new business opportunities versus attempting to capitalize on existing ones (Mintzberg, 1973; Lamberg et al., 2009). Although some existing businesses (such as product lines) are prone to decline because of environmental changes, it is generally inefficient and extremely difficult to rely solely on establishing new businesses in an effort to increase performance. Therefore, most successful entrepreneurial organizations are likely to deploy some of their resources to efficiently manage existing businesses, termed exploitation, and some of their resources in efforts to create new businesses, termed exploration (Murray, 1984). Although there can be a wide variance in the emphasis that organizations place on exploitation versus exploration, some type of balance between the two is usually necessary to avoid severe misfit on one of them (Gresov, 1989), constraints associated with premature lock-in (Rivkin and Siggelkow, 2006), and negative performance implications (Uotila et al. 2009; Van Looy et al., 2005). Those organizations that are capable of simultaneously exploring innovations and exploiting them are referred to as ambidextrous (Duncan, 1976; Tushman and O'Reilly, 1996).

While it appears logical to engage in both exploitation and exploration simultaneously (Greve, 2007), organizations may have difficulty finding the right balance between the two and they may not be equally adept at managing both types of processes (Ebben and Johnson, 2005; Levinthal and March, 1993). For example, managerial preferences for internally or externally derived knowledge may exist and this could influence whether the organization focuses on exploitation and exploration (Menon and Pfeffer, 2003). In addition, organizations tend to continue doing what they already know how to do by relying on routines so they may misapply existing solutions (Cohen et al., 1972) or rely on previous capabilities that have become core rigidities (Leonard-Barton, 1992). These conditions can lead to overreliance on exploration or exploitation. The general recommendation is for organizations to be flexible in seeking valuable opportunities, but then committed to their exploitation once they have been discovered (Ghemawat, 1991). Exploitation and exploration act as complements (Boumgarden et al., 2012) in that exploitation enables the organization to capture the potential returns identified with the opportunity (Hill and Rothaermel, 2003). However, too much focus on exploitation may provide short-term performance benefits but damage the organization's ability to profit from future opportunities and subsequently survive in the long run (Van Looy et al., 2005).

Part of the challenge associated with being ambidextrous is that the routines involved with exploitation are often different from and interfere with those associated with exploration (Benner and Tushman, 2003; Duncan, 1976). For example, exploitation involves working with existing knowledge (Lechner et al., 2010) and focusing on such things as seeking control, certainty, and invariance in order to extract maximum profits from existing capabilities and positions (He and Wong, 2004; March, 1991). If not managed appropriately, goals of this type can interfere with the search for and promotion of future opportunities (Benner and Tushman, 2003; Sterman et al., 1997). Moreover, when these efforts require significant change, the more institutionalized the exploitation activities are, the more resistance there is likely to be to change efforts (Giddens, 1984; Jarzabkowski, 2008). In other words, future adaptation can be impaired if the organization has adapted too well to its current environment (Levinthal, 1994). In contrast, an excessive focus on exploration can also negatively influence performance because it inhibits profiting from previously captured opportunities. For example, excessive exploration can cause the disruption of routinized processes associated with exploitation, thereby causing inefficiencies (Hannan and Freeman, 1984).

In addition, newer organizations may not have sufficient resources to easily and productively engage in both exploitation and exploration at the same time (March, 1991). Therefore, it is particularly important for these organizations to be ambidextrous in regards to accomplishing both exploitation and exploration (Mahoney and Pandian, 1992; Penrose, 1959; Van Looy et al., 2005). Using organizational resources for exploitation and exploration efforts can lead to a sustainable competitive advantage (Sirmon et al., 2007). However, it can be difficult switching between these efforts because organizational members who benefit from the current power structure of the organization are not inclined to risk a loss to their organizational standing as the organization transforms from one mode to the other (Pfeffer, 1992).

One option to enhance the ability to be ambidextrous is to isolate exploration and exploitation activities either temporally or spatially (Benner and Tushman, 2003; Christensen and Bower, 1996; Nickerson and Zenger, 2002). Along these lines, Thompson (1967) suggested that organizations isolate their technical cores from external uncertainty in order to improve efficiency, while separately dealing with that uncertainty outside of the technical core in order to enhance adaptation of the organization. This type of decoupling can increase flexibility (Doz and Kosonen, 2010). In a similar fashion, managers can try to develop the parts of the organization that have achieved successful exploration and need to operate in an exploitative manner to enhance performance. Simultaneously, managers can strengthen exploration efforts, such as developing new technologies, while using a different set of competences (Danneels, 2008). Another approach is to move between exploitation and exploration over time such that the organization vacillates between the two as needed, thereby lessening any negative effects from concurrent engagement (Boumgarden et al., 2012). In addition, semi-structures can be used to enable simultaneous actions associated with efficiency and exploration (Brown and Eisenhardt, 1998). These structures can be designed to provide some guidance for efficiency purposes and some flexibility for adjustment when engaging in exploration. Isolation, vacillation, and semi-structures can enable organizations to enhance their ambidexterity, and subsequently improve performance (Boumgarden et al., 2012; Eisenhardt et al., 2010).

Ambidexterity therefore represents an important moderator of the association between EO and measures of organizational performance. The relationship between EO and performance will be constrained by the degree to which EO is balanced by the continued maintenance of exploitative capabilities. If EO is not balanced with exploitative capabilities, then the organization will potentially remain in an exploratory mode, and will fail to exploit existing capacity. While the addition of new businesses and the development of new opportunities can add to top line growth (e.g. Rauch et al., 2009; Zahra, 1996), the literature on ambidexterity suggests that economic efficiency and long run survival will depend upon the ability to successfully exploit newly built capabilities. Therefore, ambidexterity is expected to positively moderate the association between EO and diverse measures of organizational performance such as sales growth, financial performance and organizational survival.

6.   CONCLUSION

The question of how to design management practices that will support entrepreneurial behavior within organizations has now been examined across a range of contexts. This literature has suggested several core 'success factors', which support an EO and corporate entrepreneurial performance. These factors can be understood as HR architecture elements on the one hand, and organizational environment factors on the other. It is also clear that these elements are somewhat interdependent. Investments in HRM will have a reciprocal relationship with the culture that both supports and is reinforced by those investments. The employee-organization relationship and the formal employment contracts that are used are both likely to reflect organizational cultures, and reinforce them.

While there have now been a number of empirical and conceptual studies of these interesting relationships, several potential avenues remain for further development. For example, research has tended to focus on one or other of these sets of factors. Research on the CEAI, for example, tends not to take a very detailed look at HRM systems, while research on HR systems tends to overlook culture and leadership issues. What is much needed is research that incorporates both of these dimensions simultaneously. We do not know, for example, the extent to which they are empirically distinct from one another, nor their incremental contribution to predicting entrepreneurial outcomes.

The micro-processes underlying the association between HRM practices and EO or corporate entrepreneurial outcomes have received only limited attention to date. There is evidence that investments in HRM influence the creation of knowledge sharing networks, which in turn impact learning and innovation (e.g. Collins and Smith, 2006; Collins and Clark, 2003; Kang et al., 2007). What is needed is more focused research on ways in which individual practices influence the ability and willingness of employees to accept risk and make innovative, entrepreneurial contributions. For example, how do extrinsic and intrinsic rewards and incentives impact entrepreneurial behaviors in organizations? What are the individual characteristics required to support entrepreneurial actions, and how are these identified or nurtured? To what extent can formal employee participation systems facilitate the identification and pursuit of entrepreneurial opportunities that lead organizations in new directions?

A further set of questions deserving of attention relate to the role of HRM in supporting the creation of entrepreneurial capabilities (Chadwick and Dabu, 2009). We have emphasized the creation of an EO as a mediating process. However, a second pathway for the influence of HRM on organizational outcomes is through the development of strategic capabilities (Wright et al., 2001). Capabilities are an 'intermediate good' (Amit and Schoemaker, 1993) that create value by enhancing the productivity of resources, and thereby influence more distal organizational performance metrics. Entrepreneurial capabilities include the ability to identify and evaluate opportunities, source and assimilate resources, and recombine existing resources for new applications. Therefore entrepreneurial capabilities rest on specific organizational processes in combination with intangibles such as intellectual, human and social capital and organizational culture and leadership. The complementarity between these resources and strategic processes is highly firm specific and path-dependent and therefore an important source of heterogeneity (e.g. Teece et al., 1997). The most important implication is that capabilities are influenced by investments in human resources *in combination with* other processes and technologies (Wright et al., 2001). Research on the content and form of such combinations between HR, culture, leadership and the strategic processes that support organizational entrepreneurship are sorely needed as they will offer a far more nuanced view of the relationships that have been reviewed in this chapter.

Notwithstanding these opportunities for future research, it is clear that knowledge in this field has progressed significantly over the past two decades, thanks in large part to several empirical studies that have successfully measured and quantified these relationships and subjected them to rigorous testing. We hope that our modest review may provide a basis for further thought on this important project.

REFERENCES

Amit, R. and Schoemaker, P.J.H. 1993. Strategic assets and organizational rent. *Strategic Management Journal*, 14: 33–46.

Batt, R. 2002. Managing customer services: human resource practices, quit rates, and sales growth. *Academy of Management Journal*, 45 (3): 587–597.

Becker, B.E. and Huselid, M.A. 1998. High performance work systems and firm performance: a synthesis of research and managerial implications. *Research in Personnel and Human Resources*, JAI Press.

Becker, B.E. and Huselid, M.A. 2006. Strategic human resources management: where do we go from here? *Journal of Management*, 32: 898–925.

Benner, M.J. and Tushman, M.L. 2003. Exploitation, exploration, and process management: the productivity dilemma revisited. *Academy of Management Review*, 28 (2): 238–256.

Beugelsdijk, Sjoerd 2008. Strategic human resource practices and product innovation. *Organization Studies*, 29: 821–827.

Bohlander, G. and Snell, S. 2004. *Managing Human Resources*. Cincinnati: South-Western.

Bottazzi, G., Dosi, G. and Rocchetti, G. 2001. Models of knowledge accumulation, entry regimes and patterns of industrial evolution. *Industrial and Corporate Change*, 10 (3): 609–638.

Boumgarden, P., Nickerson, J., and Zenger, T.R. 2012. Sailing into the wind: exploring the relationships among ambidexterity, vacillation, and organizational performance. *Strategic Management Journal*, 33: 587–610.

Brown, S.L. and Eisenhardt, K.M. 1998. *Competing on the Edge: Strategy as Structured Chaos*. Boston: Harvard Business School Press.

Burgelman, R.A. 1983. A model of the interaction of strategic behavior, corporate context, and the concept of strategy. *Academy of Management Review*, 8 (1): 61–70.

Burgelman, R.A. 1988. Strategy making as a social learning process: the case of internal corporate venturing. *Interfaces*, 18: 74–85.

Cascio, W.F. and Aguinis, H. 2008. Chapter 3: Staffing twenty-first-century organizations. *The Academy of Management Annals*, 2: 133–165.

Chadwick, C. and Dabu, A. 2009. Human resources, human resource management, and the competitive advantage of firms: towards a more comprehensive model of causal linkages. *Organization Science*, 20 (1): 253–272.

Chandler, G.N. and Lyon, D.W. 2009. Involvement in knowledge-acquisition activities by venture team members and venture performance. *Entrepreneurship Theory and Practice*, 33 (3): 571–592.

Chandler, G.N., Keller, C. and Lyon, D.W. 2000. Unraveling the determinants and consequences of an innovation supportive culture. *Entrepreneurship Theory and Practice*, 25 (1): 59–76.

Christensen, C.M. 1997. *The Innovator's Dilemma*. Boston, MA: Harvard Business School Press.

Christensen, C.M. and Bower, J.L. 1996. Customer power, strategic investment, and the failure of leading firms. *Strategic Management Journal*, 17 (3): 197–218.

Cohen, J. 1977. *Statistical Power Analysis for the Behavioral Science*. New York: Academic Press.

Cohen, W.M. and Levinthal, D.A. 1990. Absorptive capacity: a new perspective on learning and innovation. *Administrative Science Quarterly*, 35: 128–152.

Cohen, W.M. and Malerba, F. 2001. Is the tendency to variation a chief cause of progress? *Industrial and Corporate Change*, 10 (3): 587–608.

Cohen, M.D., March, J.G. and Olsen, J.P. 1972. A garbage can model of organizational choice. *Administrative Science Quarterly*, 17 (1): 1–25.

Collins, C.J. and Clark, K.D. 2003. Strategic human resource practices, top management team social networks, and firm performance: the role of human resource practices in creating organizational competitive advantage. *Academy of Management Journal*, 46 (6): 740–751.

Collins, C.J. and Smith, K.G. 2006. Knowledge exchange and combination: the role of human resource practices in the performance of high-technology firms. *Academy of Management Journal*, 49 (3): 544–560.

Combs, J., Liu, Y., Hall, A. and Ketchen, D. 2006. How much do high-performance work practices matter? A meta-analysis of their effects on organizational performance. *Personnel Psychology*, 59: 501–528.

Covin, J.G. and Slevin, D.P. 1989. Strategic management of small firms in hostile and benign environments. *Strategic Management Journal*, 10: 75–87.

Damanpour, F. 1991. Organizational innovation: a meta-analysis of effects of determinants and moderators. *Academy of Management Journal*, 34 (3): 555–590.

Danneels, E. 2008. Organizational antecedents of second-order competences. *Strategic Management Journal*, 29: 519–543.

DeCarolis, D.M. and Deeds, D.L. 1999. The impact of stocks and flows of organizational knowledge on firm performance: an empirical investigation of the bio-technology industry. *Strategic Management Journal*, 20: 953–968.

Delery, J.E. and Shaw, J.D. 2001. The strategic management of people in work organizations: review, synthesis, and extension. In G.R. Ferris (ed.), *Research in Personnel and Human Resources Management*, Volume 20. Stamford, CT: JAI Press, pp. 165–197.

Dierickx, I. and Cool, K. 1989. Asset stock accumulation and sustainability of competitive advantage. *Management Science*, 35 (12): 1504–1513.

Doz, Y.L. and Kosonen, M. 2010. Embedding strategic agility. *Long Range Planning*, 43: 370–382.

Duncan, R.B. 1976. The ambidextrous organization: designing dual structures for innovation. In R.H. Kilmann, L.R. Pondy and D.P. Slevin (eds), *The Management of Organization Design*, Vol. 1. Strategies and Implementation. New York: North-Holland, pp. 167–188.

Ebben, J.J. and Johnson, A.C. 2005. Efficiency, flexibility, or both? Evidence linking strategy to performance in small firms. *Strategic Management Journal*, 26: 1249–1259.

Eisenberger, R.L., Fasolo, P. and Davis-LaMastro, V. 1990. Perceived organizational support and employee diligence, commitment, and innovation. *Journal of Applied Psychology*, 75: 51–59.

Eisenhardt, K.M., Furr, N.R. and Bingham, C.B. 2010. Microfoundations of performance: balancing efficiency and flexibility in dynamic environments. *Organization Science*, 21 (6): 1263–1273.

Ghemawat, P. 1991. *Commitment: The Dynamic of Strategy.* New York: The Free Press.

Giddens, A. 1984. *The Constitution of Society.* Berkeley, CA: The University of California Press.

Grant, R.M. 1996.Toward a knowledge-based theory of the firm. *Strategic Management Journal*, 17 (Winter Special Issue): 109–122.

Gresov, C. 1989. Exploring fit and misfit with multiple contingencies. *Administrative Science Quarterly*, 34: 431–453.

Greve, H.R. 2007. Exploration and exploitation in product innovation. *Industrial and Corporate Change*, 16 (5): 945–975.

Hannan, M.T. and Freeman, J. 1984. Structural inertia and organizational change. *American Sociological Review*, 49: 149–164.

Hayton, J. 2003. Strategic human capital management in SMEs: an empirical study of entrepreneurial performance. *Human Resource Management*, 42: 375–391.

Hayton, J.C. 2005. Promoting corporate entrepreneurship through human resource management practices: a review of empirical research. *Human Resource Management Review*, 15: 21–41.

Hayton, J. and Kelley, D. 2006. A competency-based framework for promoting corporate entrepreneurship. *Human Resource Management*, 45: 407–427.

He, J. and Wang, H.C. 2009. Innovative knowledge assets and economic performance: the asymmetric roles of incentives and monitoring. *Academy of Management Journal,* 52 (5): 919–938.

He, Z. and Wong, P. 2004. Exploration vs. exploitation: an empirical test of the ambidexterity hypothesis. *Organization Science*, 15 (4): 481–494.

Hill, C.W.L. and Rothaermel, F.T. 2003. The performance of incumbent firms in the face of radical technological innovation. *Academy of Management Review*, 28 (2): 257–274.

Hisrich, R.D. and Peters, M.P. 1986. Establishing a new business venture unit within a firm. *Journal of Business Venturing,* 1, 307–322.

Hornsby, J.S., Naffziger, D.W., Kuratko, D.F. and Montagno, R.V. 1993. An interactive model of the corporate entrepreneurship process. *Entrepreneurship Theory and Practice*, Winter: 29–37.

Hornsby, J.S., Kuratko, D.F. and Montagno, R.V 1999. Perception of internal factors for corporate entrepreneurship: a comparison of Canadian and U.S. managers. *Entrepreneurship Theory and Practice*, Winter: 9–24.

Hornsby, J.S., Kuratko, D.F. and Zahra, S.A. 2002. Middle managers' perception of the internal environment for corporate entrepreneurship: assessing a measurement scale. *Journal of Business Venturing*, 17: 253–273.

Hornsby, J.S., Kuratko, D.F., Shepherd, D.A. and Bott, J.P. 2009. Managers' corporate entrepreneurial actions: examining perception and position. *Journal of Business Venturing*, 24 (3): 236–247.

Hornsby, J.S., Kuratko, D.F., Holt, D.T. and Wales, W.J. 2012. Assessing a measurement of organizational preparedness for corporate entrepreneurial behavior. *Journal of Product Innovation Management* (forthcoming, accepted 26 September 2011).

Hunter, J.E. and Schmidt, F.L. 1990. *Methods of MetaAnalysis: Correcting Error and Bias in Research Findings.* Newbury Park, CA: Sage.

Huselid, M.A. 1995. The impact of human resource management practices on turnover, productivity, and corporate financial performance. *Academy of Management Journal*, 38: 635–672.

Jarzabkowski, P. 2008. Shaping strategy as a structuration process. *Academy of Management Journal*, 51 (4): 621–650.

Kang, S.-C., Morris, S.S. and Snell, S.A. 2007. Relational archetypes, organizational learning, and value creation: extending the human resource architecture. *Academy of Management Review*, 32 (1): 236–256.

Kelley, D.J., Peters, L. and O'Connor, G.C. 2009. Intra-organizational networking for innovation-based corporate entrepreneurship. *Journal of Business Venturing*, 24 (3): 221–235.

Kogut, B. and Zander, U. 1992. Knowledge of the firm, combinative capabilities, and the replication of technology. *Organization Science*, 3: 383–397.

Kor, Y.Y. and Mahoney, J.T. 2005. How dynamics, management, and governance of resource deployments influence firm-level performance. *Strategic Management Journal*, 26: 489–496.

Kuratko, D.F., Montagno, R.V. and Hornsby, J.S. 1990. Developing an intrapreneurial assessment instrument for an effective corporate entrepreneurial environment. *Strategic Management Journal*, 11, 49–58.

Kuratko, D.F., Hornsby, J.S. and Montagno, R.V. 1999. Perception of internal factors for corporate entrepreneurship: a comparison of Canadian and U.S. managers. *Entrepreneurship Theory and Practice*, 24: 9–24.

Kuratko, D.F., Ireland, R.D. and Hornsby, J.S. 2001. Improving firm performance through entrepreneurial actions: Acordia's corporate entrepreneurship strategy. *Academy of Management Executive*, 15: 60–71.

Kuratko, D.F., Ireland, R.D., Hornsby, J.S. and Covin, J.G. 2005. A model of middle-level managers' entrepreneurial behavior. *Entrepreneurship Theory and Practice*, 29: 699–716.

Lamberg, J., Tikkanen, H., Nokelainen, T. and Suur-Inkeroinen, H. 2009. Competitive dynamics, strategic consistency, and organizational survival. *Strategic Management Journal*, 30: 45–60.

Langlois, R. and Robertson, P. 1996. *Firms, Markets and Economic Change: A Dynamic Theory of Business Institutions*. London: Routledge.

Lechner, C., Frankerberger, K. and Floyd, S.W. 2010. Task contingencies in the curvilinear relationships between intergroup networks and initiative performance. *Academy of Management Journal*, 53 (4): 865–889.

Lenox, M. and King, A. 2004. Prospects for developing absorptive capacity through internal information provision. *Strategic Management Journal*, 25: 331–345.

Leonard-Barton, D. 1992. Core capabilities and core rigidities: a paradox in managing new product development. *Strategic Management Journal*, 13: 111–125.

Lepak, D.P. and Snell, S.A. 1999. The human resource architecture: toward a theory of human capital allocation and development. *Academy of Management Review*, 24 (1): 31–48.

Lepak, D.P. and Snell, S.A. 2002. Examining the human resource architecture: the relationships among human capital, employment, and human resource configurations. *Journal of Management*, 28 (4): 517–543.

Lepak, D.P., Takeuchi, R. and Snell, S.A. 2003. Employment flexibility and firm performance: examining the interaction effects of employment mode, environmental dynamism, and technological uncertainty. *Journal of Management*, 29 (5), 681–703.

Lerner, M., Azulay, I. and Tishler, A. 2009. The role of compensation methods in corporate entrepreneurship. *International Studies of Management and Organization*, 39: 53–81.

Levinthal, D. 1994. Surviving Schumpeterian environments: an evolutionary perspective. In J.A.C. Baum and J.V. Singh (eds), *Evolutionary Dynamics of Organizations*. New York: Oxford University Press, pp. 167–178.

Levinthal, D.A. and March, J.G. 1993. The myopia of learning. *Strategic Management Journal*, 14: 95–112.

Mahoney, J.T. and Pandian, J.R. 1992. The resource-based view within the conversation of strategic management. *Strategic Management Journal*, 13: 363–380.

March, J.G. 1991. Exploration and exploitation in organizational learning. *Organization Science*, 2 (1): 71–87.

March, J.G. and Simon, H.A. 1958. *Organizations*. New York: Wiley.

Menon, T. and Pfeffer, J. 2003. Valuing internal vs. external knowledge: explaining the preference for outsiders. *Management Science*, 49 (4): 497–513.

Messersmith, J.G. and Guthrie, J.P. 2010. High performance work systems in emergent organizations: implications for firm performance. *Human Resource Management*, 49: 244–266.

Miller, D. 1983. The correlates of entrepreneurship in three types of firms. *Management Science*, 297: 770–791.

Mintzberg, H. 1973. Strategy-making in three modes. *California Management Review*, 16 (2): 44–53.

Morris, M.H., Davis, D.L. and Allen, J.W. 1994. Fostering corporate entrepreneurship: cross-cultural comparisons of the importance of individualism versus collectivism. *Journal of International Business Studies*, 25 (1): 65–89.

Murray, J.A. 1984. A concept of entrepreneurial strategy. *Strategic Management Journal*, 5 (1): 1–13.

Nadler, D., Gerstein, S. and Shaw, R. 1992. *Organizational Architecture: Designs for Changing Organizations*. San Francisco: Jossey-Bass, p. 118.

Nadler, D.A., Nadler, M.B. and Tushman, M.L. 1997. *Competing by Design: The Power of Organizational Architecture*. Oxford University Press, pp. 147–153.

Nickerson, J.A. and Zenger, T.R. 2002. Being efficiently fickle: a dynamic theory of organizational choice. *Organization Science*, 13 (5): 547–566.

Penrose, E.T. 1959. *The Theory of the Growth of the Firm*. New York: John Wiley.

Pfeffer, J. 1992. *Managing with Power*. Boston: Harvard Business School Press.

Ployhart, R.E. and Moliterno, T.P. 2011. Emergence of the human capital resource: a multilevel model. *Academy of Management Review*, 36: 127–150.

Quinn, J.B. 1985. Managing innovation: controlled chaos. *Harvard Business Review*, 63 (3): 73–84.

Rauch, A., Wiklund, J., Lumpkin, G.T., and Frese, M. 2009. Entrepreneurial orientation and business performance: an assessment of past research and suggestions for the future. *Entrepreneurship Theory and Practice*, 33 (3): 761–787.

Rivkin, J.W. and Siggelkow, N. 2006. Organizing to strategize in the face of interactions: preventing premature lock-in. *Long Range Planning*, 39: 591–614.

Rousseau, D.M. 1995. *Psychological Contracts in Organizations: Understanding Written and Unwritten Agreements*. Thousand Oaks, CA: Sage.

Sanders, W.G. and Boivie, S. 2004. Sorting things out: valuation of new firms in uncertain markets. *Strategic Management Journal*, 25: 167–186.

Sathe, V. 1989. Fostering entrepreneurship in the large diversified firm. *Organizational Dynamics*, 18: 20–32.

Sirmon, D.G., Hitt, D.G. and Ireland, R.D. 2007. Managing firm resources in dynamic environments to create value: looking inside the black box. *Academy of Management Review*, 32 (1): 273–292.

Sterman, J.D., Repenning, N.P. and Kofman, F. 1997. Unanticipated side effects of successful quality programs: exploring a paradox of organizational improvement. *Management Science*, 43 (4): 503–521.

Sun, L., Aryee, S. and Law, K.S. 2007. High-performance human resource practices, citizenship behavior, and organizational performance: a relational perspective. *Academy of Management Journal*, 50 (3): 558–577.

Sutton, R.L. 2001. The weird rules of creativity. *Harvard Business Review*, September: 94–103.

Teece, D.J., Pisano, G. and Shuen, A. 1997. Dynamic capabilities and strategic management. *Strategic Management Journal*, 18 (7): 509–533.

Thornhill, S. 2006. Knowledge, innovation and firm performance in high- and low-technology regimes. *Journal of Business Venturing*, 21 (5): 687–703.

Tsui, A. and Wang, D. 2002. Employment relationships from the employer's perspective: current research and future directions. *International Review of Industrial and Organizational Psychology*, 17: 77–114.

Tsui, A.S., Pearce, J.L., Porter, L.W. and Tripoli, A.M. 1997. Alternative approaches to the employee-organization relationship: does investment in employees pay off? *Academy of Management Journal*, 40 (5): 1089–1121.

Tushman, M.L. and C.A. O'Reilly. 1996. Ambidextrous organizations: managing evolutionary and revolutionary change. *California Management Review*, 38: 8–30.

Uotila, J., Maula, M., Keil, T. and Zahra, S.A. 2009. Exploration, exploitation, and financial performance: analysis of S&P 500 corporations. *Strategic Management Journal*, 30: 221–231.

Van Looy, B., Martens, T. and Debackere, K. 2005. Organizing for continuous innovation: on the sustainability of ambidextrous organizations. *Creativity and Innovation Management*, 14 (3): 208–221.

Von Hippel, E. 1988. *The Sources of Innovation*. New York: Oxford University Press.

Way, S.A. 2002. High performance work systems and intermediate indicators of firm performance within the US small business sector. *Journal of Management*, 28: 765–785.

Wiklund, J. and Shepherd, D. 2003. Knowledge-based resources, entrepreneurial orientation, and the performance of small and medium-sized businesses. *Strategic Management Journal*, 24: 1307–1319.

Williamson, O.E. 1975. *Markets and Hierarchies: Analysis and Antitrust Implications*. New York: Free Press.

Wolcott, R.C. and Lippitz, M.J. 2007. The four models of corporate entrepreneurship. *Sloan Management Review*, 49 (1): 75–82.

Wright, P.M. and Boswell, W.R. 2002. Desegregating HRM: a review and synthesis of micro and macro human resource management research. *Journal of Management*, 28 (3): 247–276.

Wright, P.M., MacMahan, G.C. and McWilliams, A. 1994. Human resources and sustained competitive advantage: a resource-based perspective. *International Journal of Human Resource Management*, 5 (2): 301–326.

Wright, P.M., Dunford, B. and Snell, S.A. 2001. Human resources and the resource based view of the firm. *Journal of Management*, 27: 701–721.

Youndt, M.A. and Snell, S.A. 2004. Human resource configurations, intellectual capital, and organizational performance. *Journal of Managerial Issues*, XVI (3): 337–360.

Zahra, S.A. 1991. Predictors and financial outcomes of corporate entrepreneurship: an exploratory study. *Journal of Business Venturing*, 6 (4): 259–285.

Zahra, S.A. 1996. Governance, ownership, and corporate entrepreneurship: the moderating impact of industry technological opportunities. *Academy of Management Journal*, 39 (6): 1713–1735.

Zahra, S.A., and Covin, J.G. 1995. Contextual influences on the corporate entrepreneurship-performance relationship: a longitudinal analysis. *Journal of Business Venturing*, 10: 43–58.

Zahra, S.A. and George, G. 2002. Absorptive capacity: a review, reconceptualization, and extension. *Academy of Management Review*, 27 (2): 185–203.

Zahra, S.A. and Hayton, J.C. 2008. The effect of international venturing on firm performance: the moderating influence of absorptive capacity. *Journal of Business Venturing*, 23 (2): 195–220.

Zahra, S.A., Hayton, J.C. and Salvato, C. 2004. Entrepreneurship in family versus non-family firms: a resource-based analysis of the effect of organizational culture. *Entrepreneurship Theory and Practice*, 28 (4): 363–381.

Zahra, S.A., Filatotchev, I. and Wright, M. 2009. How do threshold firms sustain corporate entrepreneurship? The role of boards and absorptive capacity. *Journal of Business Venturing*, 24: 248–260.

Zhang, Z. and Jia, M. 2010. Using social exchange theory to predict the effects of high-performance human resource practices on corporate entrepreneurship: evidence from China. *Human Resource Management*, 49: 743–765.

Zhang, Z., Wan, D. and Jia, M. 2008. Do high performance human resource practices help corporate entrepreneurship? The mediating role of organizational citizenship behavior. *Journal of High Technology Management Research*, 19 (2): 128–138.

5. Government policy and human resource development

Jonathan Winterton and Nigel Haworth

1. INTRODUCTION

This chapter considers the role of government policies in promoting training and development in general, and especially policies designed to build sustainable growth by investing in workforce skills to raise productivity and performance. It is no exaggeration to claim that competence development is now explicitly and universally at the centre of social and economic policy, and not just education, training and employment policies, to a greater degree than ever before. This policy focus has been the result of inter-related political, economic, social, technological and organizational developments, each of which is briefly considered in the next section exploring the drivers of change. After outlining the changes promoting such unprecedented interest in human capital development, the following section traces the principal policy imperatives of international organizations and the strategies they have promoted. Section 4 explores how these policy imperatives have been taken up by supra-national bodies, contrasting the experiences of the European Union (EU) and the Asia Pacific Economic Cooperation Forum (APEC). Given the diversity of constituent member states and member economies, Section 5 explores implementation by governments in each of these regions. Section 6 assesses the implications of the layered effects of global economic shift, the 2008 financial crisis and the unfolding post-2010 Eurozone sovereign debt crisis on efforts to increase human resource development (HRD). Finally some conclusions are offered on the challenges of developing policies for training and development in a rapidly changing world.

2. DRIVERS OF CHANGE

One of the most important political changes of the last 30 years was the reappearance of neo-liberal political-economy in the USA and UK in the

1980s which became globally hegemonic within a decade, making market fundamentalism central to strategies of international and supra-national institutions. Stagnating productivity in manufacturing industries and deteriorating global competitiveness, typified by 'Eurosclerosis', was blamed on macroeconomic mismanagement and over-regulation by the state, insulating enterprises from the effect of free market forces and enabling trade unions to distort labour markets and impede technological progress. Traditional Keynesian policies were seen as inadequate for responding to the emerging crisis, leading to rejection of the post-war 'Keynesian compromise' and accommodation between the institutions of capital and labour. The Keynesian welfare state gave way to a 'Schumpeterian Workfare State' (Jessop, 1992: 9) and demand-side management to secure 'full employment' was replaced by supply-side interventions to promote 'employability' (Finn, 2000).

Economic liberalization and deregulation promoted by this new politics accelerated the global shift already underway in trade between developed market economies, developing market economies and the eastern trading area (Dicken, 1992). This process of 'globalization' (removal of barriers to free trade and closer integration of national economies as defined by Stiglitz, 2002) involved increasingly higher value added activities, which, coupled with market fragmentation, further intensified global competition (De Woot, 1990). Moreover, the globalization of economic activity (Taylor and Thrift, 1986) revealed the vulnerability of labour-intensive mass production industries to imports from low-wage economies, since Taylorist production is easily replicated in newly industrialized countries (Dicken, 1992). Market fundamentalism even rendered the UK energy sector vulnerable to imports despite the long lead-time to exploitation of natural resources and the risk of sterilization of reserves (Rutledge and Wright, 2010). In a book that influenced American policy at the time, Reich (1991) argued that in the face of such globalization the competitiveness of nations depended on the capacity of citizens to enhance their skills and productive capacity.

In social terms, Sanderson (1998) highlighted the importance of world demographic shifts, including population growth in emerging economies and the ageing population in the West. World population is set to continue to grow until the standard of living of developing countries approaches that of the industrialized nations, but the population of Europe, North America and Japan will soon peak and then decline. The ageing population and continued problems of long-term and youth unemployment, present a serious risk of social divisions becoming more pronounced. Gender segregation is likely to remain a feature of both European and UK labour markets in the medium term and this has been recognized both as a barrier to economic efficiency and a factor exacerbating skills shortages, particularly in technologically based occupations within the EU (Rees, 1998).

Technological transformation has always been a catalyst of change in industrial development (Landes, 2003) and has played a particularly profound role since the development of flexible microprocessor-based innovations, widely seen as the major driver of change during the 1980s (Zuboff, 1988). Technology is both an 'engine of economic growth' (Schumpeter, 1939) and a catalyst for industrial restructuring (Hicks, 1988), so there are positive and negative impacts on employment. The microelectronics revolution (Forester, 1980) followed by an exponential growth in communication and information (Ito, 1994) and the integration of information and communication technologies (ICT) affected all aspects of economic activity (Freeman and Soete, 1994). The growth of knowledge work (Machlup, 1962) and knowledge based industries was associated with major changes in the nature of work (Ducatel et al., 2000) and the emergence of the much-predicted 'post-industrial society' (Bell, 1973), 'information society' (Freeman et al., 1993) and 'knowledge society' (Drucker, 1993). Most importantly from the point of view of human capital development, technological changes eliminated occupations and created new ones, leading to serious skills mismatches in labour markets (Handel, 2003) necessitating innovative human capital development initiatives.

In response to these external changes a range of restructuring strategies were adopted by organizations (Heugens and Schenk, 2004) including business process re-engineering (BPR), a set of internal restructuring methods popularized by Hammer and Champy (1983). Such strategies aimed to make organizational structures more flexible by replacing functional departments with smaller autonomous work units designed to undertake business processes, focussing on quality, delivery and cost imperatives in a changing market (Hammer and Stanton, 1995). Downsizing, defined as the 'conscious use of personnel reductions ... to improve ... efficiency and/or effectiveness', was also pursued independently of other forms of organizational restructuring (Budros, 1999: 70): reactively in face of recession (Ryan and Macky, 1998) and proactively as a key human resource strategy (Chadwick et al., 2004). All countries have experienced waves of restructuring at some period, and while this was particularly evident in economies with a high dependence on agriculture or primary industries, in recent years the effects have been particularly marked on manufacturing industries. Since restructuring changes the nature of occupations and the boundaries between them (Valenduc et al., 2008), it also affects the distribution of skills. Processes of deskilling, reskilling and upskilling co-exist even in the same sector (Gallie et al., 2004) and obviously have major implications for training and development. At the same time, the growth of 'atypical' work, including homeworking, casual and temporary working, sub-contracting and self-employment, in the 1990s and again since 2008 (Broughton et al., 2010) means that organizations are more reluctant to provide training and individuals find it more difficult to access learning opportunities.

It has long been recognized that developing workforce skills can have a major impact on organizational competitiveness (Lado and Wilson, 1994; Schuler and MacMillan, 1984; Schuler and Jackson, 1987) as well as on national economies (Briggs, 1987; Zidan 2001). Evidently there are specific issues of transition where countries are transforming from soviet planned economies to market economies, as well as in countries that are undergoing reconstruction after conflict, such as the states that were formerly part of Yugoslavia, or after major social changes, such as South Africa. Equally there are particular developmental issues associated with modernization, but on very different scales if one compares, for example Turkey and Vietnam, or some of the countries in sub-Saharan Africa that lack the basic essentials of water, sanitation and food. In all of these situations skill formation obviously plays a central role. Yet, many of the same problems appear in OECD countries that are unaffected by these particular issues. It appears that skills mismatches are almost universal (Manacorda and Petrongolo, 1999), that many employers are reluctant to provide training (Hoeckel, 2008) and that educational provision is often insufficiently adapted to changing labour market needs (Neugart and Schömann, 2002).

3. POLICY IMPERATIVES OF INTERNATIONAL ORGANIZATIONS

These drivers of change increasingly made the political economy of skill formation a focus of international policy, particularly during the past two decades. International organizations like the Organisation for Economic Co-operation and Development (OECD), World Trade Organization (WTO), International Monetary Fund (IMF), United Nations Development Program (UNDP) and the World Bank continued to promote free market ideas, but also increasingly emphasized the importance of state-led initiatives to develop human capital, especially for developing and transition economies (UNDP, 1990; World Bank, 1997). This focus on human capital development is reflected with unusual unanimity in policies promoted by international bodies like the OECD and the International Labour Office (ILO), as well as in the policies of regional supra-state bodies such as the European Union (EU) and the Asia-Pacific Economic Cooperation (APEC) forum.

The UNDP has been particularly influential in the Middle East, where Jordan, Kuwait, Oman, and the United Emirates all have national HRD programmes (UNDP, 2003) and the ILO recently helped draft a new employment and training plan for Bahrain. Saudi Arabia introduced initiatives to address chronic skills gaps in the indigenous population and reduce dependence on expatriates, but employers report continuing skills gaps in relation to work ethics, specialized knowledge and generic skills (Baqadir et al., 2011). Similarly, South Africa passed a Skills Development Act in 1998 as part of its Programme of Reconstruction and Development, aimed at promoting economic growth as well as reducing poverty and inequality through a National Skills Development Strategy (NSDS) (Kraak, 2005). Results in the first few years have been disappointing as the NSDS has suffered from a lack of political will in ensuring the success of an integrated approach to education and training; severe governance problems, including financial mismanagement; and serious operational problems (Kraak, 2008). Evidently skills development initiatives are not a panacea and fundamental weaknesses in labour markets can only be addressed with a sustained strategy of lifelong learning.

In the two decades after the Second World War the OECD countries enjoyed steady economic growth and stability. Unemployment oscillated with the business cycle but was below 10 million and declined steadily from 1958 with a decade of prosperity. In the watershed year of 1968 a wave of industrial action reminiscent of the 'Great Unrest' of 1910–14 spread across Europe. A steady labour shake-out accompanied the industrial action and accelerated with the oil shocks of 1973 and 1979, as productivity increases were sought to compensate for higher energy costs. Total OECD unemployment exceeded 30 million towards the end of the 1990s, despite a period of recovery between 1983 and 1990, leading to increased concern over high levels of structural and long-term unemployment.

According to the OECD Jobs Study (1994a; 1994b) rising unemployment and the persistence of low-wage jobs was the result of a gap between the need of OECD economies to adapt to changing circumstances and their capacity to do so. The proposed remedies included macro-economic policies promoting job-friendly growth; strategies to stimulate technological development and entrepreneurship; measures to increase labour market flexibility and strengthen active labour market policies; and initiatives to improve labour force skills. Subsequent OECD reports reiterated the need to upgrade workforce skills in order to increase the knowledge base and raise capacity for innovation.

There are marked differences between OECD states in terms of the 'skills equilibrium' or distribution of skills in the labour force, as well as in labour market regulation. Within the EU, the 'Continental' model, typified by Germany, is often contrasted with the 'Western' model, represented by the UK. While the first is associated with a highly skilled workforce and an emphasis on the intermediate skills developed in the world class 'dual system' (Steedman and Wagner, 1987), the second is seen as representing a 'low skills equilibrium' (Finegold and Soskice, 1988). While the higher skill level of the German workforce has been a major source of competitive advantage, the narrow specialization associated with the concept of Beruf has restricted the development of cross-functional flexibility associated with lean production found in the USA and UK (Herrigel, 1996). Anglo-American approaches to skill formation, characterized by a high proportion of low-skilled workers and a higher proportion of high-skilled than those at the intermediate skills level (in the US case, a much higher proportion of graduates) can be contrasted with the 'inverted U-shaped' distribution of the EU (and especially German) system producing more employees qualified at intermediate level. In terms of labour market regulation, the 'Anglophone' system is associated with low unemployment but more casual and precarious employment, while the continental European model is associated with a high degree of labour market regulation with correspondingly high employment security, but also high levels of unemployment. The OECD agenda appeared to be designed to 'Americanize' labour markets and simultaneously 'Europeanize' education and training systems (Winterton, 2007).

The emphasis on raising workforce skills, reiterated in subsequent OECD reports, was the result of increasing global demand for high skills (Reich, 1991) and the evidence that high skills equilibrium countries were more productive and competitive (OECD, 1998). Governments increasingly accepted the argument that the route to global economic competitiveness was through building workforce competence. Policy documents from the USA (Stuart, 1999) and the UK (White Paper, 2003) took up the argument of the need to build skills for the 21st century. Whilst recognizing the role of competence development for promoting employment, Crouch et al. (1999) criticized the OECD Jobs Strategy for its essentially supply-side focus. They argued that the contraction of the public sector coupled with productivity improvements reduces traditional demand for high skills and that the new high-skill jobs are insufficient to compensate for low-skill job losses.

The OECD Jobs Strategy was predicated upon human capital theory, which assumed that investment in human capital would encourage employers to upgrade and thereby increase demand for skills (Becker, 1964; Schultz, 1963). However, raising the educational level does not immediately create jobs: young people increasingly demand higher education but increasingly find it insufficient to guarantee access to the labour market. Subsequently the OECD began to emphasize the need for education and training to be better adapted to labour market needs, contributing to the movement towards outcome-based education and competence-based training (Mansfield, 2004). A decade on, OECD policy gave attention to the demand side and utilization of skills, proposing strategies for upgrading demand for labour and skills within local economies as a route to increasing competitiveness and improving the quality of local employment (OECD, 2008).

The continued existence of a significant proportion of the workforce in OECD countries with low qualifications is seen as a limitation to the high skills road and the growing earnings differential according to qualification (the so-called 'education premium') has led to an increasingly polarized workforce and greater social inequalities. The growth of service sector employment is often conflated with a growth in knowledge work and demand for higher skills but it is clear that only a proportion of service sector work demands higher qualifications. Cleaning offices, caring for the elderly and delivering pizzas are more typical of service sector jobs and such routinized work, as well as the persistence of Taylorist work organization in manufacturing and distribution, shows the limits to growth based on a high skills economy.

4. SUPRA-NATIONAL REGIONAL BODIES

The OECD Jobs Strategy stimulated supra-state organizations to develop coordinated regional training strategies and influenced the directions they took. The European Union (EU) and the Asia Pacific Economic Cooperation Forum (APEC) face similar challenges with globalization demanding increased education and training to raise workforce competence, productivity and competitiveness. Each region exhibits diversity in the economic conditions of member countries so global challenges are manifest differently in specific contexts. Diverse systems of education and training, labour market regulatory mechanisms and welfare regimes, mediate the implementation of supra-national strategies across regions. Moreover, there are fundamental differences in the political structures of the two supra-national organizations that lead to contrasting approaches to co-ordination of human capital development or skill formation (Haworth and Winterton, 2012). APEC is a loose forum of independent nation states founded on consensual decision-making, whereas the EU is an organization of inter-dependent nation states founded on common policy in support of an integrated market. Whereas social dialogue is a defining principle of the EU policy approach, trade unions play no role in developing regional training policy in APEC. Each is considered briefly in turn below.

Coordinated Approaches to Developing Workforce Skills in the European Union

Inevitably the EU has exhibited a greater degree of policy coordination concerning training and development than APEC, notably since the Delors White Paper Growth, Competitiveness, Employment (Commission of the European Communities, 1993). In arguing the equal importance and interdependence of these three elements, the White Paper secured consensus between member states and the social partners on the need for negotiated reform of labour markets and macroeconomic policy that would support both productivity and job creation. The agenda of modernizing social and labour market policy brought supply-side issues to the fore, and the Essen summit in December 1994 agreed on five priorities for employment policy: investment in human resources (education and training); macro-economic strategies that would encourage employment intensive patterns of growth; reductions in non-wage labour costs; moving labour market expenditure from passive to active measures; and targeting specific groups disadvantaged in the labour market.

The priorities for employment policy agreed at Essen established the conditions for the Amsterdam summit in June 1997 which committed member states to a coordinated strategy for employment. The policy reflected a redefinition of the European unemployment problem as one of a low employment rate in comparison with the USA (HM Treasury, 2001), which was seen as unsustainable given the commitment to maintaining superior levels of social protection to those of competing trading areas in North America and Asia. Such an analysis reinforced the shift from demand-side to supply-side concerns and put employability and flexibility at the centre of the debate (Winterton and Haworth, 2013). When, at a subsequent Jobs Summit in Luxembourg in November 1997, the Commission proposed a draft European Employment Strategy (EES) (Goetschy, 1999), the underpinning Employment Guidelines were structured into four pillars: employability; entrepreneurship; adaptability; and equal opportunities. Active labour market policies involved both labour market activation (welfare to work) strategies and measures to enhance employability and adaptability through providing access to opportunities for developing competences to meet labour market needs. Member States were required to prepare annual National Action Plans for Employment (NAPEs) to address the Employment Guidelines.

European policy emphasis on developing human resources to promote growth, competitiveness and employment was reiterated and reinforced at the Lisbon Summit in March 2000, which established the objective of making Europe by 2010 'the most competitive and dynamic knowledge-based economy in the world capable of sustainable economic growth with more and better jobs and greater social cohesion' (European Council 2000, para. 5). This high skills agenda was to be pursued through the Commission's Action Plan for Skills and Mobility, which emphasized the need to expand occupational mobility and skills development; to make education and training more responsive to labour market needs; and to consolidate more effective competence development strategies for workers (Commission of the European Communities, 2002). The employment targets of the EES were adjusted to support the Lisbon Strategy, setting an overall employment rate of 70 per cent (60 per cent for women) and priorities such as lifelong learning for skills and mobility in the 2001 Employment Guidelines. Following an evaluation of the experience of the first five years of the EES, the Commission proposed restructuring the Employment Guidelines to address the medium-term priorities of the Lisbon Strategy (Commission of the European Communities, 2003a, 2003b). The ten new priorities for action, or 'Ten Commandments' as they were often described, included measures to increase investment in human capital and promote opportunities for lifelong learning (Priority for Action 4).

The following year, a mid-term assessment of the Lisbon Strategy by the high-level group led by Wim Kok (2004) found progress on growth, productivity and employment disappointing and recommended changes to focus on key priorities. A streamlined and simplified Lisbon Strategy was re-launched with activities focussed on 'delivering stronger, lasting growth and creating more and better jobs' (Commission of the European Communities, 2005: 7). The EES was similarly revised and the Employment Guidelines incorporated into Integrated Guidelines for Growth and Jobs. A National Reform Programme (NRP) was developed annually by each member state in collaboration with the social partners. Replacing the NAPEs, each NRP report contained an employment chapter, and the Joint Employment Report became the Employment Chapter of the EU Annual Progress Report adopted by the Council. Eight guidelines related to employment and included actions to match labour market needs; to increase investment in human capital; and to adapt education and training to new competence needs. Two of the four priority areas identified for employment related to human capital development:

improving adaptability of workers and enterprises; and increasing investment in human capital through improving education and raising skills.

Human Capital Development Programmes in APEC

Parallel events were taking place in the APEC Forum since its creation in 1989, with the 21 economies developing regional co-operation around the Asia-Pacific region stretching from North America to New Zealand and from China to Chile. In comparison with the EU and international organizations like the OECD, the APEC secretariat in Singapore is small and mainly staffed by seconded officials from member economies. Driven by the same issues of globalization, competitiveness and market protectionism as the EU, APEC has been focussed mostly on trade, especially since the conclusion of the 1986–94 Uruguay round of trade negotiations that established the World Trade Organization (WTO). As the WTO was launched, an APEC meeting in Indonesia led to the Bogor Declaration, committing APEC economies to a trade and investment liberalization and facilitation (TILF) programme as well as other activities in economic and technical co-operation (ECOTECH). The Bogor Declaration set the targets of achieving free trade and investment in the APEC region by 2010 in the developed economies and 2020 for less developed economies.

There was tension from the outset between the TILF and ECOTECH agendas, partly because some economies are only concerned with the trade agenda, and TILF has predominated. This is important since human capital development strategies fall under the ECOTECH heading. When the 1995 Osaka Action Agenda committed APEC to pursue economic and technical cooperation, HRD was identified as a specific area of cooperation. Noting that human resource needs were both expanding and diversifying in line with the growth and dynamism of the region, eight priorities were identified:

1. providing a quality basic education;
2. analyzing the regional labour market to allow sound forecasting of trends and needs in HRD;
3. increasing the supply and enhancing the quality of managers, entrepreneurs, scientists and educators/trainers;
4. reducing skills deficiencies and unemployment by designing training programs for applications at all stages of a person's working life;
5. improving the quality of curricula, teaching methods and instructional materials for managers and other workers;
6. increasing opportunities for people seeking to gain skills; and
7. preparing organizations and individuals to remain productive in the face of rapid economic and technological changes, as stated in the Declaration on a Human Resources Development Framework, and further engage in

8. promoting HRD toward the liberalization and facilitation of trade and investment. (Ministry of Foreign Affairs of Japan, 1995)

These priorities have changed little over the years and have been coordinated by the APEC HRD Working Group, which since 2000 has run three networks: EDNET, focussed on education issues; the Labour and Social Protection Network, working on labour markets, labour-management issues and social support; and the Capacity Building Network, concerned with building management capacity in the public and private sectors.

Annual meetings of the HRD Working Group are attended by as many as 150 individuals, mostly officials from education, labour and HRD ministries or departments. The main concerns are upgrading HRD practices and improving the functioning and efficiency of education, training and production systems. These aims are seen as supporting a free market approach to maximizing economic advance through regional and global economic integration, along the lines of the WTO agenda. Unlike the EU, participants represent the interests of government and business and there is no role for trade unions.

5. ACTIONS AT THE LEVEL OF MEMBER STATES AND ECONOMIES

Both the EU and APEC are marked by diversity among their members, most obviously in terms of the size and nature of the economies involved. While such diversity creates different priorities for the countries involved and imposes constraints on the extent to which regional coordination is possible, in both cases members are nevertheless committed to common endeavours to raise workforce skills. As was noted earlier, each country has its own specific skills equilibrium and relative emphasis on high, intermediate and low skills, which is only partly explained by differences in economic structure. Deeper historical and cultural traditions are also important and are reflected in different education and training systems (Clarke and Winch, 2007), approaches to skill formation (Ashton et al., 2000; Brown, 1999) and conceptions of competence (Le Deist and Winterton, 2005). Recent studies suggest further divergence in training systems (Bosch and Charest, 2010: 3) and competence models (Winterton, 2009), presenting further difficulties for developing coordinated approaches to, for example, qualifications systems (Winterton, 2011). In addition to diversity in skill formation systems, further differences in labour market regulation and welfare regimes also impose limitations to developing a coordinated approach to investment in developing human capital. It is little surprise therefore that there are differences in how actions are actually implemented in member countries, but the nature of these differences is also interesting to compare between the EU and APEC cases.

Implementation of EU Strategies for Raising Workforce Skills by Member States

Differences in HRD implementation strategies of member states reflect diversity in education and training traditions as well as different economic imperatives. Many of the typologies and taxonomies of training systems discussed earlier distinguish school-based from enterprise or work-based systems, and differentiate between state-regulated and market-led systems. While each country has its own historical and institutional specificities, with some simplification four families can be identified in Europe: two variants of the dominant mainland European neo-corporatist model; the traditional Anglophone liberal market model; and the transitional socio-economic model associated with the new Central and Eastern European member states. The dominant continental approach to training is a state-regulated, school-based system, typified by France, which can be contrasted with the dual system variant that can be characterized as a state-regulated, work-based system, typified by Germany. Training under the dual system alternates between the workplace and vocational training school but the curricula are determined by the social partners in the world of work, rather than in the world of education. The market-led model associated with the UK can also be characterized as work-based. Most EU member states approximate to one of these three approaches, often for reasons of history as much as geography, hence Austria and Switzerland follow the German dual system, Ireland approximates to the UK market model, while Spain and Portugal have similar systems to France. Italy, traditionally with a market-led, school-based system is something of an anomaly (Winterton, 2000).

Most of the new member states that have joined the EU since 2004 also approximate to one of the three main training regimes: hence Malta and Cyprus correspond quite closely with the UK model, Slovenia and Hungary have something like the German model and all of the other new member states have a form of state-regulated, school-based vocational training. However, most new members are former Soviet states and exhibit characteristics of a transitional socio-economic model that are more a defining characteristic than their affinity to a particular mainland training system. Slovenia, which has a more developed economy as well as the closest correspondence with the German dual system, is an exception among the former Soviet states. For the remainder, even if the training regime resembles the predominant state-regulated, school-based training system, the demands of economic transition are highlighting fundamental weaknesses and many are expected to adopt a market-led system ostensibly to align training more with labour market needs but also evidently to restrain state expenditure.

The implementation of EU policies for HRD are heavily mediated by such fundamental national differences in training regimes and specific labour market needs, despite attempts to develop a coordinated approach to raising workforce skills. The diversity is evident in NRP reports designed to address the key EU priorities of Lisbon and Europe 2020 (see below). Inevitably in the older member states NRP reports describe measures to build higher level skills and support the growth of the knowledge economy, whereas in the newer member states the emphasis is more on developing capacity to support human capital development through, for example, arrangements for forecasting labour market skills needs. Aligning national qualifications frameworks with the European Qualifications Framework is a priority for promoting labour mobility to resolve skills mismatches (Le Deist and Tūtlys, 2012).

Different Modes of Engagement in APEC

National economic interests appear to determine modes of intervention and HRD interventions reflect the wider political-economic roles played by member economies in the regional economy. Member economies can be divided broadly into donors and recipients, with subsets in each of these categories. Amongst the donors are found investment, development and hegemonic strategies. Within the recipients are found basic development, transitional and hegemonic strategies. Member economies are not necessarily single identity. For example, Thailand and Malaysia display both donor and recipient characteristics. Japan is the classic example of the donor-investment intervention mode, having invested substantial funds in projects designed to improve quality management and production systems, much of which is directly orientated to the needs of Japanese foreign direct investment in the region, or users of Japanese inputs into production. Even in relatively undeveloped economies such as Papua New Guinea, Japan has invested substantially in projects to upgrade quality systems. To a lesser extent, Korea and Singapore (and also Malaysia and Thailand) have played a similar role in the region.

Canada illustrates the donor-development mode of intervention, in part because the international development arm of the Canadian government has been a leading agency in APEC human capital development. This intervention is more traditionally developmental, seeking to upgrade capacities as a goal in itself, rather than as a function of investment priorities. US interventions around basic education are another example of this approach. US intervention on labour protection and labour standards under the Clinton White House is the primary example of the donor-hegemonic intervention approach. Sustained political pressure from Washington (supported by relatively few other member economies) brought about the creation of a Labour and Social Protection Network within the Working Group. Whilst labour protection was a key issue for the most affected economies during the 1997 crisis, it was not necessarily understood in those economies in the same terms as the US, and was barely acceptable to economies such as Australia and China. It was forced through on the basis of a mixture of cajolery and, frankly, naked pressure. In East and South East Asia, Japan seeks a similar role, but encounters the burgeoning might of China in the process.

Recipient economies can be differentiated at particular times into basic development, transitional intervention and hegemonic intervention. At different times, many of the developing economies in APEC (Papua New Guinea, Peru, Philippines, Indonesia, Thailand, Malaysia, Brunei, for example) have used APEC for recipient-basic development intervention, as a means of identifying and acquiring basic capacity building for future development. Frequently, transfers have consisted of technical capacity exchanges, rather than the donation of funds. These economies bring forward projects that directly benefit aspects of their HRD. Vietnam and China (and to a much lesser extent Russia, barely active in APEC HRD circles) have used APEC HRD activities in the form of recipient-transitional interventions, as a rich source of capacity building expertise to help drive forward their internal reform processes. Ashton et al. (1999, 2002) describe a development model of skill formation in South East Asian economies. Several, including Brunei, Malaysia, Singapore, South Korea and Taiwan have initiated extensive national programmes for developing human capital. Malaysia introduced a Human Resource Development Act in 1992 and Singapore has become something of a model for skills-led economic growth in the region (Low, 2002).

It is widely understood that if China brings forward a project to the HRD Working Group, its prime purpose will be to develop Chinese capacities. It is also the case that most member economies in APEC seek to support such projects in order to gain the goodwill of China and, perhaps, some advantageous access to that market. The recipient-hegemonic mode of intervention is most obviously the case for China, which casts itself as a developing (recipient) economy in APEC HRD discussion, but clearly anticipates a time when donor economies from within its immediate periphery will be economically subordinate to China's massive commercial power. Dealing with China in the APEC process challenges other economies to consider how to use the access offered by APEC channels into China to advantage.

Australasian APEC countries have faced different challenges. For New Zealand, labour market restructuring begun by the 1991 National Government has set the agenda for skills development strategies ever since (Elkin, 1998). Australia, facing chronic skills shortages, has identified 'shortage lists', offering immigration opportunities for skilled workers in most trades as well as establishing a category of General High Skilled Migrants. The mining industry in Western Australia in particular has suffered skills shortages since 2003 and has made extensive use of 'FIFO' (fly-in-fly-out) miners from the East as well as offering opportunities for regional migration (Cameron, 2011).

6.   NEW IMPERATIVES

The current wave of restructuring is the result of the layered effects of global economic shift, the 2008 financial crisis and the Eurozone sovereign debt crisis from 2010, the separate effects of which are impossible to disentangle. However, the 2008 financial crisis, described in the International Monetary Fund's World Economic Outlook (2008: vii) as 'the deepest shock to the global financial system since the Great Depression', was so profound that it demanded an immediate policy response. Each world region was faced with new and particular challenges and while few countries were untouched, the responses of the supra-national regional bodies were quite different, as we review below.

European Responses to Economic Crises

Even before the sovereign debt crisis, the severity of the 2008 financial crisis increased unpredictability, reinforcing the need to enhance human capital and employability. In response, the EU launched the New Skills for New Jobs (European Commission, 2008) initiative, which was designed to assure a better matching of skills supply to labour market demand. Evidence that global economic shift and climate change are both more severe and permanent led to Europe 2020, a new strategy for sustainable growth and jobs, putting knowledge, innovation and green growth at the heart of EU competitiveness (European Commission, 2010a). Europe 2020 put human capital development at the heart of EU economic recovery, adding sustainability to the original goals of growth based on knowledge and innovation coupled with high employment and social cohesion (Council of the EU, 2011).

Two of the so-called 'flagship' initiatives of Europe 2020 deserve particular attention. The Agenda for New Skills and Jobs initiative (European Commission, 2010b) designed to upgrade skills and boost employability, proposed measures to improve the identification of training needs, make education and training more relevant to labour market needs, and facilitate access to opportunities for lifelong learning and guidance, as well as improving transitions between education, training and employment. The adoption of qualifications based on learning outcomes and greater validation of skills and competences acquired experientially in non-formal and informal contexts was also emphasized. The Youth on the Move initiative (European Commission, 2010c), designed to help young people achieve their full potential, focuses on reducing drop-out from school, ensuring all young people acquire basic skills to facilitate further learning and increasing opportunities to learn later in life.

Economic Crisis, APEC and HRD

Economic crisis has been a key factor in HRD's prominence in the APEC process. APEC has suffered two major international crises since its formation: the 1997 Asian Financial Crisis and the 2008 financial crisis. Both gave rise to increased unemployment, labour market dislocation, and the threat of social instability. Inevitably, each crisis provoked a two-fold focus on short term, social protection, and longer-term restructuring of labour markets and workforces. In both cases, HRD was seen inside APEC as key to creating new competitiveness that would drive growth out of the crisis.

The 1997 Asian Crisis was a shock to the APEC process. APEC's relevance to the region was widely questioned and in the immediate circumstances of the crisis, the TILF agenda appeared to offer little support for the economies most affected. On the other hand, to the extent that APEC could offer short-term support, the ECOTECH dimension was the most relevant. Hence, APEC undertook significant support work in areas such as defining HRD responses to the crisis. The most prominent intervention was undertaken by the APEC HRD Working Group in its task force on the HRD dimensions of the crisis. The task force produced case studies of the most affected economies and an overview analysis, the latter subsequently submitted to APEC leaders in their 1998 meeting.

The 2008 financial crisis similarly provided a boost for HRD activity within APEC. APEC economies were hit by the crisis to different degrees:

Japan and Russia suffered major economic downturns in 2009, whereas the Chinese economy continued to grow, albeit at a slower rate than the previous three years. Employment impacts also varied. While unemployment in most of the larger economies reached around 10 per cent, it remained below 5 per cent in Thailand, Malaysia and Singapore.

In response to the 2008 crisis, APEC leaders meeting in Singapore in 2009 defined an APEC Growth Strategy with five elements: Balanced Growth, Inclusive Growth, Sustainable Growth, Innovative Growth, and Secure Growth. The Growth Strategy demanded a new approach to the regional economy. While TILF remained central, a broader framework was developed involving, for example, recognition of energy and environmental constraints, human security issues (for example, terrorism, food security), and issues of opportunity and inclusion. On the basis of the Growth Strategy, APEC leaders believed that APEC could become a global leader in crisis response (and beyond).

The HRD Working Group responds to both education and labour APEC ministers so engaged with meetings of Education Ministers in Peru in 2008, and Labour Ministers in China in 2010. The Education Ministers emphasized capacity development in mathematics and science learning, language skill acquisition, career and technical education for lifelong learning, and a strong focus on ICT capacity. Whilst seen as important for the longer term, the more immediate labour market impacts of the crisis fell to the Labour Ministers to address in their 2010 meeting.

Preparation for the 2010 meeting involved three key outputs. First, the HRD Working Group surveyed the impact of the crisis in member economies, leading to a case study-based report. Second, the leadership of the Working Group prepared an overview technical paper on both social protection and active labour market initiatives taken in APEC economies during the first two years of the crisis. Third, based on these two outputs, a ministerial statement and associated action plan was produced, endorsed by APEC Labour Ministers as an agenda for the Working Group and as a focal point for interventions at economy level.

The background materials to the 2010 Labour Ministerial meeting identified three key areas for action. First, the employment (demand) focus emphasized actions like tax policies to promote employment growth, infrastructure developments as job creation, measures to reduce labour costs at enterprise levels, including subsidies to support continuing employment, and growth in public employment. Second, the HRD (supply) focus pointed to measures such as the development of standardized qualifications frameworks, government-industry partnerships, increased use of ICT to improve training provision, and efforts to extend capacity building for particularly vulnerable groups. The third focus was on social protection and safety nets, pointing to greater use of subsidies and severance payments, more job sharing, partnerships between government and business and improved assessment and evaluation.

The Labour Ministerial meeting outlined an action plan which sought to capture previous preparatory work and also the thrust of the APEC Growth Strategy. The direction taken by the 2010 Labour Ministerial achieved a number of ends. It conformed to the principles of the APEC Growth Strategy and promoted activities designed to improve social protection and drive increased competitiveness. Politically, it reflected the priorities expected of APEC by China. Above all, it consolidated HRD as a key element of the APEC process, underpinned by its role in crisis amelioration and improved competitiveness.

7. CONCLUSIONS

It is clear from the above account that HRD has become a central concern of international and supra-national organizations as well as governments of nation states over the past few decades. Globalization and the associated demand for increased competitiveness had already raised the profile of human capital development before the 2008 financial crisis and the 2010 Eurozone sovereign debt crisis unfolded. International organizations were already addressing the need to raise workforce skills and supra-national bodies similarly have been addressing the issue since the 1990s. Since EU member states and APEC countries have to a large extent faced similar challenges it is perhaps unsurprising that there are parallels in the initiatives promoted by these regional bodies. Equally, given the structural and organizational differences between the EU and APEC, very different policy mechanisms are to be expected.

The challenges of implementation at the level of nation states are similar in both regions and while there are major differences between the regions in terms of the role of social partner organizations, and especially the trade unions, there are other fundamental differences between nation states in both groupings that affect the extent to which and the way in which policies are implemented at national level. Most obviously each labour market regime has a particular set of challenges, and different training regimes determine the limits and possibilities of implementation strategies. In this respect, there are further parallels between the two regions, since each contains countries with different degrees of market orientation and state regulation and different types of economic development. Hence, in considering the links between globalization, competitiveness and skills formation, the High Skills project contrasted the market models of the

UK and US, the corporatist model of Germany and the state development models of Japan, Korea and Singapore (Brown et al., 2001). Clearly there is a need for more research in this area and on economies in transition and development as well as more nuanced versions of the market and corporatist models, particularly since the crises.

Certainly the need to raise workforce competence has become both more urgent and more difficult since the crises. In 2012 the OECD published a global Skills Strategy to help governments identify strengths and weaknesses in national skills systems and to promote strategies for ensuring that skills development translates into 'better jobs and better lives'. The fundamentals of the OECD skills strategy can be summarized as follows:

- Encouraging people to learn so they have the cognitive and higher level skills increasingly demanded in the labour market
- Involving social partners in education and training programmes to ensure skills formation meets labour market needs
- Encouraging mobility of skilled migrants to solve skills shortages by immigration and promoting cross-border skills policies
- Encouraging people to use their skills through introducing financial incentives to raise labour market participation and removing non-financial barriers such as inflexible working arrangements
- Retaining skilled people through encouraging later retirement and providing incentives for skilled workers to reduce emigration
- Ensuring that people use their skills effectively through improving information about skills needed and available
- Increasing demand for high-level skills through influencing competitiveness strategies to support stronger economic growth and more productive and rewarding jobs.

Noting that several countries have already published national skills strategies and others are under development, the OECD recognizes that the key challenges are associated with implementation and ensuring engagement with stakeholders at different levels. Further OECD action will offer guidance and support in developing and implementing national skills strategies. The first stage will entail country level analysis of strengths and weaknesses benchmarked against the OECD Skills Strategy as a basis for designing and evaluating policy alternatives. An assessment of the skills people have and how they are used at work will be available from October 2013 based on the OECD Survey of Adult Skills. This focus on analysing existing skills supply is an important innovation that should, with adequate demand-side analysis of future labour market needs, enable governments to develop and implement more targeted and effective skills strategies.

At the same time, as with the OECD Jobs Strategy, a number of questions remain concerning this essentially supply-side Skills Strategy in the context of a serious demand crisis. There is substantial emphasis on the need to encourage acquisition of cognitive and higher skills, yet, as the Skills Strategy recognizes, many countries have the apparently contradictory combination of increased demand for high-level skills with levels of graduate unemployment at an all-time high. Demand for high-level skills is assumed to be outstripping supply, yet the Skills Strategy also proposes ways of increasing demand for high-level skills, suggesting that a major realignment of education and training is necessary.

It is logical that the Skills Strategy deals with issues of labour mobility, skills retention and skills utilization since these may be more important than further supply-side measures. The Skills Strategy rightly acknowledges that while skills policies tend to be developed nationally, many organizations operate transnationally. The OECD proposes actions whereby one country contributes to improving the stock of skilled labour of another to reduce emigration of highly skilled individuals, but also seeks to promote mobility of highly skilled workers. There are global trade-offs between increasing the retirement age and dealing with youth unemployment as well as between reducing emigration and encouraging skilled migrant policies. Mechanisms to encourage labour market participation can ensure people with the requisite skills remain employed, but continual reports of skills shortages, skills gaps and recruitment difficulties suggest that opportunities for training and retraining are equally important. In the context of sustained economic crisis, there is a risk that enterprises and individuals will be reluctant to invest in skills, and governments facing a need to reduce public sector spending are unlikely to finance more training. Mismatches between employees' skills and job requirements are frequently reported but more effective skills utilization is limited by the persistence of Taylorist work organization and its increasing adoption in knowledge-based industries.

That the OECD is joining the voice of the ILO in calling for a wider role for the social partners is to be applauded, particularly given the evidence that trade unions can help align training with labour market needs, negotiate opportunities for training and encourage uptake of learning opportunities, especially by groups with traditionally low participation rates in training (Winterton, 2013). However, in many countries where trade unions could have most impact, their scope for action is severely limited by legal or other restrictions. Until freedom of association and basic bargaining rights are protected, trade unions can have only a marginal impact on solving the global skills challenge.

The Skills Strategy puts workforce development at the heart of OECD policies for recovery and growth, and this is also to be welcomed. However, like the mantra of 'more and better jobs' at the heart of the EU Lisbon Strategy, there is more than a little wishful thinking involved. Faced with the most sustained global economic crisis in living memory, long-term investment in high-level skills is more difficult to secure. Governments, juggling with national debt, are likely to expect companies and individuals to take more responsibility for training and development. Companies, struggling to maintain competitiveness in shrinking markets, are looking for labour efficiencies and may be reluctant to invest in other than short-term firm-specific training. Individuals, competing in the labour market for, in all probability, fewer of those long-promised 'better jobs', may prefer to take whatever jobs are on offer than to invest in upgrading their skills, particularly in countries where youth and graduate unemployment levels remain obstinately high and the labour market participation rate of older workers depressingly low. For those nations, enterprises and individuals with the resources and courage to take the high skills route, enormous competitive advantage will be gained but the choice for most is not unlimited.

REFERENCES

Ashton, D., Green, F., James, D. and Sung, J. (1999) Education and Training for Development: The Political Economy of Skill Formation in East Asian Newly Industrialised Economies, London: Routledge.

Ashton, D., Sung, J. and Turbin, J. (2000) 'Towards a framework for the comparative analysis of national systems of skill formation', International Journal of Training and Development, 4 (1): 8–25.

Ashton, D., Green, F., Sung, J. and James, D. (2002) 'The evolution of education and training strategies in Singapore, Taiwan, and South Korea: a development model of skill formation', Journal of Education and Work, 15 (1): 5–30.

Baqadir, A., Patrick, F. and Burns, G. (2011) 'Addressing the skills gap in Saudi Arabia: does vocational education address the needs of private sector employers?', Journal of Vocational Education and Training, 63 (4): 551–561.

Becker, G. (1964) Human Capital: A Theoretical and Empirical Analysis, with Special Reference to Education, New York, NY: National Bureau of Economic Research.

Bell, D. (1973) The Coming of Post-Industrial Society: A Venture in Social Forecasting, New York, NY: Basic Books.

Bosch, G. and Charest, J. (eds) (2010) Vocational Training: International Perspectives, New York, NY: Routledge.

Briggs, V.M. (1987) 'Human resource development and the formulation of national economic policy', Journal of Economic Issues, 21 (3): 1207–1240.

Broughton, A., Biletta, I. and Kullander, M. (2010) Flexible Forms of Work: 'Very Atypical' Contractual Arrangements, Dublin: Eurofound. http://www. eurofound.europa.eu/ewco/studies/tn0812019s/index.htm.

Brown, P. (1999) 'Globalisation and the political economy of high skills', Journal of Education and Work, 12 (3): 233–251.

Brown, P., Green, A. and Lauder, H. (2001) High Skills: Globalization, Competitiveness and Skill Formation, Oxford: Oxford University Press.

Budros, A. (1999) 'A conceptual framework for analyzing why organisations downsize', Organization Science, 10 (1): 69–82.

Cameron, R. (2011) 'Responding to Australia's regional skill shortages through regional skilled migration', Journal of Economic and Social Policy, 14 (3), art. 4.

Chadwick, C., Hunter, I. and Walston, S. (2004) 'Effects of downsizing practice on the performance of hospitals', Strategic Management Journal, 25 (5): 405–420.

Clarke, L. and Winch, C. (eds) (2007) Vocational Education: International Approaches, Developments and Systems, London: Routledge.

Commission of the European Communities (1993) Growth, Competitiveness, Employment: The Challenges and Ways Forward Into the 21st Century, White Paper COM(93)700, Luxembourg: Office for Official Publications of the European Communities. http://europa.eu/documentation/official-docs/white-papers/pdf/growth_wp_com_93_700_parts_a_b.pdf.

Commission of the European Communities (2002) Action Plan for Skills and Mobility, Brussels, 13.2.2002 COM(2002) 72 final. http://eur-lex.europa.eu/LexUriServ/LexUriServ.do?uri=COM:2002:0072:FIN:EN:PDF.

Commission of the European Communities (2003a) The Future of the European Employment Strategy (EES) 'A Strategy for Full Employment and Better Jobs for All', COM/2003/0006 final. http://eur-lex.europa.eu/LexUriServ/LexUriServ.do?uri=COM:2003:0006:FIN:EN:PDF.

Commission of the European Communities (2003b) Proposal for a Council Decision on Guidelines for the Employment Policies of the Member States, COM/2003/0176, 8 April. http://eur-lex.europa.eu/LexUriServ/LexUriServ.do?uri=COM:2003:0176:FIN:EN:PDF.

Commission of the European Communities (2005) Working Together for Growth and Jobs. A New Start for the Lisbon Strategy, Brussels 2.2.2005 COM(2005) 24 final. http://eur-lex.europa.eu/LexUriServ/LexUriServ.do?uri=COM:2005:0024:FIN:EN:PDF.

Council of the European Union (2011) Council Conclusions on the Role Of Education and Training in the Implementation of the 'Europe 2020' Strategy (2011/C 70/01) 04/03/11. http://eur-lex.europa.eu/LexUriServ/LexUriServ.do?uri=OJ:C:2011:070:0001:0003:EN:PDF.

Crouch, C., Finegold, D. and Sako, M. (1999) Are Skills the Answer? The Political Economy of Skills Creation in Advanced Industrial Societies, Oxford: Oxford University Press.

De Woot, P. (1990) High Technology Europe: Strategic Issues for Global Competitiveness, Oxford: Blackwell.

Dicken, P. (1992) Global Shift: The Internationalization of Economic Activity, London: Chapman (2nd edn).

Drucker, P.F. (1993) Post-Capitalist Society, Oxford: Butterworth-Heinemann.

Ducatel, K., Webster, J. and Herrmann, W. (eds) (2000) The Information Society in Europe: Work and Life in an Age of Globalization, Lanham, MA: Rowman & Littlefield.

Elkin, G. (1998) 'New Zealand human capital development and structural reform', International Journal of Training and Development, 2 (1): 60–74.

European Commission (2008) New Skills for New Jobs: Anticipating and Matching Labour Market and Skills Needs, Brussels 16/12/08 COM(2008) 868 final. http://ec.europa.eu/education/lifelong-learning-policy/doc/com868_en.pdf.

European Commission (2010a) Communication from the Commission to the European Parliament, the Council, the European Economic and Social Committee and the Committee of the Regions, Europe 2020: A Strategy for Smart, Sustainable and Inclusive Growth, Brussels 03/03/10 COM (2010) 2010 final. http://ec.europa.eu/commission_2010-014/president/news/documents/pdf/20100303_1_en.pdf.

European Commission (2010b) Communication from the Commission to the European Parliament, the Council, the European Economic and Social Committee and the Committee of the Regions, An Agenda for New Skills and Jobs: A European Contribution Towards Full Employment, Strasbourg 23/11/10 COM (2010) 682 final. http://eur-lex.europa.eu/LexUriServ/LexUriServ.do?uri=COM:2010:0682:FIN:EN:PDF.

European Commission (2010c) Communication from the Commission to the European Parliament, the Council, the European Economic and Social Committee and the Committee of the Regions, Youth on the Move: An Initiative to Unleash the Potential of Young People To Achieve Smart, Sustainable and Inclusive Growth in the European Union, COM(2010) 477 final. http://ec.europa.eu/education/yom/com_en.pdf.

European Council (2000) Conclusions, 23–24 March. http://www.europarl.europa.eu/summits/lis1_en.htm.

Finegold, D. and Soskice, D. (1988) 'The failure of training in Britain: analysis and prescription', Oxford Review of Economic Policy, 4 (3): 21–53.

Finn, D. (2000) 'From full employment to full employability: a new deal for Britain's unemployed?' International Journal of Manpower, 21 (5): 384–399.

Forester, T. (ed.) (1980) The Microelectronics Revolution, Oxford: Blackwell.

Freeman, C. and Soete, L. (1994) Work for All or Mass Unemployment? Computerised Technical Change into the 21st Century, London: Pinter.

Freeman, C., Sharp, M. and Walker, W. (1993) Technology and the Future of Europe: Global Competition and the Environment in the 1990s, London: Pinter.

Gallie, D., Felstead, A. and Green, F. (2004) 'Changing patterns of task discretion in Britain', Work, Employment & Society, 18 (2): 243–266.

Goetschy, J. (1999) 'The European Employment Strategy: genesis and development', European Journal of Industrial Relations, 5 (2): 117–137.

Hammer, M. and Champy, J. (1983) Reengineering the Corporation: A Manifesto for Business Revolution, London: Nicholas Brealey.

Hammer, M. and Stanton, S. (1995) The Re-engineering Revolution, New York: Harper Collins.

Handel, M.J. (2003) 'Skills mismatch in the labor market', Annual Review of Sociology, 29: 135–165.

Haworth, N. and Winterton, J. (2012) 'Regional integration and vocational training strategies: the EU and APEC compared', in M. Lee (ed.) Human Resource Development as We Know It: Speeches That Have Shaped the Field, London: Routledge, pp. 91–101.

Herrigel, G.B. (1996) 'Crisis in German decentralized production', European Urban and Regional Studies, 3 (1): 33–52.

Heugens, P.M. and Schenk, H. (2004) 'Rethinking corporate restructuring', Journal of Public Affairs, 4 (1): 87–101.

Hicks, D. (ed.) (1988) Is Technology Enough?, Washington, DC: American Enterprise Institute.

HM Treasury (2001) European Economic Reform: Meeting the Challenge, London: HM Treasury.

Hoeckel, K. (2008) Costs and Benefits in Vocational Education and Training, Paris: Organisation for Economic Co-operation and Development.

International Monetary Fund (2008) World Economic Outlook, October, Washington, DC. http://www.imf.org/external/pubs/ft/weo/2008/02/pdf/text. pdf.

Ito, Y. (1994) 'Information societies with strong and weak civil society traditions', in S. Splichl, A. Calabrese and C. Sparks (eds), Information Society and Civil Society: Contemporary Perspectives on the Changing World Order, West Lafayette, IN: Purdue University Press, pp. 233–253.

Jessop, B. (1992) 'Towards a Schumpeterian workfare state? Preliminary remarks on post-Fordist political economy', Studies in Political Economy, 40 (1): 7–40.

Kok, W. (ch.) (2004) Facing the Challenge: The Lisbon Strategy for Growth and Employment, Report from the High Level Group chaired by Wim Kok, November. http://ec.europa.eu/research/evaluations/pdf/archive/fp6-evidence-base/evaluation_studies_and_reports/evaluation_studies_and_reports_2004/the _lisbon_strategy_for_growth_and_employment__report_from_the_high_level_ group.pdf.

Kraak, A. (2005) 'The challenge of the "second economy" in South Africa: the contribution of skills development', Journal of Vocational Education and Training, 57 (4): 429–452.

Kraak, A. (2008) 'A critical review of the national skills development strategy in South Africa', Journal of Vocational Education and Training, 60 (1): 1–18.

Lado, A.A. and Wilson, M.C. (1994) 'Human resource systems and sustained competitive advantage: a competency-based perspective', Academy of Management Review, 19 (4): 699–727.

Landes, D.S. (2003) The Unbound Prometheus: Technological Change and Industrial Development in Western Europe from 1750 to the Present, Cambridge: Cambridge University Press (1st edition 1969).

Le Deist, F. and Tūtlys, V. (2012) 'Limits to mobility: competence and qualifications in Europe', European Journal of Training and Development, 36 (2/3): 262–285.

Le Deist, F. and Winterton, J. (2005) 'What is competence?', Human Resource Development International, 8 (1): 27–46.

Low, L. (2002) 'Globalisation and the political economy of Singapore's policy on foreign talent and high skills', Journal of Education and Work, 15 (4): 409–425.

Machlup, F. (1962) The Production and Distribution of Knowledge in the United States, Princeton, NJ: Princeton University Press.

Manacorda, M. and Petrongolo, B. (1999) 'Skill mismatch and unemployment in OECD countries', Economica, 66: 181–207.

Mansfield, B. (2004) 'Competence in transition', Journal of European Industrial Training, 28 (2/3/4): 296–309.

McCracken, M. and Winterton, J. (2006) 'What about the managers? Contradictions in lifelong learning and management development', International Journal of Training and Development, 10 (1): 55–66.

Ministry of Foreign Affairs of Japan (1995) The Osaka Action Agenda. Implementation of the Bogor Declaration. http://www.mofa.go.jp/policy/economy/apec/1995/agenda.html.

Neugart, M. and Schömann, K. (eds) (2002) Forecasting Labour Markets in OECD Countries: Measuring and Tackling Mismatches, Cheltenham, UK and Northampton, MA, USA: Edward Elgar.

OECD (1994a) The OECD Jobs Study: Evidence and Explanations. Part I: Labour Market Trends and Underlying Forces of Change, Paris: Organisation for Economic Co-operation and Development.

OECD (1994b) The OECD Jobs Study: Evidence and Explanations. Part II: The Adjustment Potential of the Labour Market, Paris: Organisation for Economic Co-operation and Development.

OECD (1998) Technology, Productivity and Job Creation: Best Policy Practices, OECD Jobs Strategy 1998 Edition, Paris: Organisation for Economic Co-operation and Development.

OECD (2008) 'Skills for competitiveness: tackling the low skilled equilibrium conceptual framework', Note by the Secretariat, 53rd Session 27–28 November, Paris: Organisation for Economic Co-operation and Development.

OECD (2012) Better Skills, Better Jobs, Better Lives: A Global Approach to Skills Policies, Paris: Organisation for Economic Co-operation and Development. http://skills.oecd.org/documents/oecdskillsstrategy.html.

Rees, T. (1998) Mainstreaming Equality in the European Union: Education, Training and Labour Market Policies, London: Routledge.

Reich, R.K. (1991) The Work of Nations: Preparing Ourselves for 21st Century Capitalism, New York, NY: Vintage.

Rutledge, I. and Wright, P. (eds) (2010) UK Energy Policy and the End of Market Fundamentalism, Oxford: Oxford University Press.

Ryan, I. and Macky, K. (1998) 'Downsizing organizations: uses, outcomes and strategies', Asia Pacific Journal of Human Resources, 36 (2): 29–45.

Sanderson, S.M. (1998) 'New approaches to strategy: new ways of thinking for the new millennium', Management Decision, 36 (1): 9–14.

Schuler, R.S. and Jackson, S.E. (1987) 'Linking competitive strategies with human resource management practices', Academy of Management Executive, 1 (3): 207–219.

Schuler, R.S. and MacMillan, I.C. (1984) 'Gaining competitive advantage through human resource management practices', Human Resource Management, 23 (3): 241–255.

Schultz, T.W. (1963) The Economic Value of Education, New York, NY: Columbia University Press.

Schumpeter, J.A. (1939) Business Cycles: A Theoretical, Historical and Statistical Analysis of the Capitalist Process, London: McGraw-Hill.

Steedman, H. and Wagner, K. (1987) 'A second look at productivity, machinery and skills in Britain and Germany', National Institute Economic Review, 122: 84–95.

Stiglitz, J. (2002) Globalization and its Discontents, New York, NY: W.W. Norton.

Stuart, L. (1999) 21st Century Skills for 21st Century Jobs, A Report of the U.S. Department of Commerce, U.S. Department of Education, U.S.

Department of Labor, National Institute for Literacy and Small Business Administration.

Taylor, M.J. and Thrift, N.J. (eds) (1986) Multinationals and the Restructuring of the World Economy, London: Croom Helm.

UNDP (1990) Human Development Report: Defining and Measuring Human Development, New York: United Nations Development Program Publications.

UNDP (2003) Arab Human Development Report, New York: United Nations Development Program Publications.

Valenduc, G., Vendramin, P., Krings, B.-J. and Nierling, L. (2008) How Restructuring is Changing Occupations. Case Study Evidence from Knowledge-Intensive, Manufacturing and Service Occupations, Leuven: HIVA (Research Institute for Work and Society).

White Paper (2003) 21st Century Skills: Realising Our Potential, Cm 5810, London: Department for Education and Skills, Department of Trade and Industry, HM Treasury and Department for Work and Pensions.

Winterton, J. (2000) 'Social dialogue over vocational training in market-led systems', International Journal of Training and Development, 4 (1): 8–23.

Winterton, J. (2007) 'Training, development and competence', in P. Boxall, J. Purcell and P. Wright (eds), The Oxford Handbook of Human Resource Management, Oxford: Oxford University Press, pp. 324–343.

Winterton, J. (2009) 'Competence across Europe: highest common factor or lowest common denominator?' Journal of European Industrial Training, 33 (8/9): 681–700.

Winterton, J. (2011) 'Competence in European policy instruments: a moving target for developing a National Qualifications Framework?' Journal of Contemporary Educational Studies, 62 (5): 72–87.

Winterton, J. (ed.) (2013) Trade Union Strategies for Developing Competence at Work: An Emerging Area for Social Dialogue, London: Routledge, forthcoming.

Winterton, J. and Forde, C. (2013) 'Europe en crise: vers un modèle heuristique de la restructuration', in F. Le Deist (ed.) Restructurations et santé au travail : tendances et perspectives, Toulouse: Octarès, pp. 27–46.

Winterton, J. and Haworth, N. (2013) 'Employability', in V. Pulignano and G. Della Rocca (eds), The Transformation of Employment Relations in Europe: Institutions and Outcomes in the Age of Globalisation, London: Routledge, forthcoming.

World Bank (1997) World Development Report 1997: The State in a Changing World, New York: Oxford University Press.

Zidan, S.S. (2001) 'The role of HRD in Economic Development', Human Resource Development Quarterly, 12 (4): 437–43.

Zuboff, S. (1988) In the Age of the Smart Machine: The Future of Work and Power, London: Heinemann.

6. Investing in labour force and skills development

John Field

1. INTRODUCTION

The OECD recently opened its skills strategy with the words: 'Skills have become the global currency of the 21st century' (OECD 2012: 3). Such language is very familiar, and the case for investing in skills is widely accepted – so much so that there is a risk of taking it for granted. In recent years, governments have sought to respond to the challenges of the global knowledge economy by paying increasing attention to skills and education. In addition, because of demographic change, most governments have acknowledged, at least formally, the importance of continuing development and learning by the existing workforce. The United Nations Population Division has estimated that in developed nations, the proportion of the population that is of working age will fall from 61 per cent in 2011 to 51 per cent in 2050, while the old-age-dependency ratio is set to grow from 12 to 48 per hundred of the working-age population (United Nations 2011: 6, 448–9). One possible strategy is to attract skilled migrants, though this is often politically controversial, and anyway migrants also grow older over time. So for many governments, as well as for many enterprises, increasing the adaptability, productivity and employability of workers, and improving their capacity for lifelong learning, presents a pressing challenge.

This is both an encouraging and a challenging context in which to explore the role of skills and development as ways of delivering sustainable national and regional growth and improving living standards and well-being. It is encouraging because it acknowledges and indeed gives enormous prominence to the role and contribution of specialists in human resource development, as well as to others who help to deliver and manage the skills and knowledge that their organization requires. At the same time, though, this visibility and promise places considerable responsibility on the shoulders of those who are charged with developing their organization's capacity; increased expectations always bring increased pressures to deliver. At national level, the same tensions play out in slightly different ways, not least because governments operate to a particular timescale and dynamic that is inevitably different from that of most organizations. In public, governments everywhere have espoused the language of life-long learning, but they are rarely able to supply the resources to sustain increases in public provision – on the contrary, many governments are unable, or unwilling, to maintain current levels of funding. Thus the state increasingly finds itself in the role of a co-ordinator and advocate, seeking to encourage and incentivize behaviour by others rather than by taking responsibility for delivering all the training and development that is required (Field 2000). Once more, though, the recognition that human capital is an indispensible strategic and policy resource brings the risk of disenchantment if for any reason the suppliers of training and development are seen to have failed.

Training and development is a vast topic, and it has become even larger with the more general adoption of the language and goals of lifelong learning. This chapter will therefore start by clarifying some of the key terms, before proceeding to an exploration of recent research on the benefits of learning for individuals as well as for organizations; this evidence is potentially important in widening the debate about skills and development, and yet it has so far received very little attention from trainers and others involved in supporting learning. I then go on to examine current policies and strategic approaches to skills development. I will then review recent research into actual practices, and how these translate into the experience of learning and development, both at the level of the workplace and for the labour force. I will then conclude by identifying a number of tensions and contradictions that need to be resolved in order to develop skills for growth.

2. DEFINING THE TERMS, MEASURING THE EVIDENCE

For most people, the language of training and skills is largely taken for granted, but in fact both terms are problematic. Leaving aside the question of translation between different languages, even within the English-speaking world there are important questions about definition. In all languages, moreover, we can distinguish between the explicit and overt meaning of a word, and the more implicit associations that it carries within a particular culture. The distinction between education and training is a rich source of humour, but if we consider the word 'training' for more than a moment, then we are brought right up against an entrenched view of training as somehow an inferior and inherently narrow activity. This may be one of the reasons why, in the English-speaking world and above all in Britain, professional associations have opted to use the word 'development' alongside or even in place of training.

Training has been defined as 'the process of acquiring the knowledge and skills related to work requirements by formal, structured or guided means' (Training Agency 1987: 14). This is rather a narrow notion of training (see the discussion in Tight 2002: 19–22). Moreover, it very much locates training within an 'acquisition' mode of learning, in contrast to current tendencies to understand learning in terms of 'participation' or 'construction' (Sfard 1998; Engeström 2001). Martyn Sloman, then a senior member of the Chartered Institute of Personnel and Development, has suggested that training must be undertaken within an organizational perspective, defining it as 'a deliberate act by the organisation' and 'an intervention designed to achieve an organisational objective' (Sloman 2003: xiv).

Training has a wide range of different meanings for different people. One British study reported that:

- The population at large had a much narrower understanding of the term than that held by most training professionals;
- For most people, training was what happened in formal, taught courses;
- Employers had a narrower definition still, largely seeing training as something that they funded or initiated;
- Activities which are self-directed or self-funded are less likely to be viewed as training;
- Understandings of training vary by level of education and other characteristics;
- For most people, the boundary between training and education is blurred and indistinct.

These popular understandings of training were, the authors noted, far more narrow and specific than the broad definitions that are used by researchers and policy makers; it follows that training levels go under-reported in many surveys (Campanelli and Channell 1994). More recent evidence from the UK Employer Skills Survey suggests that many managers do not see coaching or mentoring as forms of training (Winterbotham et al. 2011: 21).

The notion of skill at first appears relatively straightforward, at least by comparison with the idea of training. But again it has connotations that can be loaded down with cultural baggage. In Britain, the word was for long associated with status hierarchies inside the labour force; a 'skilled worker' (or, often, a 'skilled man') was someone who had completed a particular type of apprenticeship, and whose status and autonomy was often fiercely protected by trade unions. This was one reason why the Conservative Government in 1980s Britain decided to promote instead the language of competence, which it adopted as part of a wider move towards a standard-based qualifications framework that recognized specific sets of outcomes (or standards of performance) rather than signalling a rounded socialization into the culture and practices of an entire occupation (Hodkinson and Issitt 1995). Yet the language of skill, and the positive associations that it evokes, continued to be widely used. Indeed, the term has been enlarged in response to underlying changes in the economy, which have resulted in the use of the term to encompass attributes such as communication, teamwork, problem-solving, creativity and other so-called 'generic skills'. To confuse matters further, many languages use variations on the word 'competences' (*Kompetenzen, compétences*) to denote what in English would be called skills. In practice, much training is not really concerned with learning new skills – at least, not in the sense in which most people use the word. Quite a high volume of training is undertaken in order to comply with legislative requirements or regulatory frameworks, which demand that people train to a specified standard regardless of whether they already have this knowledge or not. In Britain, for example, 71 per cent of employers reported that they had provided health and safety training in 2011 (Davies et al. 2012: 113).

In recent years, the language and idea of lifelong learning has started to reshape how we see and understand skills and knowledge. In part, this has involved a new language, with many people now referring less often to the activities of training and teaching, and instead emphasizing the activities of, and forms of support for, learning. I have argued elsewhere that this discursive shift is associated with a rebalancing of responsibilities for learning, with a reduced role for the state and increases for individuals and employers, as well as with a sharpened interest in constructivist theories of knowledge creation and skills development (Field 2006). Greatly influenced by the seminal and popularly written work of Jean Lave and Etienne Wenger on situated learning, constructivist theories emphasize the ways in which workers produce and share their skills and knowledge through participation in the workplace (Lave and Wenger 2001). In this model, rather than trainers and trainees, learning occurs when a novice participant is accompanied and guided by more experienced workers from peripheral to full participation. However, employers in general are likely to understand training as involving a relatively simple transfer and acquisition of knowledge and skills between expert and novice (Winterbotham et al. 2011: 13–14).

These definitional and terminological issues help us understand why it can sometimes be challenging to agree on how skills and training should be measured. At enterprise level, Kirkpatrick's model of training evaluation has dominated the field since its first publication in the 1960s (Kirkpatrick 1967). This model proposed four 'levels' of criteria for evaluating training: reactions, or how people feel about the training they have received; learning, or what they know as a result of the training; behaviour, or what they can now do; and results, understood as the influence that the new skills and knowledge have on the organization's performance. While this model has been widely criticized in the academic literature as over-simplifying training, and presenting the outcomes as a linear sequence organized in an unproblematic hierarchy, its clarity and applicability continue to appeal to professionals in the field (Yardley and Dornan 2012). Surveys of current practice tend to confirm the view that few organizations have moved towards more creative ways of evaluating and measuring training. In the UK, for example, the most frequently used tools are post-course evaluations (commonly known as 'happy sheets'), and individual testimonies, followed by attempts to measure outcomes, and finally by assessments of the impact on key business objectives (CIPD 2011: 5). Similarly, most US training managers use only the low-effort levels of evaluation, such as measuring participant reactions and assessing their learning, with relatively few attempting to estimate the results in organizational terms or calculate the return on investment (ASTD 2010: 21).

This focus on simple evaluation tools is a rational response to the difficulties of estimating the organizational return on investment from training. The first challenge is to distinguish the effects of training from all the other factors in the workplace that might affect productivity. Very few studies have tried to separate out the impact of training from the effects of other strategic interventions, such as appraisal, profit-sharing or worker participation in decisions (for an exception see Akhtar et al. 2008). The second is to discriminate between the effects of training on the worker and the influence of the worker's characteristics on skills acquisition; economists believe, for example, that employer selection decisions are biased in favour of the most capable workers, so that employers sometimes overestimate the results of training activities (Vignoles et al. 2004). Third, at company level, there is some empirical support for the intuitive belief that low performance enterprises are less likely to train than high performance enterprises (Dearden et al. 2006; Zwick 2006). Finally, there is the question of time-scale: in most cases, a very long time period is needed to monitor the effects of training, and even if managers are willing to take the long view, the prospects of other factors intervening is therefore increased.

Economics, particularly in the form of human capital theory, has made a particular contribution to the measurement debate. Essentially, this theory states that skills and knowledge are a form of capital, and that part of this capital is the result of deliberate investment. Initially the idea was developed by Theodore Schultz as a way of exploring the economic value of education, particularly in relation to economic growth (Schultz 1961). Subsequently, the theory was developed by Gary Becker, who extended the analysis to include continuing training as well as other investments in skills, as well as developing a sophisticated cost-benefit analysis as a way of explaining educational decisions. Thus Becker distinguished, for example, between general training, which he claimed was mainly of benefit to the worker as it raised their future wages by improving their attractiveness to other employers; and firm-specific training, which he saw as more likely to benefit the employer, by raising productivity without raising wages (Becker 1993: 31–51). For Becker, this distinction meant that employers would pay for specific training, but normally general training would be paid for by the worker. He also argued that employers would invest more in those workers where they could expect the greatest return; one side effect of this pattern was lower investment in women workers, because they spent less time in the labour force than men (Becker 1993: 88).

Human capital theory has been widely criticized for what some see as its excessive individualism and its reliance on rational choice models of decision-making (Field 2003: 21–2). By treating skill as an attribute of the individual worker, and explaining all decisions as the result of rational calculations of individual rates of return, it is argued that human capital theory is deeply flawed conceptually and unable to deal with the socially embedded nature of decision-making. The theory has also been attacked for its use of over-simplified tools of measurement, such as years of schooling or the gaining of formal qualifications, which are unrelated to actual skills and abilities. Finally, it tends to present a direct linear model of investment and return, yet empirically much research on returns to education have suggested that the relationship may be multi-linear and iterative (these concerns are rehearsed in Field et al. 2000: 249–51). Nevertheless, the theory certainly has some explanatory power, and has been widely supplemented by forms of cost-benefit analysis to inform decisions about the funding of training and development activities.

3. SECURING KNOWLEDGE AND SKILLS DEVELOPMENT

Skills and their development command almost universal support. Policy makers proclaim that upskilling will lead to greater competitiveness, inclusion and cohesion, while employers and trade unions alike proclaim their support for training and development. In fact, it is virtually impossible to find anyone who opposes upskilling. In part, this arises from simple demographics. By European standards, the United Kingdom is a relatively youthful country, but even here the Government is concerned that something like four of every five people who will be in the workforce in 2020 has already completed their initial education (Department for Business, Innovation and Skills 2010: 4). The adaptability and employability of this existing workforce depends in large part on the extent to which it can continue to develop and apply new skills and abilities. For workers themselves, transitions are becoming both more numerous and often more complex, and thus more uncertain, whether they are transitions within a workplace, between workplaces, or from work into retirement. From a wider public policy perspective, a nation's presumed innovation capacities and competitiveness will also be affected. There is therefore a considerable stake for governments and for employers in developing strategies for upskilling the workforce and investing in its future potential.

Producing firm evidence of the gains from training is much easier now than it was a few years ago. However, even though our knowledge has improved, it remains patchy. Much recent research on the rates of return to learning has focused on the gains to the individual and to a lesser extent the organization (enterprise), with relatively few studies focusing on the rate of return to the nation or region. There has also been a very marked concentration on initial education. Unfortunately, economists often use the number of years of schooling as an indicator of education investment, and formal qualifications as an indicator of output. Both are very crude proxy indicators of what human resource developers are seeking to measure, and both reflect a focus on the initial education system. However, recent analyses of longitudinal data have therefore been important in turning attention towards the longer term effects of learning across the life span, and such studies have generally identified small but significant rises in earnings for adults who gain a new qualification; in the UK, there is also evidence of wage gains arising from improvements in literacy and numeracy skills. The employability benefits are even more consistently shown in this literature (Field 2012). Drawing on data from performance in standardized tests for literacy, numeracy and problem-solving skills, OECD analysts have shown a clear and linear relationship between weak skills and the likelihood of experiencing economic and social disadvantage more generally (OECD 2012: 10–11). There are also clear gains in subjective well-being as a result of upskilling (Hammond and Feinstein 2006).

Despite the policy consensus in favour of upskilling, and widespread evidence that it has both private and social benefits, there remain a number of controversies over the best ways of promoting continuing training. Particularly contested areas include the funding of training, and in particular, the question of who should pay for what? To what extent should the state intervene, whether as direct provider of learning and development, or as an enabler and incentivizer? Moreover, as well as the financing of skill formation, Busemeyer and Trampusch identify three other 'neuralgic points' of conflict: the tension between enterprise autonomy and state involvement (who controls what), the balance between school and firm in initial vocational education and training, and the relationship between the VET system and the wider educational system (Busemeyer and Trampusch 2012b: 16). In addition, when it comes to continuing skills development for the adult workforce, there is the question of what involvement public education bodies such as universities and colleges should have and on what basis.

Moreover, much policy focus has concentrated, perhaps understandably, on the areas of growth. In occupational terms, this has often led policy makers to present summaries of labour market trends that show an increase in high-skill employment, and project a continued decline of low-skilled jobs. However, as the OECD has noted, while there is indeed growth in some high-skill occupations, such as managers and scientists, the loss of traditional male unskilled jobs has been largely balanced by a growth of low-paid service jobs, often performed by women; it is the middle skill jobs that tend to experience relative declines, whether in services or in manufacturing, partly because these occupations can be transformed through computerization or even automation (OECD 2010: 24–5).

From a policy perspective, the pace of change and the degree of uncertainty in the labour market imply a focus on providing workers with robust skills and the capacity to develop new competences. This requires strong basic skills (literacy, numeracy and information technology) through initial education, or through compensatory measures for those who did not develop these basic skills earlier in life. Increasingly, governments are also seeking ways of developing what are sometimes called generic or key skills or transversal competences, such as problem-solving, team-working, communications and perhaps above all, 'learning to learn' (European Commission 2010: 10). In developing its policies for skills and employment, the European Commission continues to call for 'comprehensive lifelong learning' as a way of achieving the balance of flexible and secure employment that it describes as 'flexicurity' (European Commission 2010: 5–6).

There is also an emerging debate over the balance between supply and demand. It has been argued that particularly in Britain, public policy focuses excessively on the supply of skill, and virtually ignores other factors involved in determining productivity, such as investment strategies and work organization (Keep et al. 2006). In some countries, though, policy attention has recently widened to encompass the utilization of skills as well as their formation. This development is usually dated back to a 2001 report, in which the OECD argued that it was not enough simply to invest in improved skills; if new skills were to contribute to improved performance, it proposed that work practices must also change. This was not, the OECD stated, simply a matter of introducing new techniques and tools; it also meant 'a reorganization of work', with particular attention to such factors as employee involvement, flexible working and flatter hierarchies that favoured high performance working and technological innovation (OECD 2001: 15–16). OECD has described these features as characteristics of the 'learning organization', accompanied by human resources practices that are aligned with the goal of continuous learning and smooth internal communications (OECD 2010: 73–4).

So far, the policy implications of a focus on skills utilization are not entirely clear. For example, the Scottish Government's skills strategy has clearly identified a need to improve the demand for skilled work in the economy, as well as to enhance the utilization of the workforce's existing capabilities; but the strategy has yet to identify and develop clear interventions by government that might help to promote these desirable goals (Scottish Government 2010). Nevertheless, strategies that seek to make the best use of existing skills, as well as developing new ones, have considerable potential if they can be operationalized in concrete ways. They are likely to be particularly important for enterprises that employ significant numbers of such groups as older workers, who are likely to remain active in the labour market where their existing knowledge and competences are recognized (Canning 2011; OECD 2012: 64–72). This is, then, work in progress (Payne 2010).

4.   DEVELOPING SKILLS IN PRACTICE

Investing in skills can take a variety of forms. Particularly with the advent of interest in lifelong learning, human resource managers have started to explore a broad range of ways of developing skills. In part, this is also a response to the changing nature of work, as well as to the increasing potential of new technologies as ways of communicating information and ideas. A number of studies suggest that while face-to-face delivery remains the norm, it is increasingly being challenged by newer forms of training (CEDEFOP 2010: 65). These included blended learning, coaching, and mentoring, all of which appear to be particularly prominent in the UK but are being widely adopted across the European Union (Observatoire CEGOS 2012: 3). More radical forms of innovative learning, such as job rotation and learning circles, are used relatively rarely; however, job rotation is an important additional form of training in some countries, particularly Sweden and Austria, while learning circles are similarly important in Austria and Denmark (CEDEFOP 2010: 66).

In 2009, the most widespread forms of delivery in US organizations were classroom instruction, coaching, blended learning and mentoring, in that order (ASTD 2010: 24). While face-to-face instruction still seems to be the most common form of delivery, its importance is declining, both in absolute terms and as a proportion of the total volume of training activity. In the United States, the average share of learning time that was accounted for by instructor-led activity fell from 71 per cent in 2002 to 59 per cent in 2009 (ASTD 2010: 16–7). The use of technology rose over the same period, particularly in the form of blended learning. Although much is made of the potential of social media for supporting learning, and its use for non-work purposes is widespread among younger workers, it was estimated in 2009 that the adoption of social media tools and technologies for training and development was in its infancy (ASTD 2010: 23).

The question of how much is paid for training and by whom is a rather vexed one. There is considerable controversy over the level of investment in skills, as well as in the distribution of investment between government, workers and employers. The American Society for Training and Development (ASTD) estimated that US organizations spent $125.88 billion on employee learning and development in 2009, while in the UK, the 2011 Employer Skill Survey suggested a total spend of some £49 billion (ASTD 2010: 9; Davies et al. 2012: 123). There is a very clear size pattern. In general, large firms tend to spend more per worker on training than smaller firms (Davies et al. 2012: 124; CEDEFOP 2010: 101–4). The average spend is also higher in financial and business services than in other sectors (CEDEFOP 2010: 101–4; Davies et al. 2012: 129). Analysis of the European CVT Survey suggests an average spending by enterprises on training of under 1 per cent of total labour costs, ranging from a high of 1.9 per cent in Ireland to a low of 0.3 per cent in Greece (CEDEFOP 2010: 92). Spending in the States was proportionately higher, averaging around 2.14 per cent of payroll (ASTD 2010: 9).

Professionalization of training has developed unevenly in recent years.

Across Europe, some 15 per cent of enterprises have a training centre, 32 per cent have a dedicated training budget, and 42 per cent have a named individual with overall responsibility for training. In all these cases, larger firms were more likely to have dedicated resources, and smaller firms were less likely (CEDEFOP 2010: 38–40). As for training supply, much takes place within the private sector, which is large and fragmented, with a small number of very large providers, often providing training as one of several business services or as an addition to their main product (as in IT supply); and a very large number of small providers, including a sizeable number of sole traders who may provide training on an intermittent or part-time basis. In many countries, this disparate private sector has grown rapidly. A study conducted just before the recession in the UK noted that the number of training providers registered for value-added tax doubled between 2000 and 2008 (Simpson 2009: 10).

Estimates of the overall volume of skill development are plentiful, but often difficult to interpret. Many of the larger surveys of participation in training are based on data collected before the onset of recession in 2008. The 2005 European Continuing Vocational Training Survey found that participation rates ranged from a low of 11 per cent of the workforce in Latvia to a high of 59 per cent in the Czech Republic; the proportion of enterprises providing training ranged from 85 per cent in Denmark down to 21 per cent in Greece (CEDEFOP 2010: 19). It has been suggested that the 2005 survey also provides evidence pointing towards a degree of convergence within Europe, at least in respect of overall levels of training activity (CEDEFOP 2010: 25). In another indicator of training volume, the OECD estimated that in 2007, the average worker spent almost 60 hours in non-formal – that is, other than initial education at school or college – job-related learning; South Korea had the highest level of learning time, at almost 80 hours per worker, and Slovenia the lowest, at under 30 (OECD 2011: 367). Overall, the OECD findings suggest that an individual can expect to receive 715 hours of non-formal job-related learning across his or her working life.

Of course, these are overall figures. In practice, participation in training varies enormously across the workforce, with significant variations by sector. For example, training provision is often found to be highest in sectors involving person-to-person services. In the UK, for example, the Employer Skill Survey has shown that training levels are much higher than average in health, social care and education, followed closely by public administration and financial services; it is notably below average in agriculture, manufacturing, transport and communications (Davies et al. 2012: 110). European data also suggest that formalized arrangements for training are most common in the finance sector, followed by the gas, water and electricity industries (CEDEFOP 2010: 44).

Perhaps unsurprisingly, participation is higher in firms where collective bargaining covers training than in those where there are no joint agreements (CEDEFOP 2010: 55–7). Some governments actively involve trade unions in promoting levels of training, and ensuring its relevance. In the UK, for example, the Labour Government sought to promote investment in training by encouraging the appointment from 2000 of workplace union learning representatives (ULR); by 2009, over 10,000 union members had served for at least a period as a ULR, most of whom had never held a union office previously (Saundry et al. 2010: 12). An early study of workplace survey findings from 2004 suggested that while there was a weak positive relationship between union membership density and training levels, with very few UK unions using their bargaining role to negotiate over skills and training, the presence of ULRs appeared to make little difference to the number of workers being trained or the average duration of training (Hoque and Bacon 2008: 711–13). Later research has modified this rather pessimistic initial view, suggesting that as they have become a more accepted feature of the landscape, ULRs have helped increase awareness of and support for training and learning among union members, as well as helping support those who wished to take a course. Managers reported that in some cases, ULRs have also helped develop new courses, particularly in basic skills areas such as literacy, computing and numeracy (Saundry et al. 2010).

Participation also varies by worker characteristics. Age is a major factor, with participation falling rapidly over the life course (Boateng 2009: 3). According to OECD data, older people also receive the lowest number of hours of continuing training (OECD 2011: 367). Immigrant workers experience lower levels of training than the average (Rosenbladt and Bilger 2011: 67). Occupational status is another factor, with participation rates rising among white collar workers, and peaking among managers and professionals (Boateng 2009: 4; Rosenbladt and Bilger 2011: 68). And it varies by prior education, with particularly low participation rates in most countries among workers with no formal qualifications (Boateng 2009: 5; OECD 2011: 377). Seen from the perspective of human capital theory, the most precarious and least skilled appear to represent a poor investment. There is some empirical support for this generalization, in the form of survey evidence on the priorities of human resource and training managers in enterprises (Observatoire CEGOS 2012: 4). In general, these patterns can be found across most countries, though the inequalities are greater in some cases than others.

Gender is also a factor that affects participation, though not necessarily

in a straightforward manner. Some evidence points to an under-represen-
tation of women. For example, in 18 of the 25 countries covered by the
OECD, men received more hours of training than women (OECD 2011:
368). However, overall figures for the UK suggest that training provision is broadly in line with the share of women in the workforce, while
female participation is slightly above that of men (Canduela et al. 2012:
47; Department for Business, Innovation and Skills 2008: 29). The same
has been found for Germany, where roughly the same proportions of men
and women participate in vocational training (43 per cent against 42 per
cent); among part-time workers in Germany, women were more likely to
undergo training than men (Rosenbladt and Bilger 2011: 65–6). These patterns can be extremely difficult to interpret and evaluate, partly because
of the persistence of gendered labour markets, arising from the tendency
of some occupations to remain predominantly female while others remain
predominantly male. There is also some evidence that some women, particularly those with caring responsibilities, tend to make different occupational choices from men, though whether this is for positive or for negative
reasons remains contentious (Hakim 1996). One analysis of data from
the European Social Survey, which controlled for such other factors as
worker and occupational characteristics, found that all other things being
equal, male workers in any given category were more likely to participate
in training than their female equivalents (Dieckhoff and Steiber 2011). For
some commentators, this is explicable in terms of human capital theory:
employers are likely to invest less in women workers because they are less
prone to stay with the firm, and therefore the return on investment will
be lower; and women workers are likely to under-invest in training if they
see themselves as secondary earners (Hakim 1996: 69, 121). In so far as
these factors cease to characterize women workers, then the human capital
argument implies that women workers will receive similar training investment to their male counterparts.

Such equity issues have a wider importance, as a number of studies
show that for people of working age, access to education is largely decided
or denied by their occupational position. Work-related learning accounts
for much participation in adult education more generally (Boateng 2009:
3). More broadly, much of the variation in participation in learning more
generally appears to be explained by transitions in the workplace (Biesta et
al. 2011: 38–40). As we have seen, moreover, participating in training has a
number of positive outcomes for individuals and organizations, as well as
for regions and nations. In adopting lifelong learning policies from the late
1990s, a number of countries insisted that their policies would promote
'lifelong learning for all', in the belief that the new economy required a
step change in skills levels across the board, and not only among a small

number of key workers (Field 2006; OECD 2012). Relatively few countries have succeeded in achieving this balanced approach to skills, though
in general, the open Nordic economies tend to be characterized by high
overall participation and low levels of inequality. Drawing on ESS data,
Dieckhoff and Steiber found that although the gender gaps were similar
in all the 25 countries studied, they appeared to be less pronounced in the
Nordic nations (Dieckhoff and Steiber 2011: 151).

A number of commentators have singled out these Northern European
nations as particularly successful, often attributing their effectiveness at
skills formation to the arrangement of institutions that are sometimes
referred to as 'co-ordinated market economies' (Green et al. 2006). Of
course, such arrangements are themselves dynamic, and must adapt to
changing circumstances. They are currently in a significant process of
adjustment as a result not only of globalized competitive pressures and
the shift away from manufacturing and primary industry, but also as
a result of Europeanization and changing political complexion of the
governments (and electorates) involved. While these change factors are
commonly acknowledged in the literature (see the essays in Busemeyer
and Trampusch 2012a), it is less often recognized that these collective skill
arrangements appear to be much stronger in strengthening initial vocational training than they are in promoting continuing skills development.

5.   TRENDS AND PROSPECTS

Skills development is widely embraced as a way of securing future success
in an uncertain economic environment. Yet although there is a strong
general consensus on the value of skills, and the need to promote learning
and development throughout working life, there is less agreement on the
priorities and methods to be adopted. Partly this is because there are real
differences of interest at stake, in a context where different parts of any
organization will have different interests, and where information about
the outcomes of training is often incomplete and unevenly shared. It is
still common for many managers to view training as a cost, rather than
as an investment; and it is also common for governments, particularly in
the more liberal economies like Britain and the USA, to separate training
programmes for vulnerable groups (such as the unemployed) from policies
for skills training in industry, which tend to view training as primarily a
private concern. This is, then, a field characterized by continuing tensions
and uncertainties.

Some of these arise from conflicts between current economic patterns
and interests on the one hand and those that we may view as desirable to

achieve sustainable growth. If policies focus on skills for high performance organizations, which may be in the long term public interest, then they will likely neglect those organizations that specialize in low cost and low quality goods and services. Yet in the actually existing economy, low skill employment may be an important driver of growth for certain regions or nations, even if its long term fortunes are highly vulnerable to competition from other low-cost regions. Moreover, I have already noted that much recent research into skills development tends to emphasize the importance of knowledge creation within work teams, which requires a very different approach to strategy and policy from traditional training responses (Felstead et al. 2009: 203–48). Research into informal learning in the workplace has demonstrated the significance of relationships of reciprocity and trust, which enable the sharing of ideas, techniques and solutions to problems. Strategies and policies that foster such conditions are likely to prove extremely challenging for many managers, and also for many trainers, who will see them as involving decisions and choices that are outside their traditional expertise. Despite improvements in recent years, moreover, human resource development still has relatively low status within many organizations. The dominant management cliché, which speaks of people as 'our most important asset', risks reinforcing a culture of cynicism unless it is supported by real substance.

A further source of tension arises from the growth and proliferation of training suppliers. The growing economic importance of learning in a global knowledge economy creates new economic opportunities for skills developers and trainers. We can see this in the rapidly expanding number of private providers in the UK (Simpson 2009). The 'third sector' of voluntary and charitable organizations is also extremely active in many countries in providing training. In this ever more complex and crowded market place, quality assurance becomes a crucial issue. Among other 'kitemarks', the continuing development of specifications through the International Standards Organization is a particularly important example of a wider development. Most recently, the ISO has approved basic requirements for providers of learning services in non-formal education and training, ISO 29990:2010. Its underlying aim is to enhance transparency and allow comparison on a worldwide basis of learning services. However, this too is a crowded field. Within the EU, Member States and the European Commission have been working to establish a European Quality Assurance Reference Framework (EQAVET) to promote and monitor continuous improvement of national systems of vocational education and training (VET). Whether such schemes will develop any traction in such a disparate and growing area, which at present is largely unregulated outside certain specialist areas, remains at present an open question.

Skills development is one of the main levers for survival and success in a highly competitive global market place. By the same token, it must play a central role in promoting inclusion and equality of opportunity for the most vulnerable and marginal. It is therefore a topic of interest to policy makers and researchers, as well as to those who lead enterprises and manage their workforce. As we have seen, there is also a substantial body of evidence that demonstrates the impact of training and skills development for individuals, which means that the subject is therefore of wider social interest to the public and the media. Sometimes, skills and training can be presented as 'magic bullets' which will crack a previously unsolved problem, from racism in the police to disasters on oil-rigs. Yet there is often a sense that skills and training are 'unsexy' subjects that only hit the headlines when things go wrong, or when they impinge upon an issue of wider concern, such as youth unemployment. If learners and potential learners are indeed to become a more powerful voice, as recent policy trends imply, then the degree of culture change will be very considerable indeed.

REFERENCES

Akhtar, S., Ding, D.Z. and Ge, G.L. (2008) 'Strategic HRM practices and their impact on company performance in Chinese enterprises', *Human Resource Management*, 47 (1): 15 –32.

ASTD (2010) *2010 State of the Industry Report*, Alexandria VA: ASTD.

Becker, G.S. (1993) *Human Capital: A Theoretical and Empirical Analysis*, 3rd edn (original 1964), Chicago: University of Chicago Press.

Biesta, G., Field, J., Hodkinson, P., Macleod, F. and Goodson, I. (2011) *Improving Learning through the Lifecourse*, Abingdon: Routledge.

Boateng, S.K. (2009) *Significant Country Differences in Adult Learning*, Luxembourg: Publications Office of the European Union.

Busemeyer, M.R. and Trampusch, C. (eds) (2012a) *The Political Economy of Collective Skill Formation*, Oxford: Oxford University Press.

Busemeyer, M.R. and Trampusch, C. (2012b) 'The comparative political economy of collective skill formation', in M.R. Busemeyer and C. Trampusch (eds), *The Political Economy of Collective Skill Formation*, Oxford: Oxford University Press, pp. 3–39.

Campanelli, P. and Channell, J. (1994) *Training: An Exploration of the Word and the Concept with an Analysis of the Implications for Survey Design*, London: Department of Employment.

Canduela, J., Dutton, M., Johnson, S., Lindsay, C., McQuaid, R. and Raeside, R. (2012) 'Aging, skills and participation in work-related training in Britain: assessing the position of older workers', *Work, Employment and Society*, 26 (1): 42–60.

Canning, R. (2011) 'Older workers in the hospitality industry: valuing experience and informal learning', *International Journal of Lifelong Education*, 30 (5):

667–79.CEDEFOP (2010) *Employer-provided Vocational Training in Europe*, Luxembourg: Publications Office of the European Union.

Chartered Institute of Personnel and Development (CIPD) (2011) *Learning and Talent Development: Annual Survey Report*, London: CIPD.

Davies, B., Gore, K., Winterbotham, M., Shury, J. and Vivian, D. (2012) *Employer Skills Survey 2011: UK Results*, Wath-upon-Dearne: United Kingdom Commission for Employment and Skills.

Dearden, L., Reed, H. and Van Reenan, J. (2006) 'The impact of training on productivity and wages: evidence from British panel data', *Oxford Bulletin of Economics and Statistics*, 68: 397–421.

Department for Business, Innovation and Skills (2008) *Continuing Vocational Training Survey 2005*, London: BIS.

Department for Business, Innovation and Skills (2010) *Skills for Sustainable Growth*, London: BIS.

Dieckhoff, M. and Steiber, N. (2011) 'A re-assessment of common theoretical approaches to explain gender differences in continuing training participation', *British Journal of Industrial Relations*, 49, Supplement 1: 135–57.

Engeström, Y. (2001) 'Expansive learning at work: toward an activity theoretical reconceptualization', *Journal of Education and Work*, 14 (1): 133–56.

European Commission (2010) *An Agenda for New Skills and Jobs: A European Contribution Towards Full Employment*, Luxembourg: Commission of the European Communities.

Felstead, A., Fuller, A., Jewson, N. and Unwin, L. (2009) *Improving Working as Learning*, Abingdon: Routledge.

Field, J. (2000) 'Governing the ungovernable: why lifelong learning policy promises more than it delivers', *Educational Management and Administration*, 28 (3): 249–61.

Field, J. (2003) *Social Capital*, London: Routledge.

Field, J. (2006) *Lifelong Learning and the New Educational Order*, Stoke-on-Trent: Trentham.

Field, J. (2012) 'Is lifelong learning making a difference? Research-based evidence on the impact of adult learning', in D. Aspin, J. Chapman, K. Evans and R. Bagnall (eds), *Second International Handbook of Lifelong Learning*, Dordrecht: Springer, pp. 887–897.

Field, J., Schuller, T. and Baron, S. (2000) 'Social capital and human capital revisited', in S. Baron, J. Field and T. Schuller (eds), *Social Capital: Critical Perspectives*, Oxford: Oxford University Press, pp. 243–63.

Green, A., Preston, J. and Janmaat, G. (2006) *Education, Equality and Social Cohesion: A Comparative Analysis*, Basingstoke: Palgrave.

Hakim, C. (1996) *Key Issues in Women's Work*, London: Athlone.

Hammond, C. and L. Feinstein (2006) 'Are those who flourished at school healthier adults? What role for adult education?', Research Report 17, London: Centre for Research on the Wider Benefits of Learning.

Hodkinson, P. and Issitt, M. (eds) (1995) *The Challenge of Competence: Professionalism through Vocational Education and Training*, London: Cassell.

Hoque, K. and Bacon, N. (2008) 'Trade unions, union learning representatives and employer-provided training in Britain', *British Journal of Industrial Relations*, 46 (4): 702–31.

Keep, E., Mayhew, K. and Payne, J. (2006) 'From skills revolution to productivity miracle: not as easy as it sounds', *Oxford Review of Economic Policy*, 22 (4): 539–59.

Kirkpatrick, D. L. (1967) 'Evaluation of training', in R.L. Craig and L.R. Bittel (eds), *Training and Development Handbook*, New York: McGraw-Hill, pp. 87–112.

Lave, J. and Wenger, E. (2001) *Situated Learning: Legitimate Peripheral Participation*, New York: Cambridge University Press.

Observatoire CEGOS (2012) *Enquête sur la formation professionelle en Europe*, Issy-les-Moulineaux: CEGOS.

OECD (2001) *The New Economy: Beyond the Hype*, Paris: OECD.

OECD (2010) *The OECD Innovation Strategy: Getting a Head Start on Tomorrow*, Paris: OECD.

OECD (2011) *Education at a Glance 2011*, Paris: OECD.

OECD (2012) *Better Skills, Better Jobs, Better Lives: A Strategic Approach To Skills Policies*, Paris: OECD.

Payne, J. (2010) *Skill Utilisation: Towards a Measurement and Evaluation Framework*, Cardiff: SKOPE.

Rosenbladt, B. von, and Bilger, F. (2011) *Weiterbildungsbeteiligung 2010*, Deutsche Institut für Erwachsenenbildung, Bielefeld.

Saundry, R., Hollinrake, A. and Antcliff, V. (2010) *Learning Works: Report of the 2009 Survey of Union Learning Representatives and Their Managers*, London: Trades Union Congress.

Schultz, T.W. (1961) 'Investment in human capital', *American Economic Review*, 51 (1): 1–17.

Scottish Government (2010) *Skills for Scotland*, Edinburgh: Scottish Government.

Sfard, A. (1998) 'On two metaphors for learning and the dangers of choosing just one', *Educational Researcher*, 27 (2): 4–13.

Simpson, L. (2009) *The Private Training Market in the UK*, Leicester: National Institute of Adult Continuing Education.

Sloman, M. (2003) *Training in the Age of the Learner*, London: Chartered Institute of Personnel and Development.

Tight, M. (2002) *Key Concepts in Adult Education and Training*, London: Routledge.

Training Agency (1987) *Training in Britain: A Study of Funding, Activity and Attitudes – Employers' Activities*, Sheffield: Training Agency.

United Nations (2011) *World Population Prospects: The 2010 Revision*, New York: United Nations Population Division.

Vignoles, A., Galindo-Rueda and Feinstein, L. (2004) 'The labour market impact of adult education and training: a cohort analysis', *Scottish Journal of Political Economy*, 51 (2): 266–80.

Winterbotham, M., Shury, J., Davies, B., Gore, K. and Newton, J. (2011) *Defining and Measuring Training Activity*, Wath-upon-Dearne: United Kingdom Commission for Employment and Skills.

Yardley, S. and Dornan, T. (2012) 'Kirkpatrick's levels and education evidence', *Medical Education*, 46 (1): 97–106.

Zwick, T. (2006) 'The impact of training intensity on establishment productivity', *Industrial Relations*, 45 (1): 26–46.

7. Mentorship, leadership and human resource development in Trinidad and Tobago

Christine Sahadeo and Sandra Sookram

1. INTRODUCTION

While practitioners and scholars promote the importance of mentorship in human resource development, few studies have empirically determined whether mentoring positively impacts leadership and human resource development, and if so, in what ways. According to McKimm et al. (2007), 'mentoring refers to a developmentally oriented interpersonal relationship that is typically between a more experienced individual (the mentor) and a less experienced individual (the mentee).' A number of scholars and certainly numerous practitioners have touted the importance of mentorship in promoting leader development (see, for example, McCauley et al. 2004). Even though there is widespread use of mentoring within firms, there is a lack of information when it comes to the link between human resource development and organizational development. The main objective of this study is to assess the perceptions and views of mentors and mentees in firms across various industrial sectors in Trinidad and Tobago with regard to the impact of mentorship on leadership and human resource development.

A growing body of academic and practitioner literature supports the popular perception that mentoring has considerable value to both individuals and organizations. Mentoring involves an intense, one-on-one relationship in which an experienced, senior person provides assistance to a less experienced, more junior colleague in order to enhance the latter's professional and personal development. Books and articles on mentoring began appearing in the scholarly and practitioner press in the late 1970s and early 1980s. Subsequently, interest in mentoring has steadily increased.

Entities in both the private and public sectors in Trinidad and Tobago have been using mentorship programs at various levels in the organization.

More recently the government launched a national mentorship program which encompassed five government ministries. This is in keeping with international best practice: for example the Federal government in the United States employs mentoring practices as a component of development, including comprehensive career development programs like the Senior Executive Service Candidate Development Program (SESCDP), the Executive Leadership Program (ELP) and the Presidential Management Fellowship (PMF) Program. The major function of mentoring within these programs is to promote the mentee's or protégé's development in specific areas and to facilitate successful completion of the program.

Mentorship programs are likely to be more cost-effective than traditional group-based interventions because they do not require contracted trainers, expensive keynote speakers, special classrooms, conference facilities, or other logistical resources. Since mentorship programs focus on leader development, many mentors will also improve as leaders alongside their mentees, and will most likely be better prepared to lead their own organizations.

This chapter is organized as follows. Section 2 examines mentorship in Trinidad and Tobago. Section 3 presents the theoretical framework within which this study is located. Section 4 describes the methodology and survey design and in Section 5 the survey findings are discussed. The chapter concludes with Section 6.

2.   MENTORSHIP IN TRINIDAD AND TOBAGO

Mentoring is now used by many companies to provide benefits to the mentee, mentor and the organization. Further, in the international arena special focus has been placed on mentoring for women to facilitate an improvement in the number of females at the corporate level.

Various interviews and surveys alike indicate that, compared with their male peers, high potential women are over-mentored, under-sponsored, and not advancing in their organizations. Without sponsorship, women are not only less likely than men to be appointed to top roles, but may also be more reluctant to go for them. Organizations such as Scotiabank have established sponsorship programs such as Advancement of Women (AoW) to facilitate the promotion of high-potential women.

The Association of Female Executives of Trinidad & Tobago (AFETT) was formed in 2002 with a vision to 'Make Women Winners', by exposing them to networking opportunities, leadership training and business ideas. Currently, AFETT draws inspiration from over 100 successful companies which represent its active and diverse membership. Their pledge is to keep their program of activities relevant to the changing needs of female professionals in Trinidad and Tobago.

One of the largest conglomerates in Trinidad and Tobago (now with branches and subsidiaries throughout Trinidad and Tobago) the Neal and Massy Group of Companies commenced operations in 1922. The success of the group is steeped in its successful mentorship program, initiated from its start by the founders of the organization, and it has a long history of mentorship. One of its founders, Harry Neal, on the retirement of co-founder Charles Massy in 1965, said, 'I have hired good people, and I am quite confident that they will do a good job. If need be give me a call.' This statement speaks volumes about the type of leadership practiced by the founders. Understanding the importance of experience, Neal again shared the importance of networking and mentoring when he said,

> I pick the best brains from all the top foreign executives who we deal with, that's the best education you can get. The important thing is to talk with people who are experienced and they have a track record in the particular industry. You do not have to reinvent the wheel yourself. You copy and learn from it.

The former Chief Executive Officer, Bernard Dulal-Whiteway, attributed the culture and success of the group to its founders and their legacy of values which were nurtured by successive employees. According to *Our Legacy, A History of the Neal and Massy Group of Companies* (in-house publication), 'For over three and a half decades, Charles Massy's legacy of mentorship and informal coaching played an important part in solidifying the leadership traits of the next generation of managers and securing the success of Neal and Massy'.

Another publicly listed company, Trinidad Cement Limited (TCL), has a very formal system of mentoring, which is part of the human resource function of the company. The detailed mentoring policy states 'TCL recognizes the value of mentoring as an instrument of organizational learning and has therefore renewed its emphasis and focus on the importance of continuous learning and improvement of its workforce through the enhancement and enrichment of its existing Mentorship Programme.' This company has branches in Barbados and Jamaica and exports to all Caribbean territories.

Many international companies which practice formal systems of mentoring have not introduced them similarly to the subsidiaries and branches that operate in Trinidad and Tobago. The origins of Unilever Caribbean Limited in Trinidad date back to 1929. The company embarked on several programs in sustainability and is very active in the community. However, information on mentoring at the company reveals that there was no formal mentoring program at Unilever Caribbean Limited. In contrast, Unilever Global has launched a series of global mentoring programs with the aim of providing leadership support, competitive advantage and secure talent for the future.

Coca-Cola Caribbean Bottlers Trinidad and Tobago Limited is a local company which makes and bottles the Coca-Cola beverage. This company has a franchise arrangement with Coca-Cola Foods, but it does not have similar human resource practices. The approach at Coca-Cola Foods includes the use of mentoring and coaching to develop their employees. Coca-Cola views coaching as enhancing performance by providing goals, techniques, practice and feedback, thereby increasing competence and the probability of success. Nonetheless, it appears that Coca-Cola Caribbean Bottlers Trinidad and Tobago Ltd has not benefited from the formal mentoring program offered by Coca-Cola Foods.

3.   THEORETICAL FRAMEWORK

3.1   The Classic or Traditional Approach to Mentoring versus the Contemporary Approach or Power Mentoring

The contemporary approach takes a long-term perspective on succession planning and organizational diversity and the process is initiated by the mentee, unlike the classic approach where succession planning is short term and initiated more by the mentor's wishes and needs. In traditional mentoring, benefits tend to be perceived as unidirectional with the mentee alone benefiting from the relationship. Traditional mentoring also leads to loyalty being organization-based. In power mentoring the focus is on complementary skills in that both mentor and mentee benefit; that is, there is reciprocity in the relationship. It also works in any type of organization of which the mentor is a part, and provides access to a powerful lineage of mentors. Further, in traditional mentoring there is the element of exclusivity, whereas in power mentoring there may be many mentors and mentoring may be termed an open relationship.

In traditional mentoring relationships, mentors support the mentee in three ways. They offer career guidance and help in their career paths. Mentors also provide emotional support and use these difficult situations as lessons, and so develop competencies in emotional intelligence. Moreover, the mentor serves as a role model who demonstrates the application of emotional competencies. In essence there are many advantages to the traditional mentoring relationship. The technique should not be discarded but should be considered as part of the power mentoring system.

The major difference is the power of choice as it gives those involved the option of relying not on one mentor but on many. Power mentoring is empowering as it can help the mentee develop better professional relationships and derive more satisfaction and meaning from his work. An interesting comparison in mentoring can be made by looking at the traditional method of mentoring at Disney. One of the most important reasons organizations support traditional mentoring relationships is to facilitate short-term succession planning for key positions. In contrast Jack Welch, the former chief executive officer of General Electric (GE) spent a lot of time developing a circle of potential successors, ensuring smooth leadership transition as well as long-term viability of GE. Jack Welch was the consummate traditional mentor and master power mentor.

There is also the so-called 'boss mentor', who is one that provides emotional and career support to the subordinate mentee within the formal and informal boundaries of the relationship. However, research suggests that the mentee's professional success depends to a large degree on the performance of the boss mentor. This type of mentoring requires a higher level of trust and loyalty as the boss often shares proprietary and personal information with the mentee.

3.2   Mentorship and Human Resource Development

Mentorship is considered an important training and development tool in the academic literature and is either a formal or informal program in many companies. Many international companies such as ScotiaBank have invested their resources in the development of formal programs designed to promote mentoring relationships as part of the human resource development strategy. Human resource development is often seen as a key to building competitive advantage through people. Mentoring encourages and supports the development of human resources, thereby creating high performing teams.

Mentees must be identified for inclusion in formal programs. In some instances certain categories of employees are selected, such as newly recruited graduates. Selection in general is determined by employee needs and the willingness of the mentee to enter into such a relationship. The developmental needs must be determined and matched with one of a carefully selected pool of mentors. Successful mentoring programs need voluntary participation of both mentor and mentee, commitment to the program and the creation of communication policies and procedures.

Generally, before the process begins it is advisable that an orientation is held to introduce the commitment needed, type of activities and budget support. A clear agreement is an essential foundation for a good mentoring relationship and includes the developmental plan, confidentiality requirement, frequency of meetings, time to be invested in mentoring activities, and the duration of the relationship. A mentoring relationship would normally conclude when the items identified in the initial agreement have been accomplished, or when mentor and mentee believe it is no longer productive to work together. A formal process includes an evaluation, follow-up and interviews with both parties to evaluate the measure of success and determine areas for improvement.

The construct of job embeddedness looks at a variety of factors that have been empirically associated with retention – these are not attitudes and tend to be organizational in nature. Inducements to stay can derive from working with groups or on certain projects that create types of commitment other than the attraction of the job or organization. For example, many companies use teams to induce attachments (Cohen and Bailey, 1997). 'Fit' is defined as an employee's perceived compatibility or comfort with an organization and with his or her environment. According to the theory, an employee's personal values, career goals, and plans for the future must 'fit' with the larger corporate culture and the demands of his or her immediate job (e.g., job knowledge, skills and abilities). In addition, a person must consider how well he or she fits the community and surrounding environment. Job embeddedness assumes that the better the fit, the higher the likelihood that the employee will feel professionally and personally tied to the organization. Mentorship can provide such an environment.

3.3 A Case for Mentoring

Many employees lack the motivation to keep growing, learning and improving in their job. Quality systems and circles were introduced to create a culture of continuous learning and improvement. Formal systems and human resource development are also presented but they are potentially costly and time-consuming. Employers complain about the lack of social skills in new recruits and even at the executive level. The survey undertaken for this study revealed that specific technical skills are less important than qualities such as listening and oral communication, adaptability, group and interpersonal effectiveness, cooperativeness and teamwork. A study which examined the elements that corporations seek when hiring MBAs yields a similar list (Nair and Ghosh, 2006). Some of the most desired capabilities and competencies include communication skills, interpersonal skills, initiative, empathy, perspective taking, rapport and cooperation. Many of these skills can only be acquired in skilful relationships such as the one that exists between mentors and mentees.

Lester et al. (2011) conducted a longitudinal field experiment in which a targeted mentorship program was examined over a six-month period to assess the development of mentees' or protégés' leader efficacy and performance. Results show that the targeted mentorship intervention increased the mentees' level of leader efficacy more than a comparison intervention that was based on a more eclectic leadership education program delivered in a group setting. Mentees' preferences for feedback and trust in the mentor served as important moderators in contributing to the development of leader efficacy.

Other research has demonstrated that emotional intelligence counts more than IQ or expertise in determining who excels at a job (see Section 3.4). With regard to outstanding leadership, emotional intelligence counts for almost everything. Many successful people confess that formal mentor relationships can jumpstart the learning curve and help a new employee succeed. Most mentor-mentee relationships are win-win and mentors can even be the bigger winners. Building a mentoring culture supports the development of employees, even those without formal training. Mentoring can be especially important for careers in which training and development are virtually non-existent.

Mentorship is considered an important training and development tool in many companies (one such company is ScotiaBank). These companies have invested resources in the development of formal programs designed to promote mentoring relationships as part of their human resource strategy. Human resource development is key to building competitive advantage through people and the creation of high-performing teams. Mentoring has been identified as an important influence in professional development in both the public and private sector.

Some of the benefits of mentoring include increased employee performance, retention, commitment to the organization, and knowledge sharing. Many companies run formal stand-alone mentoring programs to enhance career and interpersonal development. Some of the major benefits of a formal mentoring program include a structured approach, oversight, and clear and specific organizational goals. Agencies implement formal mentoring programs for different purposes. The main purpose includes the creation of a knowledge-sharing environment, helping new employees understand the culture, and advancing career development.

Informal mentoring has less structure and can occur at any time in a career. The relationship is usually initiated by the mentor or mentee. An informal mentoring relationship is initiated when a senior level employee takes a younger employee under his or her wing and provides advice and guidance to assist with current job or career goals. It can also occur when an employee seeks out a senior level employee they admire and together they work to develop a relationship. It frequently occurs where a supervisor or a senior level employee recommends a specific employee to receive mentoring.

3.4 Leadership and Emotional Intelligence

The role of emotion in organizations has received considerable scholarly attention over the past two decades (Ashforth and Humphrey, 1995; Jordan et al., 2002; Elfenbein et al., 2007). It is increasingly recognized that emotions and the way they are experienced and expressed in the work environment have a fundamental impact on a wide range of work-related outcomes (e.g. Ashkanasy and Dasborough, 2003; Goleman, 1995, 1998; Weisinger, 1998;Weiss and Cropanzano, 1996). Emotions are subjective experiences that are most often experienced in social interactions and shared with others (Feldman and Rime, 1991). The expression and suppression of emotions not only shape how people feel, but also influence individuals' cognitive functioning, as well as their ability to establish and maintain effective interpersonal relationships (Liu et al. 2011).

Great leaders ignite our passion and inspire the best in us. Although we sometimes refer to great leaders as creators of vision and strategy, great leadership works through the emotions. Leadership is not domination, but the art of persuading persons to work towards a common goal. Our emotional intelligence determines our potential for learning and is based on five elements, namely self-awareness, motivation, self-regulation, empathy and adeptness in relationships. Our emotional competence determines how much of that potential is translated into on-the-job capabilities. Emotional competence is intertwined with job performance. Developing one's competence leads to improved performance. Being high in emotional intelligence does not guarantee that a person would have learned these competencies, it only means that the person may have a high potential to learn them. Human resource development must therefore embrace these capabilities.

A mentor shares experience as a means of influencing and persuading the mentee toward a path of success. Mentorship is relationship-based and involves high levels of feedback, commendations and even criticism. An artful critique can be one of the most helpful messages a mentor can make and still focus on the issue. In these situations a mentor must be sensitive and empathetic and be attuned to the impact of what is being communicated. Great learning will only take place when the mentor is attuned to the emotional needs of the mentee and is aware of his or her own emotional positioning. As such great leaders should be emotionally intelligent.

In the survey conducted for this study, one of the questions asked was whether mentors should have special skills, and more particularly whether they should be emotionally intelligent. All the respondents supported the need for an emotionally intelligent leader. All respondents similarly concurred that mentorship encourages and supports human resource development.

The cost effectiveness of emotional intelligence is still relatively new in business and some managers find it difficult to accept. Many leaders still feel that their work demands their heads and not their hearts. Many leaders also feel that the display of empathy or compassion for their employees does not allow them to be emotionally aloof enough to make hard decisions.

Drawing on years of research, it has now been advanced that the leader's mood and attendant behaviours have enormous effects on bottom-line performance. In other words, before leaders can devote attention to setting strategy, fixing budgets, or hiring staff, they must first attend to the impact of their moods and behaviours (Goleman et al. 2002). To help them do this several authors, including Goleman, introduced a five-step process of self-reflection and planning. Goleman (1995) recommends that working through this process helps leaders determine how their emotional leadership drives the moods and actions of their organizations and how their behaviours can be adjusted accordingly. Mentorship can provide guidance on issues such as reconciling company values with commercial imperatives and consideration of the effect of compensation policy on morale and organizational effectiveness.

In a later book, *Working with Emotional Intelligence*, Goleman (1998) maps these skills into the realms of work and career. He defines emotional intelligence as awareness of one's own feelings and knowing one's emotional state. It permits one to express feelings appropriately and therefore communicate effectively. Self-awareness allows us to take an emotional upset into account before acting on the powerful impulses it generates, that is, to manage our emotional responses. Emotional hijacking occurs when emotions express themselves in words and deeds before the individual has actually identified their nature or even their presence. Leaders should never want to experience this situation. No one can manage feelings of which he or she is unaware.

Great leaders must master the art of self-awareness if they are to be successful mentors and coaches. Being aware of our own feelings allows us to perceive the feelings of others accurately. It also affords the high level of empathy necessary for successful relationships. Empathy, in Goldman's view, underlies many interpersonal aptitudes like teamwork, persuasion, and leadership. Empathy forges emotional connection, and tends to bond people together even more deeply than shared beliefs and ideas. The real underpinning for successful mentor-mentee relationships is the emotionally intelligent mentor.

3.5   Coaching versus Mentoring

Coaching is a relationship activity designed to increase performance. Coaching is generally informal and occurs between the boss and the employee, whereas mentoring is a more formal process, based on a one-to-one relationship with someone distant in the organization. Mentorship is considered an important training and development tool and is linked to mobility and career enhancement. In recent years special emphasis has been placed on the mentoring of females, as previously mentioned, and their advancement to leadership positions. Coaching is a relationship activity designed to increase performance. It includes interaction between two levels of employees with the purpose of enhancing performance, increasing accountability, renewing commitment and facilitating continual learning. There are several types of coaching including modeling, instructing, enhancing performance, problem solving and inspiration and support. This allows a flexible approach to different coaching situations.

4.   METHODOLOGY AND RESEARCH DESIGN

A targeted survey was conducted on mentors and mentees originating from companies in both the public and the private sector. In selecting the sample, international companies operating in Trinidad with subsidiaries or branches in the Caribbean were also considered. Additionally, an effort was made to include the major revenue-generating sectors such as energy, financial services and distributive trades.

Specific questionnaires were developed for mentors and mentees. The survey instrument for the mentees (see Appendix I) consisted of 11 questions, while the questionnaire aimed at mentors (see Appendix II) comprised 14 questions. Questionnaires for both the mentors and mentees contained open-ended and closed questions. The questionnaires were self-administered in June 2012 and were sent to firms along with a letter of introduction and intent to the Human Resource Director/Manager of the selected firms.

Broadly, the areas of focus in the questionnaire included the issue of formal or informal mentoring processes and differences if any in the outcomes, the skills and training requirements for mentors from the perspectives of both mentors and mentees. The evaluation of the importance of the emotionally intelligent leader, the impact of such a leader on the mentee and the overall benefits to the mentee, mentor and the organization were examined.

5.   DISCUSSION OF RESULTS

Responses were received from six mentors and twenty-nine mentees. Fifty four per cent of the firms were from the energy and petrochemical sector, 34 per cent from the financial services sector and 12 per cent from 'other' industrial sectors in the economy.

At one end of the scale mentorship was a very formal system supported by contracts between mentors and mentees, and at the other end the mentorship programs were very informal arrangements whereby the company only acted as a facilitator for interested parties, that is, those wanting to be mentored and those keen on sharing their time and experiences. One company, which had a very formal system, offered the program only to young professionals with less than five years work experience. In addition, sessions were arranged between mentors and mentees, and the mentorship process was formalized only after meetings if parties agreed to work together.

In some instances there was a formal process of selecting and monitoring mentors. Where confidential feedback signalled a need to review the relationship, the mentor was replaced if necessary. A total review of the program was done on an annual basis. These organizations saw themselves as learning organizations with a quality system of continuous improvement.

5.1   Time Mentored

Almost all of the companies surveyed focused the mentorship program towards graduate trainees. It appears that there was no formal arrangement for employees who did not enter via the graduate route. This appears to be a major shortcoming but may in fact be overcome by the informal mentoring process. The results of the survey reveal that most of the mentees were in programs (76 per cent) that operated from between one and three years (Figure 7.1). Most healthy mentoring relationships do not continue indefinitely. Closure that is planned for is easier to deal with but presents its own challenges. Knowing the right time to end a mentoring relationship is an important feature of a formal mentoring program. Giving participants a timeframe assists in the setting and realizing of goals within the given time. 'Without an end date, participant may find that the relationship has outlived its usefulness but still feel pressure to continue'

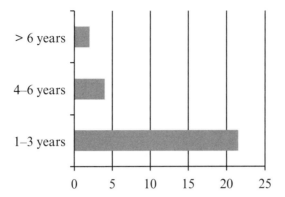

Figure 7.1   Number of years of mentorship

(Ensher and Murphy, (2005). Mentoring relationships come to an end when the company's mentoring program cycle ends with a formal event, distribution of a certificate of participation and acknowledgement of participation in the program. 'Without that formal event they might not have brought the relationship to closure or acknowledged their accomplishment and mutual appreciation' (Zachary 2000).

5.2   Mentorship – A Formal Process in the Organization

One third of the mentors surveyed indicated that their companies had a formal mentorship program in place. Many companies indicated that formal mentoring programs were costly and tended not to be all-embracing. Organizations often expend a large amount of resources on formal mentoring programs, when instead perhaps they should be using these resources on creating an infrastructure that enables mentoring relationships to grow and thrive organically. 'Research clearly shows that spontaneously developed or informal mentoring relationships are, on a whole, more effective than those developed under the auspices of formal programmes' (Ensher and Murphy, 2005).

5.3   Training for Mentors

Where organizations had a formal mentorship process in place, the human resource department provided training for mentors. Approximately 67 per cent of the mentors indicated that their organizations had a formal training program in place (Figure 7.2). Getting a formal mentoring program off the ground requires adequate pre-screening and a careful selection of

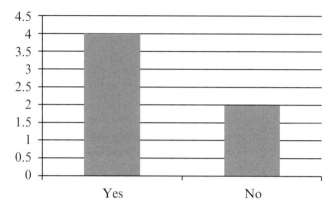

Figure 7.2   Training for mentors

mentors. Appropriate pairing, enhanced training and support for mentors are key components of a successful mentoring program. 'The mentoring agreement is, in essence, a learning contract that defines the objectives, strategies, resources, timeline, and evaluation methodology of the relationship. Mentoring is the quintessential expression of self-directed learning' (Zachary, 2005). Goleman et al. (2002) state that 'the crux of leadership development that works is self-directed learning.'

5.4   Benefit to the Company

Figure 7.3 shows that 79 per cent of the mentees believed that their organizations benefited from the mentorship provided. They stated that it provided avenues for establishing career and workplace protocols. Mentors indicated that they were also better equipped to implement company policies as the training enhanced their development and improved productivity and efficiencies. 'Past research has provided a great deal of compelling evidence that organizations benefit from providing an environment where mentoring can flourish. Another benefit is greater organizational productivity' (Ensher and Murphy, 2005).

5.5   Impact on Turnover of Employees

Of the mentors surveyed, at least 50 per cent believed that mentorship had a positive influence on employee turnover (Figure 7.4). In the main, companies are concerned about what it takes to attract and retain talented employees. Moreover companies recognize that there are huge costs associated with a high turnover rate. In a survey of 15,000 employees in a

■Yes ■No ■Don't Know

Figure 7.3   Benefit of mentoring to the company

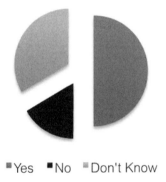

■Yes ■No ■Don't Know

Figure 7.4   Impact of mentorship on employee turnover

wide range of industries it was found that 'working with great people and relationships' was the major driver of employee retention (Ensher and Murphy, 2005). This was primarily due to mentees' shared experience with their mentors and it also assisted with their career development.

5.6   Impact of Mentorship on Succession Planning

The mentorship process had a positive impact on retention of employees and had considerable positive impact on the companies' turnover. Employees trained by very experienced mentors helped mentees to acquire greater knowledge and experience in the company's operations and culture. One of the most important reasons organizations support

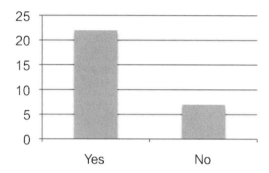

Figure 7.5   Should mentors be emotionally intelligent?

traditional mentoring relationships is to facilitate short-term succession planning for key positions. Power mentoring takes it a step further as it focuses on long-term succession planning at all levels in the organization. Results from the survey indicate that the mentors unanimously agreed that the mentorship program in place impacted on succession planning.

5.7   The Emotionally intelligent Mentor

Many companies usually embark on a formal process for the selection of mentors. Whereas the pairing of mentors and mentees was more fluid, the actual selection of mentors was quite formal. Companies recognized that training for mentors was critical to the success of the program and encouraged and supported the process. Some companies were more formal and allowed the mentees to request a change of mentor if the relationship was not a good fit. Formal annual assessments also contribute to the correction of unsuitable pairing of mentors and mentees and prevent any destructive or unproductive results. Of the 29 mentees surveyed, 76 per cent thought that mentors should be emotionally intelligent (Figure 7.5). Understandably, the case for the emotionally intelligent mentor is based on the mentor having and enhancing core competencies such as 'the ability to handle one's own emotions, understanding as well as recognizing the emotions of others and the ability to delay gratification' (Goleman et al., 2002).

5.8   Career at the Company

Almost all respondents agreed that mentorship increased job embeddedness, that is, promoted or encouraged employees to stay with the

■Yes ■No

Figure 7.6   Does mentorship encourage a career at the organization?

organization. Because most of the mentees were recent graduates the survey did not benefit from the views of long-term employees. Nonetheless, in most instances (90 per cent) the positive impact of the experience encouraged the employees to make a career at the organization (Figure 7.6). This contributed to the employees' feeling that they were a part of the organization, its culture and an overall better fit. Reseach shows conclusively that mentors provide two major forms of assistance to the mentee: emotional support and career help (Hezlett and Gibson 2005). Mentors furnish many types of career support by offering challenges and growth opportunites, career advice and access to learning opportunities and resources.

5.9   Feedback Mechanism

The results suggest that the feedback mechanism was not very efficient and it resulted in mentees not attaining their full potential. Sixty-two per cent of the respondents revealed that there was no formal feedback mechanism in place for the mentorship program in which they were participating. Data from the questionnaire show that very often mentors were too busy or the stress of the job made it almost impossible to complete the process. Mentees were very skeptical of the companies in those circumstances as they felt the company was not very honest in keeping with their commitment. A bigger issue was incompatibility between the mentor and mentee which resulted in a breakdown in communication and feedback. Companies with a more formal process had a more positive outlook on the feedback and maximized the benefits of the program.

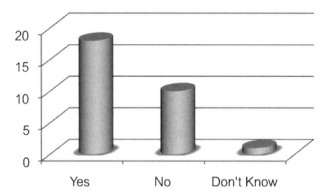

Figure 7.7   Feedback mechanism on mentorship programme

6. CONCLUSION

The survey showed conclusively that both formal and informal mentorship programs resulted in substantial benefits to all parties: the mentor, mentee and the company. Most of the mentors identified mentoring as one of the most efficient and cost-effective methods of human resource development. It was observed that emotional intelligence was still not fully integrated as a leadership competency, but it was recognized that it was a key requirement for a successful mentor and the mentor-mentee relationship.

Companies also recognized the many benefits, including reduction in staff turnover and improvement in succession planning, of a mentorship program. It was also acknowledged that it helped in the improvement of the levels of communication, teamwork and career enhancement. The results obtained from the survey should provide a significant basis for the implementation of mentorship programs in other organizations in Trinidad and Tobago.

ACKNOWLEDGEMENT

We would like to thank the mentors, mentees and organizations for participating in the survey.

BIBLIOGRAPHY

Ashforth, Blake E., and Ronald H. Humphrey. 1995. Emotion in the workplace; a reappraisal. *Human Relations*, 48 (2): 97–125. doi: 10.1177/001872679504800201.

Ashkanasy, N.M and M.E. Dasborough. 2003. Emotional awareness and emotional intelligence in leadership teaching. *Journal of Education for Business*, 79 (1): 18–22. doi:10.1080/08832320309599082.

Cohen, Susan G., and Diane E. Bailey. 1997. What makes teams work: group effectiveness research from the shop floor to the executive suite. *Journal of Management*, 23 (3): 239–290.

Elfenbein, H.A., Der Foo, M., White, J., Hoon Tan, H. and V. Chuan Aik. 2007. Reading your counterpart: the benefit of emotion recognition accuracy in negotiation. *Journal of Nonverbal Behavior*, 31 (4): 205–23.

Ensher, Ellen and Susan Murphy. 2005. *Power Mentoring. How Successful Mentors and Proteges Get the Most out of their Relationships.* Jossey-Bass.

Feldman, R.S. and Rime, B. 1991. *Fundamentals of Nonverbal Behavior.* Cambridge University Press.

Goleman, D. 1995. *Emotional Intelligence: Why It Can Matter More Than IQ.* Bantam Books.

Goleman, D. 1998. *Working with Emotional Intelligence.* Bantam Dell.

Goleman, D., Boyatzis, R. and A. Mckee. 2002. *Primal Leadership – Learning to Lead with Emotional Intelligence.* Harvard Business School Press.

Harvey, M., McIntyre, N., Thompson Heames, J., and M. Moeller. 2009. Mentoring global female managers in the global marketplace: traditional, reverse, and reciprocal mentoring. *The International Journal of Human Resource Management*, 20 (6): 1344–1361. doi: 10.1080/09585190902909863.

Hezlett, S.A. and S.K. Gibson. 2005. Mentoring and human resource development: where we are and where we need to go. *Advances in Developing Human Resources*, 7 (4): 446–469. doi: 10.1177/1523422305279667.

Johns, R., Mc Namara, J. and Z. Moses. 2012. Marketing and branding implications of a corporate service program: the case of women's group mentoring. *International Journal of Evidence Based Coaching and Mentoring,* 10 (1): 74–88.

Jordan, P.J., Ashkanasy, N.M. and C.E. J. Hartels. 2002. Emotional intelligence as a moderator of emotional and behavioral reactions to job insecurity. URL accessed on 14 June 2012. http://en.wikipedia.org/wiki/Neal_Ashkanasy.

Lester, P.B., Hannah, S.T., Harms, P.D., Vogelsang, G.R. and Avolio, B.J. (2011) Mentoring impact on leader efficacy development: a field experiment. *Academy of Management Learning & Education*, 10 (3): 409–429. doi:10.5465/amle.2010.0047.

Liu, Y., Xu, J., Weitz, B.A. 2011. The role of emotional expression and mentoring in internship learning. *Academy of Management Learning and Education*, 10 (1): 94–110.

McCauley, C.D., Charles J.P., Drath, W.H., Hughes, R.L., Mc Guire, J.B., O'Connor, P.M.G. and E. Van Velsor. 2004. Interdependent leadership in organizations: evidence from six case studies. A Center for Creative Leadership Report. Available at: http://www.ccl.org/leadership/pdf/research/interdependentLeadership.pdf.

McKimm, J., Jollie, C. and M. Hatter (2007). Mentoring: theory and practice. NHSE/Imperial College School of Medicine. Available at: http://www.faculty.

londondeanery.ac.uk/e-learning/feedback/files/Mentoring_Theory_and_Prac tice.pdf.

Nair, S.K. and Ghosh, S. 2006. Factors affecting the placement prospects of MBA students: an exploratory study, *Vision*, 10 (1): 41–49.

Opayemi, R. 2012. Psychosocial factors predisposing university undergraduates to mentoring relationships. *IFE Psychologia,* 20 (1): 70–86.

Perween, Sajida. 2008. Mentoring survey report. Centres for Excellence in Teacher Training. Available at: www2.warwick.ac.uk/study/.../mentor.../men-toring_survey_report.pdf.

Ramaswami, A. and G.F. Dreher. 2010. Dynamics of mentoring relationships in India: a qualitative, exploratory study. *Human Resource Management*, 49 (3): 501–530. doi: 10.1002/hrm.20363.

Silet, K.A, Asquith, P. and M. Fleming. 2010. A national survey of mentoring programs for KL2 scholars. *Clinical and Translational Science*, 3 (6): 299–304. doi:10.1111/j.1752-8062.2010.00237.

Weisinger, Hendrie. 1998. *Emotional Intelligence at Work.* Jossey Bass.

Weiss, H.M. and R. Cropanzano. 1996. Affective events theory: a theoretical discussion of the structure, causes and consequences of affective experiences at work. *Research in Organizational Behavior*, 19: 1–74.

Zachary, Lois J. 2000. *The Mentor's Guide.* John Wiley.

Zachary, Lois J. 2005. *Creating a Mentoring Culture – The Organization's Guide.* Jossey Bass.

APPENDIX

Questionnaire (for *Mentee*) on Mentorship and Human Resource Development in the Caribbean

Please tick where necessary.

1. Name (optional) _____
2.
   a. Type of company:
   ☐ Publicly Traded
   ☐ Privately Owned

   b. Industry type:
   ☐ Energy and Petrochemical
   ☐ Manufacturing
   ☐ Transportation
   ☐ Financial services
   ☐ Trade
   ☐ Other

3. How long have you been mentored?
   ☐ 1-3 years
   ☐ 4-6 years
   ☐ >6 years

4. How would you describe the experience?

   _____
   _____
   _____

5. Has the Company benefited from the mentorship program?
   ☐ Yes   ☐ No
   If 'yes', please provide details

   _____
   _____
   _____

6. Would the experience shared with your mentor assist you in making a career at the organization?
   ☐ Yes   ☐ No

7. How has mentorship assisted you in your development?

8. Is there a formal feedback mechanism for the mentorship at the company?
   ☐ Yes   ☐ No
   If yes, please provide details:

9. Do you believe that the mentorship program has improved the morale of staff and the firm's competitive advantage?
   ☐ Yes   ☐ No

10. In your opinion, has the mentorship program impacted positively on the organization?
    ☐ Yes   ☐ No

11. Do you believe that mentors should have special skills and be what is termed as *'emotionally intelligent'*?
    ☐ Yes   ☐ No
    If yes, what special skills do you recommend that mentors should possess:

Questionnaire (for Mentor) on Mentorship and Human Resource Development in the Caribbean

Please tick where necessary

1. Name (optional) _____

2.
   a. Type of company
   ☐ Publicly Traded
   ☐ Privately Owned

b. Industry type
☐ Energy and Petrochemical
☐ Manufacturing
☐ Transportation
☐ Financial services
☐ Trade
☐ Other

3. Is mentorship a formal process in the organization?
   ☐ Yes   ☐ No

   Please provide details of the process

   _____
   _____
   _____

4. Is there training for mentors?
   ☐Yes   ☐ No

5. Do you believe that mentors should have special skills and be what
   is termed as *'emotionally intelligent'*?
   ☐ Yes   ☐ No

   If yes, what special skills should mentors possess?

   _____
   _____
   _____

6. How has mentorship impacted on human resource development?

   _____
   _____
   _____

7. Has mentorship impacted on turnover of employees?
   ☐ Yes   ☐ No

8. Has mentorship impacted on succession planning?
   ☐ Yes   ☐ No

9. Is there a formal feedback mechanism?
    □ Yes   □ No
    If yes, please provide details:

    _____
    _____
    _____

10. Do you believe that the mentorship program has improved the
    morale of staff and the firm's competitive advantage?
    □ Yes   □ No

11. Has the mentorship program impacted positively on the
    organization?
    □ Yes   □ No

12. Has the mentorship program assisted in human resource
    development?
    □ Yes   □ No
    If yes, please provide details:

    _____
    _____
    _____

13. Has the Company benefited from the mentorship program?
    □ Yes   □ No
    If so, please provide details

    _____
    _____
    _____

14. How has the mentorship program impacted on the culture of the
    organization?

    _____
    _____
    _____

8. Employee voice, partnership and performance

Stewart Johnstone and Adrian Wilkinson

1. INTRODUCTION

This chapter explores how employee voice and partnership contribute to the goals of HRM. It consists of three main sections. Given the contested nature of HRM, we begin Section 2 by outlining our interpretation of HRM as an overarching term for the management of work and the employment relationship, rather than as a specific approach to labour management. We then consider the aims of HRM and suggest that these goals can be conceived as a mix of human, resource, and management-focused dimensions. A key concern is the shifting balance between these three dimensions, and in particular the extent to which attempts at professionalization of the management of HR have led to an increasing focus upon a narrow conceptualization of the resource dimension, with less emphasis upon the human aspects of work and employment. The potential challenges of such approaches form the focus of Section 3, which examines employee voice as a process which potentially contributes to addressing imbalances in the employment relationship. Voice can act as a means for workers to defend their interests, but it can also potentially benefit employers in managing conflict as well as eliciting cooperation and greater commitment from the workforce as part of a high performance work system. A potential challenge, however, is the legitimacy and sustainability of voice mechanisms which only focus upon one or the other, and which may fail due to their one-sided concerns.

The final section therefore examines recent debates concerning partnership and mutual gains. A central assumption of this agenda is that it is possible to reconcile the countervailing efficiency and social pressures which characterize the employment relationship by recognizing the plurality of interests, and uniting these around the goal of a successful enterprise. However, this is believed to require new forms of organizational relationships and governance processes, as well as an equitable division of the gains. The chapter concludes by considering how these contribute to the theory and practice of contemporary HRM.

2.   HUMAN RESOURCE MANAGEMENT AND EMPLOYEE VOICE

Before we can examine the relationship between HRM, employee voice and partnership, it is important at the outset to outline our interpretation of HRM, given the inherent ambiguity of the term (Guest, 1991). There are well established debates concerning the distinction between HRM and personnel management which will not be repeated in detail here (Marchington and Wilkinson, 2012), though the contested nature of HRM warrants a brief discussion. The definition of HRM offered by Storey emphasizes a particular set of policies now often identified with 'high-commitment management' or 'high-performance work systems':

> Human resource management is a distinctive approach to employment management which seeks to achieve competitive advantage through the strategic deployment of a highly committed and capable workforce, using an integrated array of cultural, structural and personnel techniques. (Storey, 1995: 5).

From this perspective, HRM can be distinguished from other related notions such as industrial relations or personnel management in several respects. These include a belief that human resources influence competitiveness and in turn require strategic attention, as well as the day to day involvement and support of line managers. Effective HR is also believed to be concerned with more than just developing and enforcing rules and procedures; the aim is to create a culture of consensus, flexibility and commitment rather than merely compliance with rules (Storey, 2007).

In contrast, a broader and more inclusive definition is provided by Boxall and Purcell:

> HRM includes anything and everything associated with the management of employment relationships in the firm. We do not associate HRM solely with a high-commitment model of labour-management or with any particular ideology or style of management. (Boxall and Purcell, 2000: 184)

From this point of view, HRM covers all employee groups, incorporates a variety of management styles, and is concerned with a range of issues relating to the management of work and people, both collectively and individually. (Boxall and Purcell, 2008)

Lewin (2008) defines HRM as the attraction, retention, utilization, motivation, rewarding and disciplining of employees in organizations – in short, the management of people at work. This seems like a good definition, which is broad and less subject to fashion. However, he also notes that HRM as a label conveys the shift in terms of a greater emphasis on people as a resource whose active management can positively contribute to organizational success. In this sense HRM is not necessarily neutral in tone but has a particular aspirational quality (see Wilkinson and Redman, 2013).

Despite the contested nature of HRM and range of conceptualizations – variously labelled high-performance management, high-commitment management, best practice HRM or high-involvement management – most convey the basic message that the adoption of HRM practices pays in terms of where it matters most, the bottom line (Huselid, 1995; Pfeffer, 1994; Guest et al., 2012) Employee voice is typically included as a central component of any such system. However, commentators also note that individual work practices have no effect on economic performance but

the adoption of a *coherent and integrated system* of innovative practices, including extensive recruiting and careful selection, flexible job definitions and problem-solving teams, gainsharing-type compensation plans, employment security and extensive labour–management communication, substantially improves productivity and quality outcomes (Ichniowski et al., 1996, p. 319)

The general argument is that piecemeal take-up of HR practices means that many employers potentially miss out on the benefits to be gained from a more integrated approach to HRM (Marchington and Wilkinson, 2012). Thus such collections of reinforcing HR practices have begun to be referred to as a 'bundle', and the task of HR managers is to identify and implement such a bundle which would typically include mechanisms for employee voice (Lengnick-Hall et al., 2009; Wilkinson and Redman, 2013).

It is perhaps most useful to view HRM as an overarching term which captures the gamut of issues and processes related to the management of work and people in organizations (Boxall and Purcell, 2008). However, before we can explore the extent to which employee voice and partnership helps meet the goals of HRM, it is important to firstly consider the main aims of HRM. Drawing from the framework of Wilkinson et al. it is proposed that these goals can be examined across three main dimensions: (a) a human focus, (b) a resource focus, and (c) a management focus (Wilkinson et al., 2009; Wilkinson et al., 2012).

A Human Focus

HRM has a longstanding concern with a human focus, placing a strong emphasis on employee rights, needs and wellbeing. In the late nineteenth century in the US and Europe, several companies began to offer various welfare amenities to workers such as medical care, housing and recreational facilities, driven by various business, social and religious motives (Kaufman, 2007). The human perspective is evident in contemporary developments in the areas of occupational health and safety and grievance management, as well as concerns such as work design, work-life balance, and equality and diversity. A central concern of HRM is the management of the employment relationship and the implicit as well as explicit agreements that are established between individuals and organizations. From a micro standpoint, HRM is concerned with the various practices which determine the nature of this relationship, including staffing, reward and employee voice, as well as the employee's experience at work and their work-life balance. Insights from the human relations school and organizational psychology inform debates on attracting and developing a committed and engaged workforce, and the importance of employee morale, motivation and commitment (Wilkinson et al., 2009). Sometimes referred to as 'soft' HRM, the emphasis is upon the development of HR various practices to promote communication and involvement, and more recently to inculcate the desired culture, values and levels of engagement (Welbourne, 2011). A central assumption is that desired levels of employee performance are not necessarily automatically forthcoming.

From a more macro perspective, the area often referred to as employment relations has traditionally focussed upon exploring the collective processes, structures, actors and relationships associated with the governance of employment (Heery et al., 2008). The employment relations perspective recognizes that the employment relationship is neither a straightforward economic transaction nor simply a legal contract between employer and an individual employee. A particular emphasis is placed upon understanding the complex political, social and societal aspects of employment as well as the social relations of productivity (Edwards et al., 2002). While employment relations has traditionally been associated with the study of trade unions and collective bargaining (Ackers, 2012), the field is increasingly concerned with a wide range of issues including management style and practices, work organization, skills and workforce development, the impact of HRM policies, and the nature of the relationships between employers and workers, irrespective of trade union presence (Sisson, 2010).

A Resource Focus

However, HRM also has the complicated responsibility of balancing the human focus with the business needs of organizations. Increased competition and emphasis on cost-efficiency has meant changing expectations of HR. In particular there has been increasing emphasis upon 'HR business partnering' whereby HR specialists work with leaders and managers to support strategic business aims (CIPD, 2011a). To what extent can HR specialists balance the role of 'employee champion', supporting the rights and needs of employees, and that of a 'business partner' focused upon business strategy? While HRM by its very nature has a human focus, it also focuses on employees as a resource in driving performance rather than as merely a cost to be minimized. Many of the practices that are typically associated with HRM focus on improving performance and in turn enhancing the competitiveness of the firm. From a micro perspective, HRM focuses on individual practices with the aim of increasing employee ability and motivation to perform effectively. Core HR practices such as recruitment and selection, training and development, and appraisal and rewards all build and develop the talent base of the organization and close the gap on required skills, abilities, and other factors.

From a more macro perspective, a resource focus of HRM addresses the set of practices for managing the aggregate of human capital in organizations. Variations on this theme include high performance work systems, high commitment models and notions of strategic fit (Guest, 2002). Much of this literature is informed by the resource-based view of organizations as it applies to HRM (Boselie and Pauwee, 2010), where 'human resources are the productive services human beings offer the firm in terms of skills, knowledge, and reasoning and decision making abilities' (Grant, 1998: 116). This perspective highlights the importance of a firm's human resources (or 'human capital') as a potential source of competitive advantage by reversing the 'outside in' view of competitiveness with an 'inside out' focus upon exploiting internal capabilities (Barney, 1991).

A Management Focus

While much HRM research has focused on the needs and concerns of employees (as people) in organizations, as well as their potential contributions to organizational performance (as resources), an important and related subset of concerns relate to the management of the HR function itself (Wilkinson et al., 2012). The earliest roles and responsibilities of HR managers emerged firstly from industrial welfare work, and subsequently the transactional requirements of employment administration and personnel issues (Kaufman, 2007). HR professionals are now urged to adopt a more strategic set of roles that focus on managing change, building organizational culture, and becoming a partner in the business. In the 1970s Legge (1978) identified three main options for HR managers. They could seek to promote and engender the dominant economic values of the organization (conformist innovation), they could question and promote broader social values (deviant innovation) or they could act as an organizational 'problem-solver'. However, the HRM function has continued to struggle with legitimacy compared to other organizational functions (Schuler, 1989). A more recent and highly influential conceptualization of the HR function has been developed by Ulrich and colleagues as part of the quest for HR to become more strategic and explicitly supportive of business performance (Ulrich, 1998; Ulrich and Brockbank, 2005: 304). They identify five roles of the modern HR function, namely acting as employee advocate, functional expert, human capital developer, strategic partner and HR leader. Particular emphasis has been upon HR professionals becoming 'business partners'. However, the skills, knowledge, and behaviours of HR managers and leaders in this context are believed to be substantially different, and many companies are challenged with identifying and developing the next generation of HR professionals (Wilkinson et al., 2012). The CIPD in the UK identifies ten professional areas for HR. It is illustrative that while these include traditional personnel management responsibilities such as effective administration of employment (service delivery and information) and management of the relationship between the organization and its staff (employee relations) most of the others are explicitly performance-oriented. These include 'insight, strategy and solutions', 'resourcing and talent planning', 'learning and talent development', 'performance and reward', and most recently employee engagement has been incorporated as a professional area of HR practice (CIPD, 2012).

From Employee Welfare to Business Partnership

In short, the aims of HRM are inherently complex, fraught with tensions, and at times potentially contradictory. Boxall (2007) notes several 'strategic tensions' which must be carefully managed including those between worker control and commitment, short-term versus long-term business priorities, flexibility versus employment security, as well as between management prerogative and employee participation in decision making. The motives of HRM are thus both economic and socio-political as part of the quest to develop a sustainable but cost-effective and socially legitimate labour management system (Boxall, 2007). Francis and Keegan (2006) highlight the need for a more balanced HR agenda which better addresses the competing human and economic discourses of HRM. They also question the extent to which the dominant 'business partnering' discourse has further deemphasized the 'human' side of HR work in the search for improved business performance, professional status and legitimacy (Francis and Keegan, 2006). A similar sentiment is expressed by Kochan (2004: 134) who questions whether 'HR professionals have lost any semblance of credibility as a steward of the social contract because most HR professionals have lost their ability to seriously challenge or offer an independent perspective on the policies and practices of the firm'. To what extent has HR become narrowly focused upon the 'strategic partnership' at the expense of the 'softer' human dimension of HRM, and is 'business partnership' actually 'conformist innovation' (Legge, 1978)? If so might it actually be further limiting the professional credibility of the function?

Much depends on how we view the aims and priorities of HRM. Some critical commentators suggest that HRM as an ideology neglects worker interests at best, and potentially manipulates worker interests at worst (Legge, 1995; Keenoy, 1997; Willmott, 1993). Others suggest that even where employers and HR specialists do retain a genuine consideration for the human side of HRM, capitalist market forces, financialization and corporate governance inevitably mean these are subordinate to short-term cost-control imperatives. The end result, it is argued, is that employers simply cannot keep their promises (Thompson, 2003, 2011). And if modern HRM has become narrowly focused around corporate (financial) performance, as opposed to a more pluralist interpretation which acknowledges worker interests and reactions (Guest, 1999, 2002), just how can employees voice their concerns and promote their interests in the contemporary workplace? Much of this is tested during hard times such as the global financial crisis (GFC) when employer responses to meeting financial challenges clearly expose, in a number of cases, the hollowness of general statements on people being seen as resources (Peetz et al., 2011). Indeed, arguably the GFC represents a challenge not only to organizations, markets and institutions but also to our fundamental ideas and assumptions about the contemporary world of work (Zagelmeyer and Gollan, 2012).

3.   EMPLOYEE VOICE

The term employee voice is one that has become increasingly used in the field of HRM in recent years. A definition offered by Hirschman, in the context of consumer relationships, contrasted 'voice' with 'exit' and thus as 'any attempt at all to change rather than escape from an objectionable state of affairs' (1970: 30). This has been influential in the field of HRM. At an individual level, the exit-voice framework is used to suggest that unionized individuals will be less likely to quit because unionized grievance procedures provide a legitimate voice mechanism and that loyalty can affect the choice between exit and voice (Boroff and Lewin, 1997). At the organization level, Freeman and Medoff (1984) argue that unions not only provide employee voice, but that this collective voice is economically superior to exit and individual voice because of collective and majority-based decision making (see Budd et al., 2010).

Clearly interest in voice precedes the birth of HRM, with employee involvement in decision making appearing in the management literature since at least the 1930s (Handel and Levine, 2004). Much of the contemporary HR literature continues to espouse the importance of participation and voice, although often in very specific ways of getting employees to contribute more effectively to the business using their skills and knowledge (Wilkinson and Dundon, 2010). Forms of participation consequently feature in most definitions of high commitment human resource management, with Pfeffer (1994), for example, stressing the importance of information sharing, participation and empowerment as key elements of an effective work system.

A Human Focus

Historically, the most obvious institutions of voice are trade unions, which emerged as organizations to collectively represent the interests of workers who found themselves in a subordinate role as waged labour in the employment relationship (Ackers et al., 1996). From an industrial relations perspective, employers and employees have both convergent and divergent interests, and as such the possibility of both conflict and cooperation pervades the employment relationship. The employment relationship is more complex than a straightforward economic exchange or legal agreement, with significant social, political and psychological dimensions. While individual employees may possess limited power or say, by acting collectively to defend their interests as the sellers of labour, workers are potentially able to yield greater power and in turn strengthen their position in the labour market (Dundon and Rollinson, 2011). Trade union representation can therefore be viewed as a way of countering managerial unilateralism. The core mechanism for advancing employee interests was the negotiation process between employers and trade unions through collective bargaining, with establishing the 'rules of the game' the central aim of such processes. Reflecting this history, academic interest in employee voice is well established, with the work of Sidney and Beatrice Webb in the early twentieth century demonstrating interest in employee voice in the UK, as well as the writings of John R. Commons in the United States (Kaufman, 2012). Research interest in employee voice also spans a range of established social science disciplines including economics, psychology, law and industrial relations (Wilkinson et al., 2010).

Of course, voice does not occur in a vacuum but is typically influenced by a range of contextual factors including national context, industry, history, public policy, statutory regulation, management style, as well as employee desire or demand for voice. In the twentieth century UK, much of the interest in employee voice was underpinned by an industrial democracy perspective, and attempts at devising a system which addresses and counters the fundamental imbalance of power between employers and workers. Trade unions and collective bargaining remained the default choice for voice provision for most of the century, with the Donovan Commission asserting in the 1960s that 'collective bargaining is the most effective means of giving workers the right to representation in decisions affecting their working lives' (Donovan, 1968: 27). This view was reinforced by the 1970s Bullock report on industrial democracy which recommended the appointment of worker directors (Bullock, 1977). Trade unions were argued to be of economic value to both employers and employees precisely because they offered an independent voice channel for addressing potentially conflictual issues such as the determination of pay and conditions, and the resolution of discipline and grievance issues (Freeman and Medoff, 1984).

In the 1980s and 1990s we saw greater interest in managerial-led employee involvement but later in that period we also saw the emergence of increasing state regulation, particularly at a European level. According to Ackers et al. (2005), the significance of this has resulted in a continuing policy dialectic that shapes management choice for employee voice. The broader environment in the UK now seems more sympathetic to trade union recognition and individual employment rights as well as emergent collective-type regulations, such as the *European Directive on Employee Information and Consultation* (Gollan and Wilkinson, 2007). So arguably, the twenty-first century has ushered in a period of legal re-regulation, which can be divided between those policies that directly affect employee participation (European Directives for example) and those that indirectly alter the environment in which employee participation operates (the competitive environment and organizational strategies for HRM) (Dundon and Wilkinson, 2013).

A Resource Focus

The 1980s saw a discernible shift in employer and government attitudes
to trade unions as the primary conduit of employee voice, and increasing
experimentation with alternative channels of voice. Forms of voice were
changing: indirect representation through joint consultation and collective
bargaining was in decline, and trade union membership and presence were
falling. New management-initiated voice channels increasingly focused
upon direct interactions and dialogue between management and workforce, through an array of mechanisms including team briefings, quality
circles and suggestion schemes, rather than trade union representatives
(Marchington et al., 1992). They also differed in terms of the scope of
issues discussed, with employees increasingly invited to contribute ideas
on issues of business or workplace improvement rather than upon the
resolution of conflict. The degree of employee influence over decision
making – which can range from none (managerial unilateralism) through
to total influence over decisions (worker control and self-management)
– was also shifting. The escalator of participation is outlined in Figure
8.1 (Wilkinson et al., 2012). The 'employee involvement' initiatives of
the 1980s were typically focused on improving information, communication and consultation with employees, but with the employer normally
reserving the right to actually make final decisions. Employee voice could
be described as becoming increasingly 'task-centred' and concerned with
specific workplace issues, rather than 'power-centred' and concerned
with the broader regulation of employment traditionally associated with
trade union representation (Boxall and Purcell, 2008). Finally, in terms
of level, much of the voice activity was increasingly being devolved to
employer-level as opposed to national level negotiations between unions
and employers' associations which were the mainstay of previous decades.

Thus in contemporary HRM, employee voice generally refers to how
and whether employees are able to have a say over work activities and
organizational decision making issues within the organization in which
they work (Marchington, 2007; Freeman et al., 2007). The CIPD (2011b)

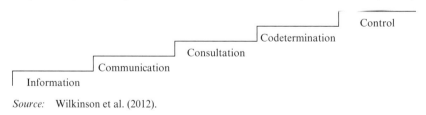

Source: Wilkinson et al. (2012).

Figure 8.1   The escalator of participation

performance outcomes, together with the pursuit of flexibility, quality and continuous improvement. In part, this could be viewed as an acknowledgement of the limitations of classical or scientific management techniques in terms of their inability to capture 'discretionary effort' or to engender desired levels of employee commitment increasingly believed to be a prerequisite for high performance outcomes. Such limitations were highlighted by human relations theorists who stressed the importance of considering social/psychological relations in the workplace, and in particular promulgated the view that employees are not motivated simply by extrinsic monetary reward but also intrinsic feelings of satisfaction and pride, of which having a say is likely to be a part (Wilkinson, 2008)

Alternatively, and in line with those who remain suspicious of HRM in general, employer-sponsored voice mechanisms could also be viewed as an attempt to substitute or avoid the union alternative. But as Strauss (2006) points out, 'voice' is a weaker term than some of the others, such as employee participation, as it does not necessarily denote influence and may be no more than spitting-in-the-wind. As the CIPD definition above states, voice can be viewed as an employer communicating with employees and listening to feedback, but this reveals little about the degree of influence or the 'power to persuade' or effect change (Greenfield and Pleasure, 1993). Voice is a necessary precursor for participation, but does not in itself lead to participation.

A Management Focus

Given the array of voice mechanisms available, HR managers typically play an important role in the choices made about employee voice, in identifying the options available, forming alliances with line managers, and devising strategies for implementation. Indeed, as Ulrich and Brockbank argue 'caring for, listening and responding to employees remains a centrepiece of HR work' (2005: 201), despite CIPD research which suggests that in practice this is far down the list of HR priorities (CIPD, 2007). Generally, a broad mix of factors shape management choice. For some, rational choice is about satisfying employee expectations, particularly when faced with tight labour markets; others equate choice with their own understanding of corporate and organizational objectives. In smaller and family-run enterprises this often relates to the personal styles and characteristics of owner-managers. Some managers may feel that they have no choice, either because employees demanded 'a say' or due to market pressures and new legislative requirements (Dundon et al., 2004). On the whole however, management decide whether or not workers have a voice, and it is managers rather than employees who often decide what mechanisms to utilize. Thus the main aim of this approach to voice reflects a management agenda concerned with increasing understanding and commitment from employees and securing an enhanced contribution to the organization. Thus, while some forms may provide employees with new channels through which their influence is enhanced, facilitating employee voice does not involve any *de jure* sharing of authority or power, so there is not necessarily always an obvious link between voice and organizational decision making. In other words it can be voice without muscle (Kaufman and Taras, 2010).

The Shifting Rationale For Employee Voice

In summary, there is an array of possible systems as well as a range of potential motives underpinning choices regarding worker voice (Wilkinson and Fay, 2011) In considering the actual and desired outcomes of voice it is useful to return to the three dimensions of HRM outlined earlier. Firstly there is the view that employees – as humans – cannot be treated in the same way as other resources in the production process such as capital equipment. Informed by companion disciplines such as political science and industrial relations, the logic is that employees have basic rights in the organizations in which they work, including the right to voice and acceptable levels of wellbeing. Voice is therefore necessary to regulate the distribution of employment outcomes between labour and the owners of capital. Voice is also required to govern and shape the rules and policies which shape the wage-effort bargain, as well as what Flanders (1965) referred to as the 'institutionalization' of conflict. From this perspective, market forces simply cannot be relied upon to deliver 'a fair day's work for a fair day's pay' (Thompson, 2003), a concern which is likely to be particularly important following the GFC. Secondly there is the view that a business case for voice exists, especially in high value added operations (Handel and Levine, 2004). However, the conceptualization of voice believed to drive the HR-performance link tends to be quite different in terms of scope and form as well as degree of influence, from the voice underpinned by democratic ideals and traditionally afforded through independent trade union representation. So voice still has multiple 'meanings' and can be interpreted in different ways. From a human perspective, voice can be viewed as a way of expressing individual or collective dissatisfaction with management action. From a resource perspective, voice can be viewed as capturing the potential contribution and expert knowledge of employees in order to improve management decision making and ultimately organizational productivity and competitiveness. A third perspective is that the two perspectives regarding voice are not necessarily mutually exclusive and that voice can be viewed as part of a mutual gains process driven by a joint commitment to organizational success (Dundon et al., 2004). The core idea is that management, unions and workers can potentially work together to use the voice process to achieve a win-win outcome (Handel and Levine, 2004). It is to the concept of partnership and mutual gains that we now turn.

4. PARTNERSHIP AND PERFORMANCE

There are long standing debates regarding the relationship between trade unions and productivity but the findings remain contested. Conceptually, two 'Faces of Unionism' were outlined by Freeman and Medoff (1984). On the one hand, the 'monopoly' perspective views unions as negative forces which distort labour market outcomes such as rates of pay. Neoclassical economics regards such interventions as undesirable, arguing that the mobility of workers and their ability to quit bad jobs in favour of better jobs combined with the workings of the 'invisible hand' are sufficient in generating an efficient system. Unions are therefore unnecessary and associated with restrictive working practices, resistance to change, conflict, industrial action and ultimately increased costs and lower profits. In short, market forces are believed to be a preferable and sufficient means of ensuring the efficient utilization of resources and unions simply hamper this endeavour.

On the other hand, the 'collective voice/institutional response' view suggests that the collective voice unions offer potentially 'elicits institutional responses which dramatically change the nature of the employment relationship and, in so doing, increase the levels of productivity and equality in many settings' (p. 2). From this perspective, trade unions are about much more than determining wage outcomes; they are also concerned with the expression of worker voice which, it is argued, can potentially make a positive contribution to the functioning of the broader economic and social system. Employers stand to gain better insights into employee views, and increased cooperation, lower levels of absenteeism and lower levels of staff turnover may result. It is proposed that unions can also 'shock' employers into adopting more innovative and productive techniques rather than focusing upon short-term cost minimization. From this point of view, the provision of voice is regarded as essential because the employment relationship is not straightforward, static, harmonious or merely economic; rather it is dynamic, indeterminate and open to interpretation. Furthermore, union voice is believed to be preferable to alternative forms such as direct voice because of the small incentives for employees, as individuals, to invest energy in promoting better conditions for all, and because individual protest could prove risky given the imbalance of power between employer and employee. Finally, in addition to influencing key labour outcomes such as rates of pay, unions are also associated with the development of fair processes believed to be necessary to avoid arbitrary treatment as well as the development of a satisfied and productive workforce (Freeman and Medoff, 1984). In reality, however, the monopoly and collective voice faces of unionism may operate side by side depending upon the specificities of the business environment (Hirsch, 2003).

The union productivity debate has since attracted a steady of stream of empirical scrutiny though the findings in the literature have been conflicting, revealing a range of positive, negative and zero union productivity effects (Delaney, 2008). Addison and Hirsch (1989: 79) conclude that 'the average productivity effect is probably quite small, and indeed it is just as likely to be negative as positive'. Interestingly Kuhn (1998: 1048) reveals that 'most estimates are positive, with the negative effects largely confined to industries and periods known for their conflictual management-union relations'. In an attempt to synthesize the disparate quantitative evidence, a meta-analysis conducted by Doucouliagios and Laroche (2003) reveals an overall near-zero association between unions and productivity. However, some differences can be found when examined at national or sectoral level. For example, an overall negative association between unions and productivity is identified in the UK and Japan, but a positive association in the US in general, as well as in US manufacturing. Nevertheless, they also acknowledge that to some extent the variation in the association between unions and productivity is due to differences in the nature of the study rather than differences in the actual union-productivity effect (Doucouliagios and Laroche, 2003).

Indeed there are several limitations to the analysis of unions and productivity despite the use of sophisticated statistical techniques. Quantitative analyses may reveal little about the nature of union-management relations, which is not surprising given the different models and types of union and unionism that exist, as well as the range of options available to management in their dealings with unions. The simple presence of unions reveals little about how either side operates or the nature of the interactions. Such studies also risk underplaying and offering limited explanations regarding the relevance of other contextual contingencies. Quantitative union productivity studies do not neatly explain economically successful countries, such as Sweden and Germany, which exhibit strong and embedded traditions of trade union representation. Yet Freeman and Medoff (1984) emphasize the importance of these contingencies, acknowledging that union productivity effects will vary across workplaces, rather than claiming universalistic union effects. As Edwards and Sengupta (2010) note, institutions such as unions thus have mixed potentials; while unions can perhaps impose restrictive practices they might also provide a form of effective workplace governance. As they state, 'Institutions do not create a fixed pattern of constraints and opportunities within which firms make choices . . . firms interact with the environment in complex ways' (Edwards and Sengupta, 2010: 393).

Indeed, they suggest that asking whether unions raise performance might actually be the wrong question, as it deemphasizes investigating the complexities and dynamics of processes rather than raw statistical associations. In many respects this reflects the limitations of the mainstream HR-performance research which also reveals little about the nature of the 'idiosyncratic competencies' or 'black boxes' which are believed to underpin the RBV (resource-based view) perspective on the HR-performance link (Becker et al., 1997; Purcell, 1999).

One potentially important moderator identified in the union-productivity literature is the nature of the relationship forged between management and unions as well as the overall employment relations climate. In this regard, the notion of workplace 'partnership' between management and unions resulted in distinctive and vociferous debates regarding the future of employee voice in the UK and attracted significant policy attention in the 1990s (Acas, 2003; DTI, 1998; IPA, 1997; TUC, 1999). Though the exact meaning of partnership remains contested (Ackers et al., 2005; Ackers and Payne, 1998; Dietz, 2004; Guest and Peccei, 2001; Stuart and Martinez-Lucio, 2004), it is generally associated with an attempt to shift from adversarial to more cooperative relations between unions and management (Johnstone et al., 2009). A central theme is the attempt to reconcile the countervailing efficiency and social pressures which characterize the employment relationship by galvanizing all parties around a joint interest in the success of the enterprise (Martinez-Lucio and Stuart, 2002). Partnership aligns with the increasing recognition of the need to manage address the several strategic tensions (Boxall, 2007) and to consider HR outcomes in terms of mutuality and sustainability in the long-term rather than just short-term economic expediencies (Guest, 2002, 2007; Peel and Boxall, 2005).

Johnstone et al. (2009) explore the academic and policy definitions of partnership. They suggest that academic definitions of partnership have focused upon identifying the principles, practices, processes, values and outcomes associated with partnership working and typically these include notions of mutuality and reciprocity (Marchington, 1998; Guest and Peccei, 1998, 2001), suggesting a return to more pluralist conceptualizations of HRM. More practical definitions are offered by the Trade Union

Table 8.1   Definitions of partnership

Partnership element	IPA	TUC	Classification
A joint declaration of commitment to organizational success	Y	Y	Values (Marchington, 1998) Commitment (IPA, 1997)
Mutual recognition of the legitimate role and interests of management, employees and trade unions where present	Y	Y	Values (Marchington, 1998) Commitment (IPA, 1997)
Commitment and effort to develop and sustain trust between the organization's constituencies	Y	Implicit	Values (Marchington, 1998) Commitment (IPA, 1997)
Means for sharing information (IPA)/Transparency (TUC)	Y	Y	Process
Consultation and employee involvement, with representative arrangements for an 'independent employee voice' (IPA)/ Transparency (TUC)	Y	Y	Process
Policies to balance flexibility with employment security (IPA/TUC)	Y	Y	Outcome
Sharing organizational success (IPA)	Y	–	Outcome
Adding value (TUC)	Implicit	Y	Outcome
Improving the quality of working life (TUC)	Implicit	Y	Outcome

Source: Johnstone et al. (2009: 262).

Congress (TUC) and Involvement and Participation Association (IPA) centred around the 'building blocks' of partnership. These include joint commitments between employers and the workforce to organizational success, mutual legitimacy, consultation, and balancing employment security and flexibility (IPA, 1997; TUC, 1999).

Interestingly, both the IPA and TUC include outcomes as part of their definition of partnership. However, it is stressed by Johnstone et al. (2009: 262) that it is important not to conflate partnership processes with employment relations outcomes. Employment relations outcomes (such as employment security or adding value) may be thought of as aspirations rather than components of working in partnership *per se*. Partnership may represent an aspiration to achieve these outcomes, irrespective of whether or not they are achieved.

Johnstone et al. (2009) therefore propose that a more useful definition would focus upon the practices and processes associated with partnership. Employee voice is central to all definitions of partnership and in theory this may involve a mix of direct participation, representative participation and financial involvement (Guest and Peccei, 2001). However, most policy and organizational definitions associate partnership primarily with representative voice mechanisms (IPA, 1997; TUC, 1999), normally (but not always) involving trade unions. The emphasis upon collective representation is important given the decline in representative mechanisms and collective regulation over the last 30 years (Kerseley et al., 2006). In terms of processes, partnership is associated with a particular approach to organizational decision making and actor relationships. In terms of voice provision, a partnership approach to decision making is typically described as a 'joint problem solving approach' (Dietz, 2004; Haynes and Allen, 2001). Key principles include early consultation and some degree of influence over decision making, as opposed to last minute discussions which afford limited opportunity for meaningful input or where decisions are presented as a *fait accompli*. In terms of the escalator of participation discussed earlier (Wilkinson et al., 2012), partnership working places great emphasis upon extensive information and consultation, but not necessarily joint decision making (Oxenbridge and Brown, 2004; Terry, 2003). Partnership is also associated with a change in the relationship between employers and worker representatives, with a particular emphasis upon developing trust, openness, mutual legitimacy and a commitment to business success (Dietz, 2004; Guest and Peccei, 2001; Martinez-Lucio and Stuart, 2005). While there is likely to be some variety within this general framework, it is suggested that these are the practices and processes which underpin a prima facie case of partnership and are likely to be mutually reinforcing (see Johnstone et al., 2009).

The surge of interest in partnership in the UK in 1990s can be attributed to a combination of factors. Firstly, partnership was a key part of the 1997 New Labour government strategy to 'modernize' employment relations. Inspired by 'Third Way' principles (Giddens, 1998), partnership was believed to offer an alternative to macho management and arms-length or adversarial relations between unions and management. The focus was upon identifying a form of governance somewhere between old style social democracy on the one hand, and free market neoliberalism on the other. Political interest in – and state sponsorship of – partnership could therefore be viewed both as a pragmatic attempt to recast union-management relations, as well as an ideology concerned with balancing economic concerns with broader social and societal values (Johnstone et al., 2011).

Partnership also chimed with European-style employment relations, and in particular the language of 'social partnership' associated with Germanic nations. Ferner and Hyman (1998) suggested that social partnership has three main components: a societal recognition of the differences in the interests of workers and employees; acceptance and encouragement of the representation of these different interests; and a commitment to the effective regulation of work and the labour market. In this sense partnership represented a return to a pluralist perspective on the conduct and regulation of employment relations, in contrast to the unitarist undertones of HRM and employee involvement of the previous decade. Elements of partnership discourse also chimed with an influential literature emerging from the United States, drawing on the 1980s strategic choice debate. In their 1994 book *The Mutual Gains Enterprise* Kochan and Osterman (1994: 46) argued that:

> Achieving and sustaining competitive advantage for human resources requires the strong support of multiple stakeholders in an organization . . . employees must commit their energies to meeting the economic objectives of the enterprise . . . in return owners (shareholders) must share the economic returns with employees and invest those returns in ways that promote the long-run economic security of the workforce.

Importantly, Kochan and Osterman (1994) acknowledge parallels between their conceptualization of the 'mutual gains enterprise', and what many others have labelled 'high performance' or 'high commitment' in the HRM literature. However, they argue that they prefer the term mutual gains because it emphasizes the centrality of multiple stakeholders. Their argument is based on the view that the New Deal system of industrial relations devised by Roosevelt in the 1930s in the US has been failing. Again, it is argued that this is due to generally adversarial union management relationships based upon legalistic contractual compliance and conflict resolution where unions are recognized, as well as union avoidance where they are not, leaving little scope for fostering cooperative relations.

This can be related to earlier theories of collective bargaining and in particular the distinction between distributive and integrative bargaining developed by Walton and McKersie (1965). Distributive bargaining has the function of resolving pure conflicts of interests and aims to allocate fixed sums of resources (dividing the pie) and hence often has a 'zero-sum' outcome. Tactics centre on developing the negotiators' relative power, convincing the other party of the first party's power and resolution, modifying the other party's expectations, closely guarding information, and preventing the other side from using the same tactics. Integrative bargaining, by contrast, aims to identify common or complementary interests and to solve problems which confront both parties. The aim is to work towards achieving joint gains (expanding the size of the pie) and identifying opportunities for 'win-win' outcomes. Tactics include exchanging information, exploring underlying interests and engagement in problem solving techniques. In short, partnership is about 'management and unions working together to produce a bigger pie as well as fighting over the size of their slices' (Freeman and Medoff, 1984:. 165). Partnership is thus concerned both with employment relations processes and with business and employment outcomes (Johnstone et al., 2009).

Given the decline in trade union representation, research has assessed the potential of partnership as a union revitalization strategy (Haynes and Allen, 2001; Heery, 2002; Wills, 2004), as well as the extent to which partnership results in mutual gains outcomes (Guest and Peccei, 2001; Martinez-Lucio and Stuart, 2005; Oxenbridge and Brown, 2004; Roche and Geary, 2002; Stuart and Martinez-Lucio, 2004; Terry and Smith, 2003). In contrast to the literature on HR-performance links and union-productivity effects, the research on union management partnership consists mainly of qualitative case studies (see Johnstone et al., 2009 for a detailed review). Much of the emphasis is upon the outcomes for trade unions and to a lesser extent the implications for workers. Early empirical studies revealed mixed results, with the more positive studies revealing a range of benefits including stronger workplace union organization, enhanced union legitimacy and improved processes of information and consultation (Haynes and Allen, 2001; Wills, 2004). Critical studies, on the other hand, suggested that the realities of partnership were work intensification, job insecurity and limited union effectiveness in defending member interests (Kelly, 2004; Tailby et al., 2004). Further research has since suggested that the outcomes of partnership are contingent upon a range of variables including underlying management and union strategies, as well as rationale for partnership and the way in which it has been implemented (Heery, 2002; Heery et al., 2004; Roche and Geary, 2002; Samuel, 2007; Wills, 2004). Important distinctions have been made between different types of partnership including formal/ informal, union/non-union, and private/public sector arrangements, and typologies of partnerships have been developed (Kelly, 2004; Oxenbridge and Brown, 2004; Wray, 2004), making generalizations difficult (Johnstone et al., 2009).

Assessing the outcomes of partnership is therefore complex. Perhaps the greatest limitation of the industrial relations literature, despite present-ing qualitative case study evidence, is the tendency to nevertheless focus upon raw quantitative labour outcomes, and to overlook the more subtle processes and qualitative aims of partnership. However, partnership outcomes, like many HR outcomes, are notoriously difficult to quantify. Partnership is about much more than just examining quantitative labour/business outcomes; partnership can be viewed more broadly as an attempt to reconfigure voice mechanisms and recast employment relations in light of the demise of old style joint regulation (Stuart and Martinez-Lucio, 2004; Terry, 2003), as well as the birth of more unitarist and individual-istic HRM. A narrow focus on labour outcomes such as number of job losses or dismissals reveals little about the process-oriented dynamics of employee voice, the overall quality of actor relationships or the general climate of employment relations which are important in themselves (Johnstone et al., 2011).

A further complexity in evaluating partnership outcomes is a lack of agreement regarding what partnership is expected to achieve, or how to set appropriate measurements for success. Consequently, outcomes are too easily offset against benchmarks which are either quite vague (e.g. increas-ing transparency, enhancing training and development, creating a better quality of working life), or highly ambitious such as the renaissance of the union movement as the default mechanism for employee voice (Johnstone et al., 2011). In addition, few UK studies have considered the implications of partnership from the perspective of line managers or HR specialists with academic research focusing primarily on assessing the labour out-comes. Interestingly, where employer benefits have been addressed, the conclusion has been that the 'balance of advantage' tends to be skewed in favour of the employer (Guest and Peccei, 2001). Guest and Peccei term this 'constrained mutuality' but conclude that 'partnership can lead to potential benefits for all the partners (2001: 233). Again, much depends on how 'successful' partnership is defined and what it is expected to achieve, but it seems unrealistic to expect that long-term partnerships will lead to harmonious, consensual and conflict-free workplaces (Terry and Smith, 2003). Industrial conflict is not in itself evidence of the 'failure' of partner-ship. It also seems unrealistic to suggest that partnership will lead to per-fectly apportioned division of 'mutual gains', with benefits flowing equally and harmoniously to all parties; indeed it is difficult to imagine what such a situation would look like (Johnstone et al., 2011). Yet in a study of workplace partnership in the Republic of Ireland, Roche (2009: 26) concluded that there was no 'major asymmetry with respect to the balance of mutuality or advantage in partnership'. Nevertheless, concerns remain about the legitimacy or sustainability of a partnership where benefits are

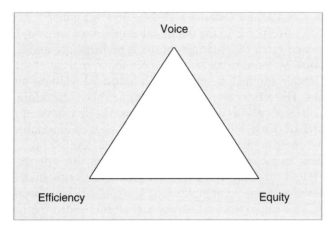

Source: Budd (2004: 30).

Figure 8.2   Efficiency, equity and voice

perceived by unions or employees to be lop-sided in favour of employers (Guest and Peccei, 2001). For some, lop-sided outcomes create a challenge of legitimacy (Boxall and Purcell, 2008; Evans et al., 2012). An alternative view is that where employees are already entirely aware of the imbalance of power in the labour market, they have come to accept practices which are perceived to be skewed in favour of the employer (Geary and Trif, 2011). What is clear is that the achievement and assessment of 'mutual gains' remains complex, not least because of a lack of agreement regarding what mutual gains look like in practice.

The arguments of Budd (2004) are instructive in this respect. Budd suggests that to make progress, we need to firstly return to considerations regarding the fundamental objectives of the employment relationship. Starting with the classical economic view of the employment relationship, in which capital wants to increase profits and workers want higher wages, he argues that equity and voice are equally important objectives. A narrow economic focus, he suggests, must be balanced with employees' entitlement to fair treatment and wellbeing at work (equity), as well as the opportunity to have meaningful input into workplace decisions (voice) (Figure 8.2). He argues that extreme positions of either dimension are both undesirable and untenable and that the aim should be to strike a balance. Budd thus brings us back to old British industrial relations debates between pluralists and radicals regarding appropriate political processes as well as the division of economic outcomes.

As with Kochan and Osterman (1994), Budd's argument can also be interpreted as a response to the dominant emphasis of unitarist US HRM on narrow and often short-termist business performance and 'efficiency' criteria. Equally, it also rejects a narrow economic analysis of the implications for labour adopted in some British industrial relations analyses of partnership. The efficiency/equity/voice framework is therefore valuable given that it explicitly sets out three dimensions that have run through this long debate. First, efficiency matters because it creates stable employment at the company level and growth at national level, for the benefit of shareholders, employees and society. It therefore aligns with the resource focus of HRM, and the current global economic crisis underlines the importance of sustainable organizations and job creation. Second, equity matters because employees and society care about the distribution of benefits, and again this aligns with the human focus of HRM. Finally, voice matters because in a democratic society employees should have some say over how decisions are made, for its own sake as part of human dignity and democratic ideals. Voice, Budd argues, is intrinsically important as an end in itself irrespective of the actual outcomes (Johnstone et al., 2011).

Budd suggests that efficiency, equity and voice 'provide the dimensions for evaluating social partnerships' (Budd, 2004: 120). The framework was applied in a study by Johnstone et al. (2011) of partnership in the UK financial services sector, which revealed how several decisions were better than they could otherwise have been for staff, and that the dialogue afforded through the partnership approach had resulted in several compromises to the benefit of employees by mitigating the negative impact of decisions (equity). There was evidence to suggest that without the voice afforded through the early consultation and mutual legitimacy afforded by partnership dialogue, management decisions may have been more focused on short-term efficiency, with scant regard for the short- or long-term equity outcomes. Interestingly management acknowledged that decisions based solely on 'profit-maximizing' and 'efficiency' are often inefficient in the long term because they are met with staff resistance and union opposition, whereas compromises which may appear to be less efficient in the short term, are actually more efficient in the long term because of their greater legitimacy and acceptability. To varying extents, partnership facilitated dialogue and voice, which promoted more considered decision making, the moderation of business decisions, and the moderation of the worst effects for employees (Johnstone et al., 2011). In other words, managers acknowledged that often there was a sound business case for equity and that the concepts are not mutually exclusive. Partnership may be unable to perfectly 'balance' the objectives of the employment relationship; indeed it is difficult to imagine what a balance would actually look like. However, the voice process afforded through partnership often led to outcomes which were more balanced than they otherwise would have been, and this is a central component of the pluralist ethic, where the aim is one of levelling the playing field (Clegg, 1975). Thus a strong, genuine partnership may 'shock' management into addressing the 'strategic tensions' than pervade HRM, and encourage longer-term thinking in relation to their business strategies, and related HRM and employment policies, potentially leading to better management and improved organizational performance. Partnership may also present one way of addressing the 'representation gap' (Towers, 1997), while trying to balance the distribution of outcomes for workers and organizations.

5. CONCLUSION

As we move away from Taylorist approaches and the emphasis in HR on high-performance work practices that deliver flexibility and quality, this has led to experimentation with a whole cocktail of methods for sharing information and consulting with employees, involving employees in workplace decision making, and soliciting feedback (Boxall and Purcell, 2008). This has taken place alongside union decline and an inability of traditional mechanisms to perform, partly because they are absent from many workplaces, and partly because they are seen as not delivering to employees or employers. So the real world is reflected in academic research, which has significantly broadened the scope of research on employee voice and participation in organizations. Employee voice is being redefined in ways that go beyond the exit-voice framework's focus on expressing dissatisfaction (Dundon et al., 2004; Wilkinson et al., 2004) and the importance of voice in high-performance work systems has drawn management and behavioural scholars into the research domain on voice (Dundon and Gollan, 2007; Budd et al., 2010). Yet reconciling economic and social dimensions of work and employment continue to remain problematic as the current controversies surrounding the GFC illustrate. The quest for labour-management partnership is potentially a form of governance which can regulate the various tensions between efficiency, equity and voice. However, models of partnership may need to be developed for different sectors and groups of workers rather than assuming a one size fits all approach, and may also need to be integrated into a broader and supportive HR system to achieve mutual gains.

REFERENCES

Acas 2003. *Acas Annual Report and Resource Accounts*. London: Acas.

Ackers, P. 2012. Rethinking the employment relationship: a neo-pluralist critique of British industrial relations orthodoxy. *The International Journal of Human Resource Management*, forthcoming.

Ackers, P. and Payne, J. 1998. British trade unions and social partnership: rhetoric, reality and strategy. *The International Journal of Human Resource Management*, 9 (3): 529–549.

Ackers, P., Smith, C. and Smith, P. 1996. *The New Workplace and Trade Unionism*. Routledge.

Ackers, P., Marchington, M., Wilkinson, A. and Dundon, T. 2005. Partnership and voice, with or without trade unions: changing UK management approaches to organisational participation. In M. Stuart and M. Martinez-Lucio (eds), *Partnership and Modernisation in Employment Relations*. London: Routledge, pp. 23–45.

Addison, J.T. and Hirsch, B.T. 1989. Union effects on productivity, profits, and growth: has the long run arrived? *Journal of Labor Economics*, 72–105.

Barney, J., 1991. Firm resources and sustained competitive advantage. *Journal of Management*, 17 (1): 99–120.

Becker, B.E., Huselid, M.A., Pickus, P.S., and Spratt, M.F. 1997. HR as a source of shareholder value: research and recommendations. *Human Resource Management*, 36 (1), 39–47.

Boroff, K. and Lewin, D. 1997. Loyalty, voice and intent to exit a union firm: a conceptual and empirical analysis. *Industrial and Labour Relations Review*, 51 (1): 50–63.

Boselie, P. and Paauwe, J. 2010. Human resource management and the resource-based view. In A. Wilkinson, N. Bacon, T. Redman and S. Snell (eds), *The SAGE Handbook of Human Resource Management*. London: Sage.

Boxall, P. and Purcell, J. 2000. Strategic human resource management: where have we come from and where should we be going? *International Journal of Management Reviews*, 2 (2): 183–203.

Boxall, P. and Purcell, J. 2008. *Strategy and Human Resource Management*. Palgrave.

Budd, J.W. 2004. *Employment with a Human Face*. ILR Press.

Budd, J.W., Gollan, P.J. and Wilkinson, A. 2010. New approaches to employee voice and participation in organizations. *Human Relations*, 63 (3): 303–310.

Bullock, A. 1977. *Report on the Committee of Inquiry on Industrial Democracy*. Cmnd 6706.

CIPD 2007. *The Changing HR Function: Transforming HR*. London: CIPD.

CIPD 2011a. *HR Business Partnering, Factsheet*, http://www.cipd.co.uk/hr-resources/factsheets/hr-business-partnering.aspx, accessed 23 July 2012.

CIPD 2011b. *Employee Voice, Factsheet*. http://www.cipd.co.uk/hr-resources/factsheets/employee-voice.aspx, accessed 23 July 2012.

CIPD 2012. *The HR Profession Map* http://www.cipd.co.uk/cipd-hr-profession/hr-profession-map/, accessed 23 July 2012.

Clegg, H.A. 1975. Pluralism in industrial relations. *British Journal of Industrial Relations*, 13 (3): 309–316.

Delaney, J. 2008. Industrial relations and business performance. In Blyton et al., *The Sage Handbook of Industrial Relations*. Sage.

Dietz, G. 2004. Partnership and the development of trust in British workplaces. *Human Resource Management Journal*, 14 (1): 5–24.

Donovan, T. 1968. *Report of the Royal Commission on Trade Unions and Employers Associations*. Cmnd 3623.

Doucouliagios, C. and Laroche, P. 2003. What do unions do to productivity? A meta-analysis. *Industrial Relations: A Journal of Economy and Society*, 42 (4): 650–691.

DTI 1998. *Fairness at Work*. Cmnd 3968. London: DTI.

Dundon, T. and Rollinson, D. 2011. *Understanding Employment Relations*. Second edition. McGraw-Hill Higher Education.

Dundon, T. and Wilkinson, A. 2013. Employee participation. In A. Wilkinson and T. Redman (eds), *Contemporary Human Resource Management*. FT Prentice Hall.

Dundon, T., Wilkinson, A., Marchington, M. and Ackers, P. 2004. The meanings and purpose of employee voice. *International Journal of Human Resource Management*, 15 (September): 1150–1171.

Edwards, P. and Sengupta, S. 2010. Industrial relations and economic performance. In T. Colling and M. Terry (eds), *Industrial Relations: Theory and Practice* (3rd edn). Chichester: Wiley, pp. 378–397.

Edwards, P., Bélanger, J., and Wright, M. 2002. The social relations of productivity: a longitudinal and comparative study of aluminium smelters. *Relations industrielles*, 57 (2).

Evans, C., Harvey, G. and Turnbull, P. 2012. When partnerships don't 'match-up': an evaluation of labour-management partnerships in the automotive components and civil aviation industries. *Human Resource Management Journal*, 22 (1): 60–75.

Ferner, A. and Hyman, R. 1998. *Industrial Relations in the New Europe*, Oxford: Blackwell.

Flanders, A. 1965. *Industrial Relations – What Is Wrong With The System?* Faber and Faber.

Francis, H. and Keegan, A. 2006. The changing face of HRM: in search of balance. *Human Resource Management Journal*, 16 (3): 231–249.

Freeman, R. and Medoff, J. 1984. *What Do Unions Do?* Basic Books.

Freeman, R., Boxall, P. and Haynes, P. (eds) 2007. *What Workers Say: Employee Voice in the Anglo-American Workplace*. New York: Cornell University Press.

Geary, J. and Trif, A. 2011. Workplace partnership and the balance of advantage: a critical case analysis. *British Journal of Industrial Relations*, 49, s44–s69.

Giddens, A. 1998. *The Third Way*. Oxford: Polity Press.

Gollan, P.J. and Wilkinson, A. 2007. Contemporary developments in information and consultation. *The International Journal of Human Resource Management*, 18 (7): 1133–1144.

Grant, R.M. 1998. *Contemporary Strategy Analysis*, 3rd edn. Blackwell.

Greenfield, A. and Pleasure, R. 1993. Representatives of their own choosing: finding workers' voice in the legitimacy and power of their unions. In B. Kaufman and M. Kleiner (eds), *Employee Representation: Alternatives and Future Directions*. Madison, WI: IRRS.

Guest, D. 1991. Personnel management: the end of orthodoxy? *British Journal of Industrial Relations*, 29 (2): 149–175.

Guest, D. 1999. Human resource management: the workers' verdict. *Human Resource Management Journal*, 9 (3): 5–25.

Guest, D. 2002. Human resource management, corporate performance and employee wellbeing: building the worker into HRM. *Journal of Industrial Relations*, 44 (3): 335–358.

Guest, D. 2007. Human resource management and the worker: towards a new psychological contract? In P. Boxall, J. Purcell and P. Wright (eds), *The Oxford Handbook of Human Resource Management*. Oxford: Oxford University Press, 128–46.

Guest, D. and Peccei, R. 1998. *The Partnership Company: Benchmarks for the Future*. London: Involvement and Participation Association.

Guest, D. and Peccei, R. 2001. Partnership at work: mutuality and the balance of advantage. *British Journal of Industrial Relations*, 39 (2): 207–236.

Guest, D., Paauwe, J. and Wright, P. (eds) (2012), *HRM and Performance: Achievements and Challenges*, Wiley.

Handel, M.J. and Levine, D.I. 2004. Editors' introduction: the effects of new work practices on workers. *Industrial Relations: A Journal of Economy and Society*, 43 (1): 1–43.

Haynes, P. and Allen, M. 2001. Partnership as union strategy: a preliminary evaluation. *Employee Relations*, 23 (2): 164–187.

Heery, E. 2002. Partnership versus organising: alternative futures for British trade unionism. *Industrial Relations Journal*, 33 (1): 20–35.

Heery, E., Conley, H., Delbridge, R. and Stewart, P. 2004. Seeking partnership for the contingent workforce. In M. Martinez-Lucio and M. Stuart (eds), *Partnership and Modernisation in Employment Relations*. London: Routledge, pp. 274–302.

Heery, E., Bacon, N., Blyton, P. and Fiortio, J. 2008. Introduction: the field of industrial relations. In P. Blyton, N. Bacon, J. Fiortio and E. Heery, *Sage Handbook of Industrial Relations*. London: Sage, pp. 1–32.

Hirsch, B. 2003. What do unions do for economic performance. IZA Discussion Paper 892, October.

Hirschman, A. 1970. *Exit, Voice and Loyalty: Responses to Decline in Firms, Organizations and States*. Cambridge: Harvard University Press.

Huselid, M.A. 1995. The impact of human resource management practices on turnover, and productivity, and corporate financial performance. *Academy of Management Journal*, 38 (3): 635–672.

Ichniowski, C. et al. 1996. What works at work: overview and assessment. *Industrial Relations: A Journal of Economy and Society*, 35 (3): 299–333.

IPA 1997. *Towards Industrial Partnership*. London: IPA.

Johnstone, S., Ackers, P. and Wilkinson, A., 2009. The British partnership phenomenon: a ten year review. *Human Resource Management Journal*, 19 (3): 260–279.

Johnstone, S., Wilkinson, A. and Ackers, P. 2011. Applying Budd's model to partnership. *Economic and Industrial Democracy*, 32 (2): 307–328.

Kaufman, B. 2007. The development of HRM in historical and international context. In P. Boxall, J. Purcell and P. Wright (eds), *The Oxford Handbook of HRM*. OUP.

Kaufman, B. 2012. History of the British industrial relations field reconsidered: getting from the Webbs to the new employment relations paradigm. *British Journal of Industrial Relations*, forthcoming.

Kaufman, B. and Taras, D. 2010. Employee participation through non-union forms of employee representation. In A. Wilkinson, P. Gollan, M. Marchington and D. Lewin (eds), *The Oxford Handbook of Participation in Organizations*. Oxford: Oxford University Press.

Keenoy, T. 1997. HRMism and the languages of re-presentation. *Journal of Management Studies*, 34 (5): 825–841.

Kelly, J. 2004. Social partnership arrangements in Britain. *Industrial Relations*, 43 (1): 267–292.

Kochan, T.A. 2004. Restoring trust in the human resource management profession. *Asia Pacific Journal of Human Resources*, 42 (2): 132–146.

Kochan, T. and Osterman, P. 1994. *The Mutual Gains Enterprise: Forging a Winning Partnership among Labor, Management and Government*. Boston, MA: Harvard Business School Press.

Kuhn, P. 1998. Unions and the economy: what we know; what we should know. *Canadian Journal of Economics*, 31 (November): 1033–56.

Lawler, E. 1986. *High Involvement Management: Participative Strategies for Improving Organizational Performance*. Jossey Bass.

Legge, K. 1978. *Power, Innovation and Problem-solving in Personnel Management*. London: McGraw-Hill.

Legge, K. 1995. *Human Resource Management: Rhetorics and Realities*. Macmillan.

Lengnick-Hall, M.L. et al. 2009. Strategic human resource management: the evolution of the field. *Human Resource Management Review*, 19 (2): 64–85.

Lewin, D. 2008. Human resource management in the 21st century. In C. Wankel (ed.), *21st Century Management: A Reference Handbook*. London: Sage, pp. 56–64.

Marchington, M. 1998. Partnership in context: towards a European model. In P. Sparrow and M. Marchington (eds), *Human Resource Management: The New Agenda*. London: FT Pitman.

Marchington, M. 2007. Employee voice system. In P. Boxall, J. Purcell and P. Wright (eds), *The Oxford Handbook of Human Resource Management*. Oxford, Oxford University Press, 50 (1), 65–74.

Marchington, M. and Wilkinson, A. 2012. *Human Resource Management at Work*. London: CIPD.

Marchington, M., Goodman, J., Wilkinson, A. and Ackers, P. 1992. *New Developments in Employee Involvement*. Sheffield: Employment Department Research 2.

Martinez-Lucio, M. and Stuart, M. 2002. Assessing partnership: the prospects for, and challenges of, modernisation. *Employee Relations*, 24 (3): 252–261.

Martinez-Lucio, M. and Stuart, M. 2005. Partnership and new industrial relations in a risk society: an age of shotgun weddings and marriages of convenience? *Work, Employment and Society*, 19 (4): 797–817.

Oxenbridge, S. and Brown, W. 2004. Achieving a new equilibrium: the stability of co-operative employer-union relationship. *Industrial Relations Journal*, 35 (5): 388–402.

Peel, S. and Boxall, P. 2005. When is contracting preferable to employment? An exploration of management and worker perspectives. *Journal of Management Studies*, 42, 1675–97.

Peetz, D., Frost, A. and Le Queux, S. 2011. The GFC and employment relations. In A. Wilkinson and K. Townsend (eds), *The Future of Employment Relations: New Paradigms, New Developments*, Basingstoke: Palgrave MacMillan.

Pfeffer, J. 1994. *The Human Equation*. Harvard Business School Press.

Purcell, J. 1999. Best practice and best fit: chimera or cul de sac? *Human Resource Management Journal*, 9 (3): 26–41.

Roche, W.K. 2009. Who gains from workplace partnership? *The International Journal of Human Resource Management*, 20 (1): 1–33.

Roche, W. and Geary, J. 2002. Advocates, critics and union involvement in partnership. *British Journal of Industrial Relations*, 40 (4): 659–688.

Samuel, P.J. 2007. Partnership consultation and employer domination in two British life and pension firms. *Work, Employment and Society*, 21 (3): 459.

Schuler, R.S. 1989. Strategic human resource management and industrial relations. *Human Relations*, 42 (2): 157–184.

Sisson, K. 2010. *Employment Relations Matters*. Warwick. http://www2.warwick.ac.uk/fac/soc/wbs/research/irru/erm/, last accessed 23 July 2012.

Storey, J. 1995. Human resource management: still marching on or marching out? In J. Storey (ed.), *Human Resource Management: A Critical Text*. London: Routledge.

Storey, J. 2007. *Human Resource Management: A Critical Text*. London: Thomson.

Strauss, G. 2006. Worker participation? Some under-considered issues. *Industrial Relations: A Journal of Economy and Society*, 45 (4): 778–803.

Stuart, M. and Martinez-Lucio, M. 2004. *Partnership and Modernisation in Employment Relations*. London: Routledge.

Tailby, S., Richardson, M., Stewart, P., Danford, A. and Upchurch, M. 2004. Partnership at work and worker participation: an NHS case study. *Industrial Relations Journal*, 35 (5): 403–418.

Terry, M. 2003. Can 'partnership' reverse the decline of British trade unions? *Work, Employment and Society*, 17 (3): 459–472.

Terry, M. and Smith, J. 2003. *Evaluation of Partnership at Work Fund*. Employment Relations Research No. 17, London: DTI.

Thompson, P. 2003. Disconnected capitalism: or why employers can't keep their side of the bargain. *Work, Employment & Society*, 17 (2): 359–378.

Thompson, P. 2011. The trouble with HRM. *Human Resource Management Journal*, 21 (4): 355–367.

Towers, B. 1997. *Representation Gap*. Oxford: Oxford University Press.

TUC 1999. *Partners for Progress: Next Steps for the New Unionism*. London: TUC.

Ulrich, D. 1998. A new mandate for human resources. *Harvard Business Review*, January: 125–135.

Ulrich, Dave, and Brockbank, W. 2005. *The HR Value Proposition*. Harvard Business School Press.

Walton, R.E. 1985. From control to commitment in the workplace. *Harvard Business Review*, March–April.

Walton, R.E. and McKersie, R.B. 1965. *A Behavioural Theory of Labor Negotiations*. London: McGraw-Hill.

Welbourne, T. 2011. Engaged in what? A role-based perspective for the future of employee engagement. In A. Wilkinson and K. Townsend (eds), *The Future of Employment Relations: New Paradigms, New Developments*, Basingstoke: Palgrave MacMillan.

Wilkinson, A. 2008. Empowerment. In S. Clegg and J. Bailey (eds), *Encyclopaedia of Organizational Studies*. London, NY: Sage, pp. 441–442.

Wilkinson, A., and Dundon, T. 2010. Direct employee participation. In A. Wilkinson, Paul J. Gollan, Michael Marchington, and D. Lewin (eds),

Oxford Handbook of Participation in Organizations. Oxford: Oxford University Press.

Wilkinson, A. and Fay, C. 2011. New times for employee voice? *Human Resource Management*, 50 (1): 65–74.

Wilkinson, A. and Redman, T. 2013. *Contemporary Human Resource Management*. Financial Times/ Prentice Hall.

Wilkinson, A., Dundon, T., Marchington, M. and Ackers, P. 2004. Changing patterns of employee voice. *Journal of Industrial Relations*, 46 (3): 298–322.

Wilkinson, A., N. Bacon, T. Redman and S. 2009. *The SAGE Handbook of Human Resource Management*, Sage.

Wilkinson, A., Gollan, P., Marchington, M. and Lewin D. 2010. Conceptualising employee participation in organisations. In A. Wilkinson, P. Gollan, M. Marchington and D. Lewin (eds), *The Oxford Handbook of Participation in Organisations*. Oxford: Oxford University Press, pp. 1–25.

Wilkinson, A., Johnstone, S. and Townsend, K. 2012. Changing patterns of human resource management in construction. *Construction Management and Economics*, forthcoming.

Willmott, H. 1993. Strength is ignorance; slavery is freedom: managing culture in modern organizations. *Journal of Management Studies*, 30 (4): 515–552.

Wills, J. 2004. Trade unionism and partnership in practice: evidence from the Barclays-Unifi agreement. *Industrial Relations Journal*, 35 (4): 329–343.

Wray, D. 2004. Management and union motives in the negotiation of partnership: a case study of the process and outcome at an engineering company. In M. Stuart and M. Martinez-Lucio (eds), *Partnership and Modernisation in Employment Relations*. London: Routledge, pp. 190–215.

Zagelmeyer, S. and Gollan, P.J. 2012. Exploring terra incognita: preliminary reflections on the impact of the global financial crisis upon human resource management. *The International Journal of Human Resource Management*, July: 37–41.

9. Employee attitudes, HR practices and organizational performance: what's the evidence?

Yanqing Lai and George Saridakis

1. INTRODUCTION

Employee attitude constitutes an important factor of the organizational performance process. In particular, organizational commitment and job satisfaction are the two important employee attitudes that have been commonly studied and empirically assessed in the organizational behaviour and labour economics literature. This literature suggests that positive employee attitudes, such as higher levels of organizational commitment and job satisfaction, are associated with higher levels of financial performance, labour productivity and other related organizational outcomes (e.g. Porter et al., 1974; Mathieu and Zajac, 1990; Ostroff, 1992; Hackett et al., 1994; Swailes, 2002; Schneider et al., 2003; Luchak and Gellatly, 2007; Brown et al., 2010; Suliman and Al-Junaibi, 2010). Hence, it is important to researchers, policy makers and business owners and managers to analyse and implement appropriate human resource (HR) strategies that enhance employee attitudes and workplace perceptions which in turn improve organizational performance. In this chapter we provide an analysis of this literature and highlight the key contributions and debates that emerge from studying the relationship between employee attitudes, HR practices and organizational performance (e.g. Becker et al., 1997; Purcell et al., 2003; Wright and Nishii, 2006).

Looking at employee attitudes, organizational commitment is critical to organizational performance since it reflects employees' supportive attitudes towards the organization (e.g. Baotham et al., 2010; Zeinabadi, 2010). Many authors (e.g. Sims and Keon, 1999; O'Fallon and Butterfield, 2005; Eby et al., 1999; Lacity et al., 2008) suggest that high levels of organizational commitment may create a work environment that encourages employees to reason and behave ethically through social process and workplace norms, and help firms experience additional benefits through positive interactions among employees (Valentine et al., 2011). Suliman and Al-Junaibi (2010) argue that the importance of organizational commitment comes from a belief that if properly managed through, for example, appropriate HR practices, it may lead to positive employee reactions such as improved job performance, reduced absenteeism and turnover. Westover et al. (2010) find that an organization that has highly committed employees is able to achieve long-term and enduring improvement in organizational performance.

Job satisfaction has also received attention in the employee attitude-performance literature. The primary argument here tends to suggest that job satisfaction is an indicator of organizational outcomes (Ostroff, 1992). In other words, employees who experience high levels of job satisfaction achieve higher levels of performance than those who have lower levels of job satisfaction (Ackfeldt and Wong, 2006). Some researchers (e.g. Gross and Etzioni, 1985; Ostroff, 1992; Ilies et al., 2006) find that satisfied employees improve organizational performance because they tend to work harder than frustrated ones. In short, promoting job satisfaction enhances individuals' performance in the organization and in turn, this boosts overall organizational performance.

However, studies designed to investigate the relationship between employee attitudes, such as organizational commitment, and job satisfaction and organizational outcomes are often connected to human resource management (HRM)-performance research (e.g. Guest, 1987; Beer et al., 1984; Boxall and Steeneveld, 1999; Steijin, 2002; Wright et al., 2003; Bradley et al., 2004; Saridakis et al., 2008; Brown et al., 2010; Storey et al., 2010; Saridakis et al., 2012). Dyer and Reeves (1995), for example, suggest an essential causal chain of HRM-performance relationship by positing four levels of organizational outcomes: (i) human resource reactions or employee reactions (affective, cognitive and behaviour); (ii) organizational outcomes (productivity, quality, efficiencies); (iii) financial performance; and (iv) market based outcomes (i.e. market value). Consequently, if the assumed cause-and-effect relationship between HRM and organizational performance exists, employee reactions (e.g. employee attitudes and the subsequent behaviours) may act as a mediating mechanism within this framework. According to this proposition, we consider the economic and HRM literature on employee attitudes/behaviours with a focus on organizational commitment and job satisfaction and organizational performance. The chapter is of particular relevance for scholars of economics, management and organization interested in understanding the relationship between organizational commitment/job satisfaction, individual performance and organizational performance.

The chapter is structured as follows. Section 2 presents a detailed explanation regarding the mediating role of employee responses within the HRM-performance diagram. Section 3 explains the construct of two important employee attitudes: organizational commitment and job satisfaction, and the possible statistical relation between them. Section 4 discusses the primary HRM models and framework in the literature, and its association with employee attitudes. Section 5 examines the way in which organizational commitment/job satisfaction is linked to employee behaviours, in particular, employee turnover/turnover intention and organizational citizenship behaviours. The subsequent effect of employee behaviours (employee turnover/turnover intention and organizational citizenship behaviours) on organizational performance is examined in Section 6. Section 7 discusses the predominate research methods that have been used in existing studies. Section 8 concludes the chapter.

2. EMPLOYEE REACTIONS: THE 'BLACK BOX' THAT LINKS HRM AND ORGANIZATIONAL PERFORMANCE?

HRM-Performance Relationship

Broadly, the study of HRM is mainly involved in the selection that organizations make from numerous policies, practices and structures for managing employees (Sisson, 1990; Boxall and Purcell, 2003). In strategic terms, HRM is conceptualized through developing a collection of HR practices so as to improve organizational performance and outcomes. Therefore, identifying and examining the nature of relationship between HRM and organizational performance has been a central focus of attention in the literature for more than three decades. A substantial amount of research finds that HRM is positively associated with various organizational performance outcomes (Boselie et al., 2005; Wright et al., 2005; Combs et al., 2006), including financial performance and labour productivity (Brown et al., 2010), market value (Huselid, 1995) and operational measures of performance (MacDuffie, 1995). Additionally, Saridakis et al. (2008) find that British small firms with informal work structures are more likely to experience employment tribunal claims than large firms, and also lose at a tribunal. However, in spite of a well-established HRM-performance relationship in empirical research, what is still missing is a theory about how HRM and performance are linked (Guest, 1997). Researchers argue HR practices may not directly influence organizational performance

(Becker and Huselid, 2006); instead, there are mediating variables through which HRM practices are converted to performance (Edgar and Geare, 2009). Researchers have referred to this as the 'black box' issue, and have required theories and studies on the mediating mechanisms through which HRM affects organizational performance (Becker and Gerhart, 1996; Wright and Gardner, 2003).

Employee Attitudes and Behaviours: the Mediator Mechanisms?

Becker et al. (1997) suggest that in order to study the most immediate outcome of HR practices, it would be better to examine employee reactions and outcomes first. Thus, it is argued that HR practices operate through employee skills, motivation and work design, resulting in behavioural outcomes (e.g. productivity, and discretional effect) and eventually financial performance. Hence, the casual link between HRM and organizational performance appears to start with attention on the response of employees (Wright et al., 2003; Legge, 2005; Macky and Boxall, 2007; Paauwe, 2009). Boselie et al. (2005) explain that HRM interventions should be further examined to increase our understanding of HRM-related outcomes, which are typically manifested in shifts in employee attitudes and behaviours. In other words, HRM leads to employee responses before the organization observes an impact on firm performance. Hence, employee reactions to HR practices lie at the heart of HRM-performance relationship, because the linkage between employee reactions and their subsequent behaviour is critically significant.

According to Dyer and Reeves (1995), the first causal chain of HRM-performance relationship is HRM-related outcomes or employee reactions, which can be further divided into three levels: cognitive, affective and behavioural response. Cognition is a process of thought in which an individual first becomes aware of stimuli, evaluates the significance of the stimuli and then thinks of possible behavioural reactions (Scherer, 1999). Affective responses (or emotion) are immediate reactions to external stimuli that are of importance to individuals and are short in duration (Frijda, 1988; Gray and Watson, 2001). Hence, cognition reflects one's mind and affective reactions (or emotion) mirror one's heart. There is a reciprocal relationship between cognition and emotion – emotion affects cognition, cognition elicits emotion (Lazarus, 1991). Together, cognition and emotion create attitudes that contain positive, negative, or mixed elements (Piderit, 2000), which leads to behavioural responses (or one's deeds) (Smollan, 2006). In a word, employee behaviours are the outcomes of cognition and emotion.

The relationship between cognitive, affective and behavioural responses

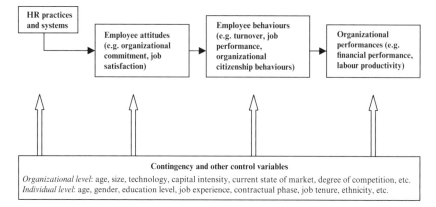

*Figure 9.1   Relationship between HR practices, employee attitudes and
              organizational performance*

suggests that employee attitudes resulting from cognitive and affective
reactions (minds and heart) cannot directly influence organizational performance on their own: employees must also behave (deeds) appropriately.
Researchers (e.g. Heskett et al., 1997; Rucci et al., 1998) found that positive employee attitudes lead to positive employee behaviours towards customers, which increase the customer retention and eventually contributed
to financial performance (e.g. sales and profitability) and organizational
growth. Koys (2001) suggests that employee behaviours are more likely to
directly impact on organizational performance than employee attitudes,
especially when the notion of organizational performance is associated
with profitability and customer attitudes. Therefore, it can be argued (see
Figure 9.1) that employee attitudes such as organizational commitment
and job satisfaction cause employee behavioural outcomes like turnover,
job performance and organizational citizenship behaviours, which in turn
lead to organizational performance (e.g. financial performance and labour
productivity).[1]

In this framework, HR practices and systems cannot directly intervene
in firm performance. Instead, their effective functioning is realized via
employees' perceptions, interpretations and reactions. The most immediate employee response towards these HR practices is employee attitudes,
including organizational commitment and job satisfaction. We turn to
discuss these concepts in the next section.

3. EMPLOYEE ATTITUDES: ORGANIZATIONAL COMMITMENT AND JOB SATISFACTION

The Concept of Organizational Commitment

The concept of organizational commitment has a long history within the organization literature (Becker, 1960), evolving from a single to a multidimensional construct. The notion of organizational commitment as a single construct was based on the work of Mowday and his colleagues (Mowday et al., 1982; Cohen, 2003), by perceiving it as a behaviour rather than an attitude (Nijhof et al., 1998). Mowday et al. (1982: 20) defined organizational commitment as 'the relative strength of an individual's identification with and involvement in a particular organization', and then further characterized it by three factors: (i) a belief in and acceptance of organizational goals and values; (ii) a willingness to exert effort toward organizational goal accomplishment; and (iii) a strong desire to maintain membership. A high level of organizational commitment is viewed as equivalent with positive feelings to an organization and its values, which essentially evaluate the degree of congruence between values and beliefs of individuals and the organization (Swailes, 2002). However, the concept has been widely recognized and examined as a multidimensional construct in the 20 years since Allen and Meyer's pioneering work (1990). They developed a three-component model by breaking organizational commitment into three dimensions: affective commitment, continuance commitment and normative commitment. This is the so-called three-component model of organizational commitment.

Affective commitment is defined as an acceptance and internalization of the organizational goals and values, a willingness to exert significant efforts on the organization's behalf, and an emotional attachment to the organization (Mowday et al., 1979; Allen and Meyer, 1990). Individuals that have a high level of affective commitment are expected to engage in the behaviours that are geared towards organizational goals and objectives (Mayer and Schoorman, 1992; Suliman, 2002), and work for organizational benefits and well-being. Continuance commitment represents a psychological attachment to an organization that is associated with one's perceived value of accrued investment and one's perceived effect on opportunities for exit (Meyer and Allen, 1984; Allen and Meyer, 1990). This type of organizational commitment reflects an individual's desire to continue working for the current organization, which is largely determined by perceived benefits/rewards resulting from staying or perceived costs caused by leaving. Finally, Wiener (1982: 471) defined commitment as 'totality of internalised normative pressures to act in a way which meets organisational goals and interest', because 'they believe it is the right and moral thing to do'. This is consistent with the concept of normative commitment, which reflects a generalized sense of internal obligation to the organization for which one works (Yao and Wang, 2006). In other words, normative-committed employees are willing to dedicate and devote themselves to their organization because they feel responsible for its success. These three streams of organizational commitment share one common characteristic: the reflection of a psychological state (want, need and ought, respectively) of an employee vis-à-vis the organization (Allen and Meyer, 1990; Solinger et al., 2008), through encouraging individuals to pursue courses of action that benefit the organization (Gardner et al., 2011).

Empirically, organizational commitment has been treated as an attitude-based variable, and originally operationalized through the organizational commitment questionnaire (OCQ) and turnover (Mowday et al., 1982; Tett and Meyer, 1993). It is typically measured by seeking employees' responses to questions like 'I find that my values and the organization's are very similar'. The answers are usually rated on a five-point scale from 1 (strongly disagree) to 5 (strongly agree). Allen and Meyer (1990) combined attitudes, behaviour and binding economic actions in the measurement of commitment, and designed measures for each component of organizational commitment (affective commitment scale, continuance commitment scale, and normative commitment scale), which have been widely used in empirical studies (Ketch and and Strawser, 1998; Kallbers and Cenker, 2007).

The Concept of Job Satisfaction

Job satisfaction is defined as a pleasurable emotional state that results from the valuation of one's work (Locke, 1976). It includes characteristics related to the job itself (e.g. pay and promotion) and work environment (Gonzalez and Garazo, 2006). Therefore, it is a concept that has been assessed with two facets, intrinsic job satisfaction (e.g. received from the job itself) and extrinsic job satisfaction (e.g. work condition and policies, and praise) (Babin and Boles, 1998; O'Neil and Mone, 1998; Pepe, 2010; Singh and Loncar, 2010). In other words, job satisfaction is an individual's feeling about the job and the attitudes he/she has towards various aspects or facets of the job. In addition, it is an attitude and perception that may consequently impact on the degree of fit between an employee and the organization (Ivancevich and Matteson, 2002; Spector, 1997). Individuals experiencing high levels of job satisfaction are more likely to work harder and better than frustrated and unhappy ones (Ackfeldt and Wong, 2006).

In the organizational behaviour literature, job satisfaction is operationalized either as an individual's score across several items that comprise an overall job satisfaction scale, or as scores for multiple facets of satisfaction, such as sense of achievement, influence over the job and job security (Brown and Peterson, 1993; Spector, 1997). Therefore, job satisfaction is considered as a construct with multiple facets (Weiss, 2002), and an individual can be more or less satisfied with his/her job, pay, workplace, and so forth.

In most empirical studies, job satisfaction is measured by self-reported, subjective assessments at the individual level, which is assumed to be a satisfactory empirical approximation to individual utility (Frey and Stutzer, 2002). Items like 'All in all, I am satisfied with my job', 'In general, I like working at my company', and 'In general, I don't like my job' are rated on a seven-point scale or five-point scale from 1 (strongly disagree) to 7 or 5 (strongly agree), and an overall job satisfaction index is generated after reverse scoring one time and averaging the items' scores (see Cammann et al., 1983; Rich, 1997; Valentine et al., 2011). The job description index (JDI) (Smith et al., 1969) and job satisfaction survey (JSS) are examples of measurement of job satisfaction in terms of examining the multiple facets of satisfaction, including pay, promotion, supervision etc.

The Link between Organizational Commitment and Job Satisfaction

Most of the literature has argued that organizational commitment and job satisfaction are inextricably linked, and an increase in a level of one leads to a higher level of the other. The interest in exploring this relationship began with their presumed role in predicting labour turnover (William and Hazer, 1986; Farkas and Tetrick, 1989). So far, four alternative models of job satisfaction-organizational commitment relationship have been proposed and examined in empirical studies: (i) job satisfaction is an antecedent of organizational commitment; (ii) organizational commitment is an antecedent of job satisfaction; (iii) job satisfaction and organizational commitment are reciprocally related; and (iv) job satisfaction and organizational commitment are independent.

Job satisfaction is an antecedent of organizational commitment
Job satisfaction is a more immediate affective response to various facets of job and work environment. Therefore, it would develop faster after an individual joined the organization (Cramer, 1996; Zeinabadi, 2010). On the other hand, organizational commitment is slower to develop because it is based not only on the job but also on aspects of the employing

organization such as its goals and values (Porter et al., 1974). According to Bagozzi's (1992) 'attitude-intention-behaviour' model, behaviour is a copying activity that results from an individual's appraisal of a situation and subsequent emotional response. Accordingly, job satisfaction represents an appraisal of the different work environment while organizational commitment is perceived as a positive emotional response to the positive appraisal of work (Zeinabadi, 2010). In this case, job satisfaction should lead to organizational commitment. The bulk of empirical research has reached the same conclusion. For instance, a meta-analysis of 59 empirical studies finds that organizational commitment is primarily a consequence rather than an antecedent of job satisfaction (Brown and Peterson, 1993; Jones et al., 2007). Also, Yang (2008) finds that job satisfaction displays the strongest correlation with affective commitment, which is line with some previous work (Baker, 1992; Lo and Lam, 2002).

Organizational commitment is an antecedent of job satisfaction
According to self-perception theory, Bateman and Strasser (1984) argue that organizational commitment may result in increased job satisfaction because commitment might initiate a rationalization process in which attitudes are made consistent with behaviours. The concept of organizational commitment reflects a sense of attachment and belonging (Meyer and Allen, 1997). When an individual has this possessive feeling towards the organization, they would have a high level of general satisfaction, which in turn influences job satisfaction (Van Dyne and Pierce, 2004). Bateman and Strasser (1984) find that earlier organizational commitment and later job satisfaction are significantly positive while the relationship between prior job satisfaction and subsequent organizational commitment is not statistically significant. Moreover, Lu et al. (2007) observe that organizational commitment has the strongest impact on Chinese nurses' job satisfaction.

Job satisfaction and organizational commitment are reciprocally related
Several studies have reported a reciprocal relationship between organizational commitment and job satisfaction. Farkas and Tetrick (1989) found a cyclical, or possibly a reciprocal, relationship between job satisfaction and organizational commitment in an organization. Lance (1991) and Mathieu (1991) also obtain a similar finding but report an asymmetrical relationship between job satisfaction and organizational commitment. Likewise, Lincoln and Kalleberg (1990) find a significant reciprocal relationship between organizational commitment and job satisfaction in the US and Japan.

Table 9.1   Summary of major studies regarding the relationship between organizational commitment and job satisfaction

Relationship	Representative publications
Job satisfaction leads to organizational commitment	Mobley, 1977; Price and Mueller, 1981; Bluedorn, 1982; Mathieu, 1991; Shin and Reyes, 1995; Gaertner, 1999; Testa, 2001; Yang and Chang, 2007; Jones et al., 2007; Zeinabadi, 2010
Organizational commitment leads to job satisfaction	Bateman and Strasser, 1984; Curry et al., 1986; Poznanski and Bline, 1997; Lu et al., 2007
Reciprocal relationship	Farkas and Tetrick, 1989; Lance, 1991; Mathieu, 1991; Martin and Bennet, 1996; Saridakis et al., 2009
Organizational commitment and job satisfaction are independent	Anderson and Williams, 1992; Curry et al., 1986; Martin and Bennett, 1996; Cramer, 1996

Source: Johnstone et al. (2009: 262).

Job satisfaction and organizational commitment are independent

Just a few studies have found organizational commitment and job satisfaction are not statistically significantly related. Cramer (1996), for example, found that increasing job satisfaction is unlikely to lead to greater organizational commitment, and vice versa. This is consistent with Curry et al.'s (1986) and Anderson and William's (1992) findings. The result can be partially explained by different measures for organizational commitment and job satisfaction, and different study environments (Martin and Bennett, 1996).

The proposition that 'job satisfaction precedes organizational commitment' has dominated the studies of the job satisfaction-organizational commitment relationship (see Table 9.1). On the other hand, the relationship between job satisfaction and organizational commitment remains debatable, not only because of the disparity of empirical findings, but also due to methodological issues. Saridakis et al. (2009) raise concern about using relatively small sample sizes and ignoring the endogenous nature of the variables, which might lead to biased estimates of the two effects. By applying micro-econometric techniques to correct the potential endogeneity caused by omitted variables and simultaneity and using a large dataset (WERS 2004), they confirm the proposition and found that job satisfaction was not an exogenous variable.

Thus, it is argued that organizational commitment and job satisfaction may lead to a happy, committed and productive workforce that contributes to enhance firm performance. Some commentators (e.g. Organ, 1977; O'Reilly and Chatman, 1986; Balfour and Wechsler, 1991; Ostroff, 1992; Konovsky and Pugh, 1994) suggest that commitment and satisfaction can be predicted on a reciprocal, exchange-based relationship between an individual and the organization. Employees develop a sense of attachment and belonging to the organization mainly based on the perception that the organization appreciates and values them in terms of satisfying their needs and providing a hospitable and socially satisfying place to work (Balfour and Wechsler, 1991; Allen et al., 2003; Snape and Redman, 2003). Also, individuals accorded some manner of social gift by organizations would experience satisfaction and feel an obligation to reciprocate, usually in the form of better job performance and work behaviours (Ostroff, 1992). The most common mechanism that has been used by organizations for generating and enhancing this reciprocity relationship is to develop appropriate HRM policies and practices, which will be discussed in following section.

4. ORGANIZATIONAL COMMITMENT, JOB SATISFACTION AND HRM

HRM Models

Human resource management (HRM) has been described as a concept with two distinct versions: 'soft' and 'hard' depending on whether the emphasis is placed on the human or the resource. Soft HRM is associated with the human relations movement. McGregor (1960: 326) suggest that 'man will exercise self-direction and self-control in the service of objectives to which he is committed'. In other words, if an individual is assumed to achieve self-fulfilment through work, the organization should use the potential of its human capital in terms of fostering individual growth and development. Eventually, it meets not only the needs of the organization (i.e. higher levels of performance), but also of the individual (i.e. psychical and psychological needs). Soft HRM is also usually equated with the concept of a 'high commitment work system' (Walton, 1985), which is designed to elicit employees' commitment so that their behaviours are self-regulated rather than controlled by sanctions and pressure within the organization (Wood, 1996: 41). The affection and commitment to the organization are generated if employees are trusted, if they are offered training and development opportunities, and if they are given autonomy and control over their work (Guest, 1987; Hendry and Pettigrew, 1990; Purcell and Ahlstrand, 1994).

The hard HRM model reflects the notion of tight strategic control, and emphasizes 'the quantitative, calculative and business-strategic aspects of managing the "headcount resource" in as "rational" a way as for any other factor of production' (Storey, 1992: 29). Hard HRM stresses the significance of 'strategic fit', in terms of closely linking HR practices and systems to the organization's strategic objectives (external fit) and being coherent among themselves (internal fit) (Baird and Meshoulam, 1988; Hendry and Pettigrew, 1986). Under this model, the control usually comes through the performance management system (i.e. appraisal) and tight control over individual activities (Guest, 1995). Therefore, employees are managed on a much more instrumental basis under the hard HRM model than under the soft HRM model.

Many researchers and commentators have used this soft-hard dichotomy in HRM to categorize approaches to managing the workforce, leading to the multi-disciplinary treatment of HRM. However, the dominant school of thought seems to employ a contingent framework (e.g. HRM in relation to business strategy or external environment) and the resource-based view (RBV) of the firm (Boselie et al., 2005). The contingent framework tends to be consistent with the hard HRM model because the 'external fit' indicates that HR strategy should be contingent upon business strategies, responding accurately and effectively to the environment and complementing other systems. On the other hand, the RBV argues that the added value to the organization is through the utilization and development of internal resources, which is essentially embodied in its employees. HR practices and systems create the human capital pool and stimulate subsequent reactions and behaviours that influence organizational outcomes (Boxall and Steeneveld, 1999). Therefore, the RBV tends to reflect the developmental-humanist principle of the soft HRM model.

It seems impossible to incorporate the soft and hard models (e.g. apply contingency theory and RBV) into one single HRM model because they are predicated on divergent and opposing theoretical principles. However, empirical research has found no pure example of either model exists in reality. By reviewing 104 HRM-related studies from 1994 to 2003, Boselie et al. (2005) conclude that the top four HR practices are training and development (soft HRM), contingent pay and reward schemes (hard HRM), performance management (including appraisal) (hard HRM) and careful recruitment and selection (soft HRM). They consider that organizations usually adopt an integrated and coherent bundle of mutually reinforcing practices rather than a single 'best practice'.

HR Practices and Employee Attitudes

In organizations, HR practices and systems are considered as mediating mechanisms between HRM strategy and HRM outcomes (e.g. employee response and reactions). HRM strategy has been classified into different categories (Sheppeck and Militello, 2000; Guest, 1997) or dimensions (Sivasubramaniam and Kroeck, 1995; Guest, 1997), but all strategies are developed to accomplish the same organizational objectives via different HR practices and systems. The impact of HR practices on employee attitudes and behaviours (especially employee commitment) has been the central focus throughout the history of HRM literature. Many authors (e.g. Steijin, 2002; Wright et al., 2003; Bradley et al., 2004; Zaleska and De Menezes, 2007; Kuvaas, 2008) have suggested that HR practices can positively affect employee attitudes and behaviours, which has the potential to result in improved organizational performance. What matters most to the organization is the human and social resource that is held by its employees (Boselie et al., 2005), and it is the HR practices that play a role in 'building the human capital pool and stimulate the kinds of human behaviours that actually constitute an advantage' (Boxall and Steeneveld, 1999: 445). Recently, Saridakis et al. (2012) show that formal HR practices may be unnecessary in SMEs that benefit from high employee satisfaction and positive employment relations within a context of informality, but HR practices may potentially improve effort and performance among underperforming SMEs with low employee satisfaction.

HRM Model: AMO Framework

Though various systems of HRM practices have been developed and most scholars have agreed that HR practices should comprise a set of mutually reinforcing or synergistic practices (Dyer and Reeves, 1995). More recently, the so-called 'AMO' framework proposed by Appelbaum et al. (2000) has attracted most attention and it has been widely cited in this field since its emergence (Boselie et al., 2005). HR practices that intend to improve the knowledge, skills and abilities of the employees refer to the dimension 'A' (for ability). These include recruiting and selection, training and personal development, and other practices to enhance the competencies of the workforce. Motivation-enhancing ('M') practices encourage employees to perform task related behaviour (in-role behaviours) and exhibit discretionary behaviour (extra-role behaviours), and also discourage counterproductive behaviours (e.g. theft, sabotage). Incentive payment schemes and performance-related reward (e.g. profit-sharing schemes), and performance management systems (e.g. appraisal) are primarily designed for, and aim at, managing employee behaviour in this way. Pfeffer (1998) suggest that motivation-enhancing practices can not only attract high-quality workforce but also motivate employees to stay and elicit extra effort at work. Empowerment enhancing practices function to provide opportunity ('O') to participate in decision-making with respect to work and organizational outcomes. Information sharing regarding organizational issues (e.g. financial performance, investment strategy and staffing plan), granting discretion and authority on the job, and regular communication and meeting with senior or line managers are all included in this dimension.

Since HRM is viewed as a collection of multiple and discrete practices (Boselie et al., 2005), dimensions are expected to be overlapped among practices. The primary purpose of training investment is to build the requisite skill base, but it may also communicate a commitment to the employees that elicits motivation (Lepak et al., 2005). Similarly, participation programmes aim at providing opportunity but can also build employees' knowledge and motivation.

The Relationship between AMO Framework and Employee Attitudes

Positive relationship?

The three subcategories within the AMO framework demonstrate that organizations are committed to employees in the long term, are willing to invest in them and care about their welfare and development (Allen et al., 2003; Snape and Redman, 2010), which has a positive impact on employees' observation of organizational actions and discretionary behaviours (Sun et al., 2007). The training investment may increase employees' perception that organizations value their current and future contribution and thus elicit a high level of organizational commitment (especially affective and normative commitment) (Meyer and Allen, 1997; Marchington and Wilkinson, 2005). The motivation-enhancing and empowerment-enhancing practices are usually used to lead to an increase in organizational commitment because employees feel that they are trusted, valued and respected by their employers. This strengthens shared perceptions of congruence between employees and organizational value, integrates employees into the life of the organization and increases employees' identification with the organization (Arthur, 1994; Long, 1980; Meyer and Herscovitch, 2001). Gardner et al. (2007) find that the motivation and opportunity focused bundles of HR practices are positively related to affective commitment and negatively related to turnover. Brown et al. (2010) also observe that HR practices focused on employee information and communication, employee involvement and participation, and employee trust have a positive impact on affective commitment and loyalty among British workplaces, which eventually lead to better financial performance and labour productivity.

Similarly, these HR practices may also lead to a positive impact on job satisfaction. Some authors (e.g. Mathieu and Zajac, 1990; Ting, 1997; Baotham et al., 2010) propose that individuals who are satisfied with different aspects of their job are more likely to develop positive attitudes at work, leading to a high level of job satisfaction. The construct of job satisfaction reflects the degree to which the job itself and the work environment meet the expectations and requirements of employees, such as amount of pay, training, using initiative at work, influence and decision-making over the job, all of which can be detected within the AMO framework. Therefore, it is expected that skill-enhancing, motivation-enhancing and empowerment-enhancing practices will create a high level of job satisfaction. Steijin (2002) and Bradley et al. (2004) find that HR pay practices positively influence job satisfaction. Bauer (2004) and Hunjra et al. (2011) find that empowerment-enhancing practices affect job satisfaction positively and significantly. Guest (2002) suggests that a desirable scope of opportunities to participate combined with a proper incentive scheme may lead to intrinsic and extrinsic rewards for employees, resulting in a higher level of job satisfaction.

Insignificant or negative relationship?
HR policies and HR practices are two distinctive constructs. The former is the organization's stated intention with respect to employee management activities as perceived by management. The latter is the actual, functioning and observable activities (Wright and Boswell, 2002; Boselie et al., 2005) as experienced by employees, which are expected to influence their responses in terms of commitment and satisfaction. According to Van den Berg et al. (1999: 302), HR policies and systems '. . . are meaningless until the individual perceives them as something important to her or his organizational well-being'. Therefore, HR practices may not affect employee attitudes positively because employees may perceive them in a different way from that expected by management. For instance, individuals usually expect training programmes to help them become some kind of generalist eventually, while the organization usually aims at creating the workforce that it needs, composed of individuals who do their jobs in such a way as to improve organizational performance. Similarly, empowerment enhancing practices are supposed to take individuals' interests into account; however, they are usually accompanied in reality by curtailing of career opportunities and development. This is consistent with Legge's (2005)

juxtaposition of HRM 'rhetoric' with organizational 'reality'. According to Truss et al. (1997), the rhetoric adopted by organizations embraces the tenets of the soft HRM model, while the reality experienced by employees is more concerned with strategic control (hard model), due to the interests of the organization prevailing over interests of employees. Therefore, if an individual views HR practices as operationalized in order to achieve organizational interests and objectives at the expense of employees', then positive attitudes and high levels of organizational commitment and job satisfaction may not be achieved.

It has also been argued that skill-enhancing practices may have no or even a negative impact on employee attitudes, especially with continuance commitment. The degree of continuance commitment is largely dependent on the availability of alternative employment. Improved knowledge, skills and abilities are expected to increase the marketability of employees, leading to a low level of continuance commitment and eventually a rise of voluntary turnover (e.g. Williamson et al., 1975; Oatey, 1970; Benson et al., 2004). Wright and Kehoe (2007) argue that incentive payment schemes and financial rewards could not positively impact continuance commitment unless they are at a level that will require employees to take a pay cut if they leave the organization. Wright and Nishii (2006) suggest that before performing any behaviour at work, individuals will perceive, interpret and react to HR practice, largely based on influences from previous experiences. For example, an employee who has experienced exploitation from a previous employer may not elicit commitment and job satisfaction from a subsequent employee's profit-sharing programme, because he/she simply perceives it as one more way to exploit the workforce (Wright and Kehoe, 2007). On the other hand, an individual who had a positive work experience may interpret the same programme in altruistic way. Therefore, HR practice serve as a communication mechanism to employees and is interpreted through each individual's personal lens (Bowen and Ostroff, 2004) and then reflected in their attitudes, which in turn determines subsequent behaviours that may have a direct impact on organizational performance.

5. EMPLOYEE ATTITUDES AND EMPLOYEE BEHAVIOURS

Organizational Commitment, Job Satisfaction and Employee Behaviours

There is a significant body of work connecting employee attitudes and employee behaviours with organizational outcomes. Most of this literature tends to focus on the two most important employee attitudes

– organizational commitment and/or job satisfaction, and examines the subsequent impact on a number of employee behaviours and outcomes, especially employee turnover/turnover intention and organizational citizenship behaviours (e.g Podsakoff et al., 1996; Griffeth et al., 2000; Meyer et al., 2002; Snape and Redman, 2003; Foote and Tang, 2008; Valeau et al., 2010). Although studies show some evidence of inconsistency in their results, there are mainly strong patterns of agreement suggesting that a high level of organizational commitment and job satisfaction leads to lower actual turnover/turnover intention, and results in more presence of organizational citizenship behaviours within the organization. This section first introduces the concept of employee turnover/turnover intention and organizational citizenship behaviours, and then explains their link to each component of organizational commitment and job satisfaction.

Employee Turnover or Turnover Intention

Employee turnover is described as 'individual movement across the membership boundary of an organization' (Price, 2001: 600). It is important to differentiate voluntary turnover from involuntary turnover because they are caused by different variables and reasons. Voluntary turnover happens when an individual decides to cease membership of the organization (Morrell et al., 2001). Under March and Simon's (1958) model, employees' decision-making behaviour – 'decision not to participate' is equated to employees' voluntary turnover. Apparently, employee turnover based on employee attitude that is constructed on the basis of a psychological process is more closely linked to voluntary turnover, because it focuses on the mutual relations of employees' turnover behaviour, including organizational commitment and job satisfaction (Zheng et al., 2010).

Unlike voluntary employee turnover, turnover intention is not explicit. Mobley et al. (1978) suggested that turnover intention is subjected to the individual's perception and relies upon the evaluation of job alternatives. According to Sousa-Poza and Henneberger (2002: 1), turnover intent reflects the possibility that an individual will leave the current job within some specified time period. Therefore, turnover intention is a statement about a specific behaviour of interest (Berndt, 1981), which can lead to the likelihood of termination and actual turnover. A number of researchers (e.g. Hom et al., 1992; Griffeth et al., 2000) have suggested that turnover intention is the immediate precursor to actual turnover. Most empirical studies measure employee turnover intention or intention to quit by collecting data at employee level, mainly because employee level information reflects the behaviour of employees and the decision they make that may influence organizational performance (Brown et al., 2010).

Organizational Citizenship Behaviours

Employee behaviours have differed conceptually between in-role (task-dependent behaviour) and extra-role (individual behaviours beyond what they are expected to do) (Brief and Motowidlo, 1986; Organ, 1988). Organizational citizenship behaviour studies the extra-role behaviour that is concerned about promoting the welfare of individuals, groups and organizations (Brief and Motowidlo, 1986); that is performed voluntarily and contributes to organizational effectiveness (George and Brief, 1992); and that is beyond the formally prescribed role (Organ, 1988). Organ (1988:4) defined it as 'individual behaviour that is discretionary, not directly or explicitly recognised by the formal reward system and that in aggregate promotes the affective functioning of the organization'.

Organ (1988) proposes five dimensions of organizational citizenship behaviours that have been most widely recognized and used in this field. These include conscientiousness, altruism, civic virtue, sportsmanship and courtesy. *Conscientiousness* represents in-role behaviours (e.g. task performance) beyond the minimum required levels. *Altruism* means individuals give help to others in the organization, which is associated with pro-social behaviours. *Civic virtue* reflects employees' participation in political life (e.g. decision-making process) responsibly in the firm. *Sportsmanship* suggests people have no complaints but positive attitudes. *Courtesy* means individuals treat other with respect. Turnipseed and Rassuli (2005) illuminate these notions as cooperation with peers, performing duties without complaints, punctuality, voluntarily helping others, using time efficiently, conserving resources, sharing ideas and positively representing the organization.

The Relationship between Organizational Commitment and Employee Behaviours

Affective commitment and employee turnover

Employees who have a high level of affective commitment are more likely to stay with the organization because they want to, rather than because they have to or ought to (Meyer and Allen, 1991). Affective commitment reflects the strength of the bond between the values and beliefs of an individual and of an organization, which is closely connected to the identification base of commitment (Becker et al., 1996; Meyer et al., 2004). The strong degree of personal identification indicates unwillingness to leave the current employer (Greenberg and Baron, 2000; Gallie et al., 2001; Suliman and Al-Junaibi, 2010). Affective commitment serves as a powerful source leading to employee retention/turnover and fulfilling the organizational mission (Agarwal and Ramaswami, 1993; Buciuniene and Skkudiene, 2009), and negatively affects labour turnover and turnover intention. Therefore, affective-committed employees tend to maintain affiliation with the organization. Researchers (e.g. Suliman and Illes, 2000; Stallworth, 2004) suggest that affective commitment is the best single predictor of intention to leave or actually leave the organization.

Affective commitment and organizational citizenship behaviour

An individual with a high level of affective commitment would be keen to accept organizational values and goals, and also would be more willing to work towards organizational goals and objectives (Peng and Chiu, 2010), in terms of attending work regularly, performing tasks to the best of their ability and putting extra effort into helping others out (e.g. altruism) (Meyer and Allen, 1991). Some authors (e.g. Mael and Ashforth, 1992; Dutton et al., 1994; Bartel, 2001) suggest that affective-committed employees view themselves as integral to the collective and link their fates with that of the organization. As the identification becomes more salient, these employees tend to depersonalize (Hogg and Terry, 2000) and deemphasize self-interest in place of organizational interests and values. This is consistent with the concept of organizational citizenship behaviours, which also reflects a personal involvement in or personal self-sacrifice for the benefit of the organization (Peng and Chiu, 2010; Zeinabadi, 2010). Hence, affective commitment is expected to be positively associated with organizational citizenship behaviours.

Continuance commitment and employee turnover

Continuance commitment is supposedly negatively linked to absenteeism, and excessive absenteeism can lead to termination with the organization (Mayer and Schoorman, 1992; Meyer et al., 2002). This kind of behavioural outcome is expected to be manifested in subsequent labour retention and turnover (Porter et al., 1974). Usually, an individual with a high level of continuance commitment chooses to stay with their current employer because they are unwilling to sacrifice the valuable resource and personal benefits offered by the current employer, or simply because they cannot be obtained elsewhere (Eagly and Chaiken, 1993; Somers and Birnbaum, 1998; Valeau et al., 2010). Arguably, continuance commitment is an attitude towards behaviour rather than towards the organization or target, which simply reflects the consideration of instrumental outcomes of a course of action: stay or go (Solinger et al., 2008). Therefore, continuance-committed employees are expected to have stronger intent to stay in the firm and be less likely to leave or quit.

Continuance commitment and job performance

Researchers (e.g. Suliman and Iles, 2000) have proposed that continuance-committed employees are unlikely to achieve high job performance, because the notion of continuance commitment is rooted in a perception of few alternatives or a feeling that the sacrifices involved in leaving outweigh the benefits. Meyer et al. (1989) suggest that continuance commitment is negatively related to performance and productivity, based on the belief that people who feel 'stacked' in an organization will not exert significant effort at work. In this case, continuance commitment is viewed as a discouraging and negative organizational aspect (Iles et al., 1996; Randall and O'Driscoll, 1997). Sethivikram et al. (1996) find that the organization may realize the reduced turnover at the expense of reduced job performance when employees' commitment to the organization is primarily based on recognition that there will be costs associated with leaving. On the other hand, Slocombe and Dougherty (1998) suggest that employees may exert considerable effort on behalf of the organization while trying to seek employment elsewhere. The rationale behind this is to receive the maximum compensation until a more desirable job is located or to preserve their reputation as good employees. In other words, continuance commitment may be positively linked to job performance. Some empirical evidence has been found in the context of Islamic culture, such as in the Arab world (Suliman and Iles, 2000) and in Pakistan (Khan et al., 2010).

Normative commitment and employee turnover

Individuals with high level of normative commitment feel that they have an obligation to stay with their organization because they think the organization has valued and treated them appropriately (Amos and Weathington, 2008). Therefore, normative commitment is expected to improve employee turnover and turnover intention. The appreciation and support received from the organization may instil a sense of reciprocity among employees (Valeau et al., 2010), resulting in another possible reciprocal behaviour: put in extra effort at work, leading to better job performance.

Normative commitment and organizational citizenship behaviours

According to Wiener (1982: 421), employees with a high level of normative commitment 'act in a way which meets organizational goals and interests'. Hence, the notion of normative commitment represents a value congruency between the employees' goals and values and organizational objectives. Individuals exhibiting these behaviours 'should make sacrifices on behalf [of the organization], and should not criticise it' (Weiner and Vardi,

1980: 86). Similarly, the construct of organizational citizenship behaviour is also embedded in a personal self-sacrifice for the benefit of the organization. Therefore, normative commitment is proposed to have a positive impact on organizational citizenship behaviours.

The Relationship between Job Satisfaction and Employee Behaviours

Job satisfaction and employee turnover

Studies regarding the job satisfaction-employee turnover nexus indicate that job satisfaction has a significant effect on employee turnover (e.g. Arnold and Feldman, 1982; Mobley, 1982; Steel, 2002; Boswell et al., 2005). A high level of job dissatisfaction usually leads to employee withdrawal, particularly in terms of voluntary turnover (employees quit the job) (Lambert et al., 2001). Arnold and Feldman (1982) suggest that job dissatisfaction reinforces employees' thoughts of leaving the organization, which leads to an evaluation of alternatives and intention to quit, and eventually the withdrawal decision and behaviour. Roznowski and Hulin (1992: 126), however, suggest that overall job satisfaction measures are 'the most informative data a manager or researcher can have for predicting employee behaviour'.

Porter et al. (1974) suggest that the link between job satisfaction and employee turnover is strongest at points in time closest to when the employment contract terminates. As employees approach the point of leaving the organization, their attitude is a more accurate predictor of subsequent behaviour such as employee turnover. The extent to which the expectation of stayers and leavers has been reached is based on the employment situation (Porter and Steers, 1973), especially the relatively common reward system (e.g. levels of pay, training etc.). In this case, the choice of staying or quitting can be viewed as a result of a process in which individuals compare their level of expectation, rather than their degree of job satisfaction solely, with the perceived realities of the job environment (Porter et al., 1974). In other words, in spite of enjoying a high level of satisfaction with the current job, an individual who approaches the end of the contract is likely to leave the organization simply because his/her expected reward package is offered somewhere else. In this case, the effect of job satisfaction on employee labour appears to be very similar to the continuance commitment.

Job satisfaction and organizational citizenship behaviours

The nature of the relationship between job satisfaction and organizational citizenship behaviours is underpinned by two principles: the theory of exchange (Konovsky and Pugh, 1994), and the concept of the psychological contract (Robinson and Morrison, 1995). Both principles share the same defining characteristic rested in the 'reciprocity rule'. Employees who experience job satisfaction are more likely to reciprocate through behaviours that contribute to the organizational objectives (Bateman and Organ, 1983; Rousseau, 1995; Mount et al., 2006; Reisel et al., 2010; Valentine et al., 2011). George (1991) argues that positive mood can be considered as an antecedent of organizational citizenship behaviours, whilst it is also a predictor of job satisfaction (Ackfeldt and Wong, 2006). Moreover, Mackenzie et al. (1998) suggest that job satisfaction is positively and directly related to extra-role job performance, which is central to organizational citizenship behaviours (Organ, 1988). Therefore, job satisfaction is predicted to have a positive impact on the development of organizational citizenship behaviours.

In sum, this section has discussed the association between employee attitudes and employee behaviours. In particular, it has focused on the effect of each component of organizational commitment and job satisfaction on employee turnover and organizational citizenship behaviours. These subsequent employee behavioural outcomes, however, may have a direct impact on organizational performance. The next section analyses the literature on this issue.

6. EMPLOYEE BEHAVIOURS AND ORGANIZATIONAL PERFORMANCE

Organizational Performance

There is a lack of consensus on the construct of organizational performance (Katz and Kahn, 1978; Ford and Schellenberg, 1982; Jobson and Schneck, 1982; Au, 1996). Organizational performance is measured through the attainment of an 'ultimate criterion' (Thorndike, 1949), such as productivity, profitability, mission accomplishment, or firm growth and stability. Management research in general has adopted a more limited empirical view by stressing the central role of accounting, financial and market outcomes (Richard et al., 2009), such as financial profit, sales and market share. The concept of organizational performance is usually closely associated with the construct of organizational effectiveness, which is a broader concept that captures it, but has a basis in organizational theory that entertains alternative performance goals (Cameron and Whetten, 1983). Therefore, performance is one type of organizational effectiveness.

Most of the research on employee attitudes examines the employee attitude-performance relationship at the individual level of analysis (e.g. Locke, 1976; Iaffaldano and Muchinskey, 1985; Ostroff, 1992; Koys, 2001; Schneider et al., 2003; Illies et al., 2006). This research has found only a relatively weak or modest relationship between attitudes and performance because of the difficulties in measuring individual performance. Others (e.g. Locke, 1976; Peters and O'Connor, 1980; Ostroff, 1992; Ryan et al., 1996) point out that individual performance can be constrained not only by situational factors such as budgetary support and time availability, but also by individual factors such as ability and personality.

On the other hand, researchers (e.g. Argyris, 1957; Likert, 1961; Ostroff, 1992; Ryan et al., 1996; Brown et al., 2010) propose that the way employees experience work in an organization may be better reflected at an organizational level, such as financial performance and labour productivity. In accounting terms, financial performance, for example profitability, is usually measured at department or organizational level. Similarly, labour productivity is considered as existing at a group, unit or organizational level (Ryan et al., 1996). Thus, organizational performance is not a simple sum of individual performance or productivity (Mahoney, 1984); rather, it reflects the combination and interaction of salient employee attitudes and behaviours, in relation to the norms of cooperation and collaboration (Isen and Baron, 1991; Jackson et al., 1995; Schneider et al., 2003). Employees that have a high level of organizational commitment and job satisfaction are more likely to engage in collaborative effort and accept organizational goals. Therefore, organizational performance is better explained by aggregated employee attitudes and behaviours. Denison (1990) finds, for example, that aggregated employee attitudes are steadily related with financial performance for five years in publicly held firms. In addition, Schneider et al. (2003) find that there is a consistent and statistically significant positive relationship over time between aggregated levels of employee satisfaction, financial performance (e.g. return on assets (ROA)) and market performance (e.g. earnings per share (EPS)).

The Relation between Employee Behaviours and Organizational Performance

Numerous authors (e.g. Roethlisberger, 1959; McGregor, 1960; Kopelman et al., 1990) suggest that an employee's well being can lead to organization performance in terms of productivity that is related to employee behaviours. Hence, from a broader perspective, organization performance is a function of employee behaviours. Mudor and Tooksoon (2011) argue that the ultimate goal of any organization is to achieve better performance through the functioning of employees because they are the ones supplying effort at all levels (Albrecht and Albrecht, 1995).

The link between employee turnover and organizational performance

The HRM literature suggests that employee turnover shows a negative sign towards organizational performance through losing firm-specific human and social capital (Dess and Shaw, 2011). A high level of employee turnover, or intention to quit, is often considered as a major contributor to lagging productivity and competitiveness in certain organizations and industries (e.g. skill-specific professions in manufacturing industries) (Phillips, 1990), primarily due to the enormous costs that relate to profit-making activities. Hutchinson et al. (1997) explain that the obvious loss in production is a consequence of the difference in production rate of an experienced, trained employee and that of an untrained, inexperienced one, and also the shortfall in knowledge of organizational objectives and customer requirements (Schneider and Bowen, 1985).

The negative relationship between employee turnover or turnover intention and organizational performance can also be understood in management accounting terms, particularly through the cost structure. Direct costs are essentially financial consequences, which include the cost caused by increased recruitment and training expenditure of the newly employed (Khilji and Wang, 2007; Mudor and Tooksoon, 2011). Therefore, assuming other cost elements remain constant, a rise in costs in training and recruitment will lead to a lower corporate profitability (Koys, 2001). A study at Sears, for example, showed that as voluntary turnover decreased, financial performance such as return on controllable assets increased (Ulrich et al., 1991).

The link between organizational citizenship behaviours and organizational performance

Organizational performance has its roots in pro-social behaviours, and is featured by the behaviours and activities that benefit individuals, work groups or the entire organization (Brief and Motowidlo, 1986). The contemporary organizational psychology studies argue that organizational citizenship behaviours have 'an accumulative position effect on organizational functioning' (Wagner and Rush, 2000:379). Podsakoff et al. (2000) suggest that organizational citizenship behaviours contribute to organizational success in terms of enhancing co-workers' productivity and managerial productivity, strengthening the organizational ability to attract and retain best workers, and enabling firms to adapt more effectively to changes. Organizational citizenship behaviour has been classified as a significant component of individual job performance (e.g. Organ and

Ryan, 1995; Podsakoff et al., 2000; LePine et al., 2002), which eventually contributes to organizational performance.

Organ et al. (2006:193) suggest that citizenship is 'more important in jobs where people work in groups, need to coordinate their activities, or are interdependent with each other than in jobs where people work independently or as individual contributors'. Ryan et al. (1996) argue that employees in a unit that share the same positive attitudes should have norms of cooperation and collaboration. The coordination and interaction among individuals is a critical element for the effective functioning of organizations, because it keeps individuals and groups working together towards the organizational goals (Roethlisberger, 1959; Podsakoff et al., 1997). The concept of organizational citizenship behaviours stresses the importance of aggregation, cooperation and interactions among individuals and groups within the organization. Therefore, organizational citizenship behaviour can help the firm manage the interdependences between members of a work unit and act as an integrative force (Cohen, 1976; Doolittle and McDonald, 1978; Koys, 2001; Ehrhart et al., 2006) and in turn, have a positive influence in group performance and organizational performance. Nielsen et al. (2010) observe that three dimensions of organizational citizenship behaviours (e.g. helping behaviours, civic virtue and sportsmanship) leads to an amplified group performance that benefits task-interdependent groups.

Some authors (e.g. Robinson and Morrison, 1995; Koys, 2001) suggest organizational citizenship behaviours have a more straightforward and direct influence in financial performance, especially in the service industries where front-line staff (e.g. sales) have direct contact with customers as organization representatives (Tsai and Su, 2011). Beyond serving customers, these employees must also practice their in-role responsibilities and elicit extra efforts to promote operational performance and maintain organizational image (Schneider and Bowen, 1993; Podsakoff et al., 1997; Podsakoff et al., 2003). This kind of behaviour, that is, embedded in a discretionary nature and beyond employees' formal role requirements, is consistent with the five dimensions of organizational citizenship behaviours (Organ, 1988; Hui et al., 1999; Koys, 2001; Tjosvold et al., 2003). Specifically, a conscientious workforce thinks beyond satisfying customer expectations from products and service delivery, which can lead to higher levels of customer retention. Altruistic employees would be helpful to both internal and external customers. Staff with civic virtue improve the quality of service and customer satisfaction by making valuable suggestions. They exhibit sportsmanship and courtesy, creating a favourable climate within the organization that spills over to customers. Walz and Niehoff (1996) report that civic virtue, sportsmanship and altruism are positively related to financial results and customer satisfaction in limited-menu restaurants. Markose and Jayachandran (2006) also find that sportsmanship, civic virtue, conscientiousness and altruism behaviours have a significant and positive impact on output performance of salesman.

7.   PREDOMINANT RESEARCH METHODS AND EMPIRICAL RESULTS

Employee attitudes (e.g. organizational commitment and job satisfaction) and the subsequent behaviours such as intention to quit and organizational citizenship behaviours are essentially self-reported, subjective concepts, and reflect an individual's perception and attitude towards the organization and his/her work. They are usually measured at the individual level and assessed using standard survey research methodology. Similarly, the construction of HR practices is based on self-reported employee and/or management questionnaires (Murphy and Zandvakili, 2000; Brown, 2004; Storey et al., 2010, Saridakis et al., 2012). Most studies in this field are conducted based on the assumption that HR practices causes employee attitudes and behaviours that can in turn influence organizational performance. The primary object of this research is to test the existence of the relationship, and also examine how they are connected. This is consistent with the characteristics of scientific method (in particular, positivism): (i) observing the significant facts in order to arrive at a hypothesis; (ii) deducing the consequence on the basis of the hypothesis; and (iii) eventually verifying and modifying the hypothesis based on the results (Russell, 1931). Indeed, much of the most dominant research design in this field is the quantitative survey method (Boselie et al., 2005).

More recently, however, some researchers (e.g. Boselie et al., 2005; Fleetwood and Hesketh, 2006; 2007) argue that there is an under-theorization[2] and lack of explanatory power in the existing HRM-performance literature. Boselie et al. (2005) use a comprehensive sample of 104 articles and find that very few studies are able to derive from a theory an explicit set of propositions, and then examine them in an appropriate research design. Moreover, Fleetwood and Hesketh (2007) show that empirical researchers are committed to positivism and the research approaches and statistical techniques of positivism may eventually generate theory. Some authors (e.g. Wright et al., 2003; Legge, 2005; Macky and Boxall, 2007; Paauwe, 2009) suggest that the role of human capital (more precisely, employee responses and reactions) may be the missing element for forming a theory that explains the way in which HRM practices influence performance. However, so far the black box has not been filled and a theory is still needed. In addition, the absence of a quantifiable, measurable and statistical link does not necessarily mean that HR practices, and employee attitudes and behaviours are not related to organizational performance. There is a possibility the relationship is merely not manifested in this kind of quantifiable and statistical link through techniques like regression analysis, because the relationship is '. . . preoccupied with prediction, which can only sustain Humean causality and emaciated explanation, (rather than) . . . the explanatory dimension which is characterised by complex causality and robust explanation . . .' (Fleetwood and Hesketh, 2007:1985–86).

Though empirical research has reported mixed findings and shown inconclusive results, the overwhelming evidence tends to support the claim that HR practices can have a positive impact on employee attitudes and employee outcomes, which in turn lead to better organizational performance (e.g. Mac Duffie, 1995; Truss et al., 1997; Meyer and Allen, 1997; Jackson and Schuler, 2000; Gardner et al., 2001; Carson, 2005; Edgar and Geare, 2005; Kuvaas, 2008; Brown et al., 2010; Baakile et al., 2011; Saridakis et al., 2012). In other words, empirical studies based on scientific research methods and approaches tend to support the proposition that employee attitudes may at least partially mediate the relationship between HR practices and employee behaviours. Also, employee attitudes and behaviours play a mediating role between HR practices and organizational outcomes, either directly or indirectly.

8.   CONCLUSION

This chapter has critically reviewed the literature on the link between employee attitudes, HR practices and organizational performance. The literature shows that positive employee attitudes, such as higher levels of organizational commitment and job satisfaction, may lead to favourable employee behaviours and responses (e.g. lower employee turnover intention, better job performance and embarking on organizational citizenship behaviours). In turn this enhances workplace performance. In addition, the purpose of developing HR practices by top management within organizations is to encourage and elicit positive employee attitudes, creating employees' perception of reciprocity, in the form of better performance and productivity. In this chapter, we have provided the theoretical explanation behind each single potential direct causal link in the HRM performance relationship: HR practices affect employee attitudes, employee attitudes lead to employee behaviours, and employee behaviours result in organizational performance.

Regarding HR practices, we discuss those within the AMO framework; we are aware, however, that there are some other HR practices such as employment security that may also be important to employees. The literature suggests that HR interventions, in the form of different HRM activities such as careful HR planning, recruitment/selection, rewards, participation and consultation, and training may not directly impact on organizational performance. Instead, they should be understood and realized through HR outcomes/reactions, which are typically manifested in shifts in employee attitudes and reactions (Boselie et al., 2005). HR outcomes or employee reactions are further divided into three levels: affective (emotion), cognitive and behavioural response. The cognition and emotion create employee attitudes, eventually leading to subsequent employee behaviours. It is expected that positive employee attitudes such as a high level of organizational commitment and job satisfaction lead to positive employee behaviours towards work (and customers), which increase employee retention, customer retention and job performance. This in turn contributes to better financial performance, organizational growth and economic prosperity.

Moreover, HR practices and systems such as skill-enhancing, motivation-enhancing and empowerment-enhancing practices embrace the tenets of the soft and hard HRM models, and are expected to have a positive impact on employees' organizational commitment and job satisfaction. However, the actual effects are largely dependent on the perception, expectation and experience of employees. In addition to this, although most organizations adopt the rhetoric of the soft model, empirical studies have shown that HRM experienced by employees within organizations is based on the concept of tight strategic direction towards organizational goals (hard model). The impact of HR interventions on employee reactions and responses differs not only from different aspects of attitudes (e.g. affective commitment, continuance commitment), but also between individuals and organizations. Accordingly, subsequent employee outcomes are expected to be distinctive as well. Therefore, the proposed framework discussed earlier and summarized in Figure 9.1 can be extended conceptually in Figure 9.2.

This theoretical framework may have important implications for businesses and policy makers. It is assumed that human capital is the root source of quality and productivity gains at the workplace; therefore, employees are the fundamental basis of organizational improvement, and appropriate HR management practices may lead to better organizational performance. Skill-enhancing practices (e.g. training and personal development programmes), motivation-enhancing practices (e.g. incentive payment schemes and performance-related rewards), and empowerment-enhancing

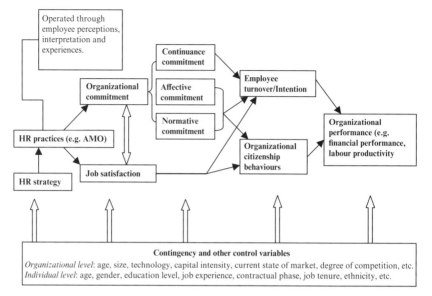

Figure 9.2   Relationship between HRM, employee attitudes/behaviours and organizational performance

practices (e.g. giving employees autonomy and discretion over work, building information sharing systems and inviting employees to discuss important organizational issues) are expected to create significant incentives for employees, leading to positive responses. Specifically, they can result in a high level of affective commitment and normative commitment because they make employees feel they are trusted, valued and respected by the organization, which will enhance the shared perception of value congruence between individual and organization, and integrate employees into the life of the organization. The motivation-enhancing and empowerment-enhancing practices can also lead to an increased level of job satisfaction since employees are offered financial incentives as well as a high level of discretion and authority on the job. A large amount of training and personal development programmes can create a more skilful and knowledgeable workforce, but also causes the departure of some skilled employees looking for better opportunities elsewhere (lower level of continuance commitment), which is expected to negatively affect organizational performance.

Affective commitment reflects a strong bond between values and beliefs of an individual and of an organization. Individuals consider themselves as integral to the collective and link their fates with that of the organization, indicating a strong desire to maintain membership with the current employer. Normative-committed employees have a generalized sense of internal obligation to the organization that they are working for, and feel responsible for its success. Continuance commitment, on the other hand, represents a psychological attachment to an organization in relation to the perceived benefits of staying or perceived costs of leaving. Apparently, affective and normative commitment represent a stronger psychological connection (want to and ought to) to the organization than continuance commitment (have to). These employees stay with the organization even in times of crisis and recession, while continuance-committed individuals leave once preferable alternatives are available or offered elsewhere. Therefore, policy makers and practitioners should focus on management practices that can enhance affective and normative commitment, creating a strong, committed and more loyal and stable workforce.

Like affective and normative commitment, job satisfaction is predicted to be negatively and positively associated with employee turnover and organizational citizenship behaviours, respectively. However, happy employees (a high level of job satisfaction) may also leave the current employer for opportunities that meet or exceed their expectations (e.g. payment or promotional opportunities). Future empirical and theoretical research in this area is needed to shed more light on these associations.

NOTES

1. In addition, Paauwe and Richardson (1997) report a list of other factors at both organizational and individual level that are controlled and examined in most of the existing empirical models.
2. Lack of theoretical understanding regarding the way in which HRM practices influence performance has been one central focus in the HRM-performance literature (e.g. Guest, 1997; Delery, 1998; Wright and Gardner, 2003; Purcell et al., 2003).

REFERENCES

Ackfeldt, A. and Wong, V. (2006). The antecedents of prosocial service behaviors: an empirical investigation. *The Service Industries Journal*, 26: 727–745.

Agarwal, S. and Ramaswami, S. (1993). Affective organisational commitment of salespeople: an expanded model. *Journal of Personal Selling and Sales Management*, 13 (2): 49–70.

Albrecht, P.M. and Albrecht, R.C.E. (1995). *Fundamentals of Human Resource*. New York: American Management Association.

Allen, N.J. and Meyer, J.P. (1990). The measurement and antecedents of affective, continuance, and normative commitment to the organisation. *Journal of Occupational Psychology*, 63: 1–18.

Allen, D.G., Shore, L.M. and Griffeth, R.W. (2003). The role of perceived organizational support and supportive human resource practices in the turnover process. *Journal of Management*, 29: 99–118.

Amos, E.A. and Weathington, B.L. (2008). An analysis of the relation between employee-organization value congruence and employee attitude. *The Journal of Psychology*, 142: 615–631.

Anderson, S.E. and Williams, L.J. (1992). Assumptions about unmeasured variables with studies of reciprocal relationships: the case of employee attitude. *Journal of Applied Psychology*, 77: 638–650.

Appelbaum, E., Bailey, T., Berg, P. and Kallenberg, A.L. (2000). *Manufacturing Advantage: Why High-Performance Work Systems Pay Off*. New York: Cornell University Press.

Argyris, C. (1957). *Integrating the Individual and the Organization*. New York: Wiley.

Arnold, H.J. and Feldman, D.C. (1982). A multivariate analysis of the determinants of job turnover. *Journal of Applied Psychology*, 76: 350–360.

Arthur, J.B. (1994). Effects of human resource systems on manufacturing performance and turnover. *Academy of Management Journal*, 29: 31–50.

Au, C. (1996). Rethinking organizational effectiveness: theoretical and methodological issues in the study of organizational effectiveness for social welfare organizations. *Administration in Social Work*, 20: 1–21.

Baakile, M. (2011). Comparative analysis of teachers' perception of equity, pay satisfaction, affective commitment and intention to turnover in Botswana. *Journal of Management Research*, 3: 1–21.

Babin, B.J. and Boles, J.S. (1998). Employee behavior in service environment: a model and test of potential differences between men and women. *Journal of Marketing*, 62: 77–91.

Bagozzi, R.P. (1992). The self-regulation of attitudes, intentions, and behavior. *Social Psychology Quarterly*, 55: 178–204.

Baird, L. and Meshoulam, I. (1988). Managing two fits of strategic human resource management. *Academy of Management Review*, 13: 116–128.

Baker, H.E. (1992). Employee socialization strategies and the presence of union representation. *Labor Studies Journal*, 17: 5–17.

Balfour, D.L. and Wechsler, B. (1991). Commitment, performance, and productivity in public organisations. *Public Productivity and Management Review*, 14 (4): 355–367.

Baotham, S., Hongkhauntod, W. and Rattanajun, S. (2010). The effects of job satisfaction and organizational commitment on voluntary turnover intentions of Thai employees in the new university. *Review of Business Research*, 10: 72–82.

Bartel, C.A. (2001). Social comparisons in boundary-spanning work: effects of community outreach on members' organizational identity and identification. *Administrative Science Quarterly*, 46: 379–413.

Bateman, T.S. and Organ, D.W. (1983). Job satisfaction and the good soldier: the relationship between affect and employee 'citizenship'. *Academy of Management Journal*, 26: 587–595.

Bateman, T.S. and Strasser, S. (1984). A longitudinal analysis of the antecedents of organizational commitment. *Academy of Management Journal*, 27: 95–112.

Bauer, T.K. (2004). High performance workplace practices and job satisfaction: evidence from Europe. *IZA Discussion Paper No. 1265*, Aug.

Becker, H.S. (1960). Notes on the concept of commitment. *American Journal of Sociology*, 66: 32–40.

Becker, B. and Gerhart, B. (1996). Effects of human resource systems on manufacturing performance and turnover. *Academy of Management Journal*, 37: 470–687.

Becker, B. and Huselid, M. (2006). Strategic human resource management: where do we go from here? *Journal of Management*, 32: 898–925.

Becker, T.E., Billings, R.S., Eveleth, D.M. and Gilbert, N.L. (1996). Foci and bases of employee commitment: implications for job performance. *Academy of Management Journal*, 39: 464–482.

Becker, B., Huselid, M., Pinckus, P. and Sparatt, M. (1997). HR as a source of shareholder value: research and recommendations. *Human Resource Management*, 36: 39–48.

Beer, M., Spector, B., Lawrence, P.R., Mills, D.Q. and Walton, R.E. (1984). A conceptual view of HRM. In *Managing Human Assets*. New York: Free Press.

Benson, G.S., Finegold, D. and Mohrman, S.A. (2004). You paid for the skills, now keep them: tuition, reimbursement and voluntary turnover. *Academy of Management Journal*, 47: 315–331.

Berndt, T. (1981). Effects of friendship on prosocial intentions and behavior. *Child Development*, 52: 636–643.

Bluedorn, A.C. (1982). A unified model of turnover from organisation. *Human Relations*, 35: 135–153.

Boselie, P., Dietz, G. and Boon, C. (2005). Commonalities and contradictions in HRM and performance research. *Human Resource Management Journal*, 15: 67–94.

Boswell, W.R., Boudreau, J.W. and Tichy, J. (2005). The relationship between employee job change and job satisfaction: the honeymoon-hangover effect. *Journal of Applied Psychology*, 90: 882–892.

Bowen, D.E. and Ostroff, C. (2004). Understanding HRM-firm performance linkages: the role of strength of the HRM system. *Academy of Management Journal*, 29: 203–221.

Boxall, P. and Purcell, J. (2003). *Strategy and Human Resource Management*. Basingstoke: Palgrave Macmillan.

Boxall, P. and Steeneveld, M. (1999). Human resource strategy and competitive advantage: a longitudinal study of engineering consultancies. *Journal of Management Studies*, 36: 443–463.

Bradley, S., Petrescu, A. and Simmons, R. (2004). The impacts of human resource management practices and pay inequality on workers' job satisfaction. Paper presented at the Western Economic Association 79th Annual Conference, Vancouver.

Brief, A.P. and Motowidlo, S.J. (1986). Prosocial organizational behaviors. *Academy of Management Review*, 11: 710–725.

Brown, D. (2004). Capital vetter – the case of human capital reporting. *People Management*, 30, September: 38–41.

Brown, S. and Peterson, R.A. (1993). Antecedents and consequences of salesperson job satisfaction: meta-analysis and assessment of causal effect. *Journal of Marketing Research*, 30: 63–77.

Brown, S., McHardy, J., McNabb, R. and Taylor, K. (2010). Workplace performance, worker commitment, and loyalty. *Journal of Economics and Management*, 20: 925–955.

Buciuniene, I. and Skudiene, V. (2009). Factors influencing salespeople motivation and relationship with the organization in b2b sector. *Engineering Economics*, 4: 79–85.

Cameron, K.S. and Whetten, D.S. (1983). *Organisational Effectiveness: A Comparison of Multiple Models*. New York: Academic Press.

Cammann, C., Fichman, M., Jenkins, G.D. and Klesh, J.R. (1983). Assessing the attitudes and perceptions of organizational members. In S. Seashore, E.E. Lawler, P.H. Mirvis, and C. Cammann (eds), *Assessing Organizational Change: A Guide to Methods, Measures, and Practices*. New York: Wiley, pp. 71–138.

Carson, C.M. (2005). A historical view of Douglas McGregor's theory Y. *Management Decision*, 43 (3): 450–460.

Cohen, E. (1976). The structural transformation of the kibbutz. In G.K. Zollschan and W. Hirsch (eds), *Social Change*. New York: Wiley, pp. 703–740.

Cohen, A. (2003). *Multiple Commitments in the Workplace: An Integrative Approach*. Mahwah, NJ: Lawrence Erlbaum Associates.

Combs, J., Liu, Y., Hall, A. and Ketchen, D. (2006). How much do high performance work practices matter? A meta-analysis of their effects on organizational performance. *Personnel Psychology*, 59: 501–528.

Cramer, D. (1996). Job satisfaction and organizational continuance commitment: a two-wave panel study. *Journal of Organizational Behavior*, 17: 389–400.

Curry, J.P., Wakefield, D.S., Price, J.L. and Mueller, C.W. (1986). On the causal ordering of job satisfaction and organizational commitment. *Academy of Management Journal*, 29: 847–858.

Delery, J.E., Gupta, N. and Shaw, J.D. (1998). Human resource management and firm performance: a systems perspective. University of Arkansas Working Paper.

Denison, D.R. (1990). *Corporate Culture and Organizational Effectiveness*. New York: Wiley.

Dess, G.G. and Shaw, J.D. (2001). Voluntary turnover, social capital, and organizational performance. *Academy of Management Review*, 26: 446–456.

Doolittle, R.J. and McDonald, D. (1978). Communication and a sense of community in a metropolitan neighborhood: a factor analytic examination. *Communication Quarterly*, 26: 2–7.

Dutton, J.E., Dukerich, J.M. and Harquail, C.V. (1994). Organizational images and member identification. *Administrative Science Quarterly*, 39: 239–263.

Dyer, L. and Reeves, T. (1995). HR strategies and firm performance: what do we know and where do we need to go. *International Journal of Human Resource Management*, 6: 656–670.

Eagly, A.H. and Chaiken, S. (1993). *The Psychology of Attitudes*. Orlando, FL: Harcourt.

Eby, L.T., Freeman, D.M., Rush, M.C. and Lance, C.E. (1999). Motivational bases of affective organizational commitment: a partial test of an integrative theoretical model. *Journal of Occupational and Organizational Psychology*, 72: 463–483.

Edgar, F. and Geare, A. (2005). HRM practice and employee attitudes: different measures-different results. *Personnel Review*, 34 (5): 534–549.

Edgar, F. and Geare, A. (2009). Inside the 'black box' and 'HRM'. *International Journal of Manpower*, 30: 220–236.

Ehrhart, M.G., Bliese, P.D. and Thomas, J.L. (2006). Unit-level OCB and unit effectiveness: examining the incremental effect of helping behavior. *Human Performance*, 19: 159–173.

Farkas, A.J. and Tetrick, L.E. (1989). A three-wave longitudinal analysis of the causal ordering of satisfaction and commitment on turnover decisions. *Journal of Applied Psychology*, 74: 855–868.

Fleetwood, S. and Hesketh, A. (2006). (Not) measuring the HRM-organisational performance link: applying critical realist meta-theory. *Organisation*, 13 (5): 677–699.

Fleetwood, S. and Hesketh, A. (2007). HRM-performance research: under-theorised and lacking explanatory power. *International Journal of Human Resource Management*, 17 (12): 1977–1993.

Foote, D.A. and Tang, T.L. (2008). Job satisfaction and organisational citizenship behaviours (OCB): does team commitment make a difference in self-directed teams? *Management Decision*, 46: 933–947.

Ford, J.D. and Schellenberg, D.A. (1982). Conceptual issues of linkage in the assessment of organizational performance. *Academy of Management Review*, 7: 49–58.

Frey, B. and Stutzer, A. (2002). What can economists learn from happiness research? *Journal of Economic Literature*, 40: 402–435.

Frijda, N. (1988). The laws of emotion. *American Psychologist*, 43: 249–359.

Gaertner, S. (1999). Structural determinants of job satisfaction and organisational commitment in turnover models. *Human Resource Management Review*, 9: 479–493.

Gallie, D., Felstead, A. and Green, F. (2001). Employer policies and organizational commitment in Britain 1992–1997. *Journal of Management Studies*, 38: 1081–1102.

Gardner, T.M., Moynihan, L.M., Park, H.J. and Wright, P.M. (2001). Beginning to unlock the black box in the HR firm performance relationship: the impact of HR practices on employee attitudes and employee outcomes. CAHRS Working Paper 01-12, Cornell, School of Industrial and Labour Relations.

Gardner, T., Moynihan, L. and Wright, P. (2007). The influence of human resource practices and collective affective organisational commitment on aggregate voluntary turnover. CAHRS Working Paper, Cornell University.

Gardner, T.M., Wright, P.M. and Moynihan, L.M. (2011). The impact of motivation, empowerment, and skill-enhancing practices on aggregate voluntary turnover: the mediating effect of collective affective commitment. *Personnel Psychology*, 64: 315–350.

George, J.M. (1991). State or trait: effects of positive mood on prosocial behaviors at work. *Journal of Applied Psychology*, 76: 299–307.

George, J.M. and Brief, A.P. (1992). Feeling good-doing good: a conceptual analysis of the mood at work – organizational spontaneity relationship. *Psychological Bulletin*, 112: 310–329.

Gonzalez, J.V. and Garazo, T.G. (2006). Structural relationship between organizational service orientation, contact employee job satisfaction and citizenship behavior. *International Journal of Service Industry Management*, 17: 23–50.

Gray, E.K. and Watson, D. (2001). Emotions, mood and temperament: similarities, difference, and a synthesis. In R. Rayne and C. Cooper (eds), *Emotions at Work: Theory, Research and Applications for Management*. Chichester: John Wiley and Sons, pp. 21–43.

Greenberg, J. and Baron, R.A. (2000). *Behavior in Organizations* (7th edn). Upper Saddle River, NJ: Prentice-Hall.

Griffeth, R.W., Hom, P.S. and Gaertner, S. (2000). A meta-analysis of antecedents and correlates of employee turnover: update, moderator tests, and research implications for the next millennium. *Journal of Management*, 26: 463–488.

Gross, E. and Etzioni, A. (1985). *Organizations in Society*. Englewood Cliffs, NJ: Prentice-Hall.

Guest, D. (1987). Human resource management and industrial relations. *Journal of Management Studies*, 24: 503–521.

Guest, D. (1995). Human resource management, trade unions and industrial relations. In J. Storey (ed.), *Human Resource Management: A Critical Text*. London: Routledge.

Guest, D.E. (1997). Human resource management and performance: a review and research agenda. *The International Journal of Human Resource Management*, 8: 263–276.

Guest, D. (2002). Human resource management, corporate performance and employee wellbeing: building the worker into HRM. *The Journal of Industrial Relations*, 44: 335–358.

Hackett, R.D., Bycio, P. and Hausdorf, P.A. (1994). Further assessments of Meyer and Allen's (1991) three-component model of organisational commitment. *Journal of Applied Psychology*, 79: 15–23.

Hendry, C. and Pettigrew, A. (1986). The practice of strategic human resource management. *Personnel Review*, 15: 3–8.

Hendry, C. and Pettigrew, A. (1990). Human resource management: an agenda for 1990s. *International Journal of Human Resource Management*, 1: 17–44.

Heskett, J.L., Sasser, W.E. and Schlesinger, L.A. (1997). *The Service Profit Chain: How Leading Companies Link Profit and Growth to Loyalty, Satisfaction, and Value*. New York: Free Press.

Hogg, M.A. and Terry, D.J. (2000). Social identity and self-categorization processes in organizational contexts. *Academy of Management Review*, 25: 121–140.

Hom, P.W. and Griffeth, R.W. (1995). *Employee Turnover*. Cincinnati, OH: South-Western.

Hom, P.W., Caranikas-Walker, F., Prussia, G.E. and Griffeth, R.W. (1992). A meta-analytical structural equations analysis of a model of employee turnover. *Journal of Applied Psychology*, 78: 890–909.

Hui, C., Law, K.S. and Chen, Z.X. (1999). A structural equation model of the effects of negative affectivity, leader-member exchange, and perceived job mobility on in-role and extra-role performance: a Chinese case. *Organizational Behavior Human Decision Processes*, 77: 3–21.

Hunjra, A.I., Haq, N.U., Akbar, S.W. and Yousaf, M. (2011). Impact of employee empowerment on job satisfaction: an empirical analysis of Pakistani Service Industry Interdisciplinary. *Journal of Contemporary Research in Business*, 2: 680–686.

Huselid, M.A. (1995). The impact of human resource management practices on turnover, productivity, and corporate financial performance. *Academy of Management Journal*, 38: 635–372.

Hutchinson, J.R., Villalobos, J.R. and Beruvides, M.G. (1997). Effects of high labour turnover in a serial assembly environment. *International Journal of Production Research*, 35: 3201–3223.

Iaffaldano, M.T. and Muchinsky, P.M. (1985). Job satisfaction and job performance: a meta analysis. *Psychological Bulletin*, 97: 251–273.

Iles, P.A., Forster, A. and Tinline, G. (1996). The changing relationship between work commitment, personal flexibility and employability: an evaluation of a field experiment in executive development. *Journal of Managerial Psychology*, 11: 18–34.

Ilies, R., Scott, B.A. and Judge, T.A. (2006). The interactive effects of personal traits and experienced states on intraindividual patterns of citizenship behavior. *Academy of Management Journal*, 49: 561–575.

Isen, A.M. and Baron, R.A. (1991). Positive affect as a factor in organizational behavior. In L.L. Cummings and B.M. Staw (eds), *Research in Organizational Behavior*. Greenwich: JAI Press, pp. 1–53.

Ivancevich, J. and Matteson, M. (2002). *Organisational Behaviour and Management* (6th edn). New York: McGraw-Hill.

Jackson, S.E. and Schuler, R.E. (2000). *Managing Human Resource: A Partnership Perspective* (7th edn). Cincinnati: South-Western College Publishing.

Jackson, L.A., Hunter, I.T. and Hodge, C.N. (1995). Physical attractiveness and intellectual competence: a meta-analytic review. *Social Psychology Quarterly*, 58: 108–122.

Jobson, J.D. and Schneck, R. (1982). Constituent views of organizational effectiveness: evidence from police organizations. *Academy of Management Journal*, 25: 25–46.

Jones, E., Chonko, L., Rangarajan, D. and Roberts, J. (2007). The role of overload on job attitudes, turnover intentions, and salesperson performance. *Journal of Business Research*, 60: 663–671.

Kallbers, L.P. and Cenker, W.J. (2007). Organizational commitment and auditors in public accounting. *Managerial Auditing Journal*, 22: 354–375.

Katz, D. and Kahn, R.L. (1978). *The Social Psychology of Organization*. New York: Wiley.

Ketch, A.A. and Strawser, J.R. (1998). The existence of multiple measures of organizational commitment and experience-related differences in a public accounting setting. *Behavioral Research in Accounting*, 10: 109–137.

Khan, M.R., Ziauddin, M., Jam, F.A. and Ramay, M.I. (2010). The impacts of organizational commitment on employee job performance. *European Journal of Social Sciences*, 15: 292–298.

Khilji, S. and Wang, X. (2007). New evidence in an old debate: investigating the relationship between HR satisfaction and turnover. *International Business Review*, 16: 377–395.

Konovsky, M.A. and Pugh, S.D. (1994). Citizenship behavior and social exchange. *Academy of Management Journal*, 37: 656–669.

Kopelman, R.E., Brief, A.P. and Guzzo, R.A. (1990). The role of climate and culture in productivity. In B. Schneider (ed.), *Organizational Climate and Culture*. San Francisco: Jossey-Bass, pp. 282–318.

Koys, D.J. (2001). The effects of employee satisfaction, organizational citizenship behavior, and turnover on organizational effectiveness: a unit-level, longitudinal study. *Personnel Psychology*, 54: 101–114.

Kuvaas, B. (2008). An exploration of how the employee-organizational relationship affects the linkage between perception of development human resource practices and employee outcomes. *Journal of Management Studies*, 45: 1–25.

Lacity, M.C., Lyer, V.V. and Rudramuniyaiah, P.S. (2008). Turnover intentions of Indian IS professionals. *Information Systems Frontiers*, 10: 225–241.

Lambert, E.G., Hogan, N.L., Barton, A. and Lubbock, S.M. (2001). The impact of job satisfaction on turnover intent: a test of a structural measurement model using a national sample of workers. *Social Science Journal*, 38: 233–251.

Lance, C.E. (1991). Evaluation of a structural model relating to job satisfaction, organizational commitment, and precursors to voluntary turnover. *Multivariate Behavioral Research*, 26: 137–162.

Lazarus, R.S. (1991). Cognition and motivation in emotion. *American Psychologist*, 46: 352–367.

Legge, K. (2005). *Human Resource Management: Rhetorics and Realities*, 10th anniversary edition. Basingstoke: Palgrave Macmillan.

Lepak, D.P., Bartol, K.M. and Erhardt, N. (2005). A contingency framework of the delivery of HR practices. *Human Resource Management Review*, 15: 139–159.

LePine, J.A., Erez, A. and Johnson, E.D. (2002). The nature and dimensionality of organizational citizenship behavior: a critical review and meta-analysis. *Journal of Applied Psychology*, 87: 52–65.

Likert, R. (1961). *New Patterns of Management*. New York: McGraw-Hill.

Lincoln, J.R. and Kalleberg, A.L. (1990). Commitment, quits and work organization: a study of U.S. and Japanese plants. *Industrial and Labor Relations Review*, 50: 738–760.

Lo, A. and Lam, T. (2002). The relationship between demographic characteristics and socialization outcomes among new employees in Hong Kong hotels. *Journal of Human Resources in Hospitality and Tourism*, 1: 1–14.

Locke, E.A. (1976). The nature of causes of job satisfaction. In M.D. Dunnette (ed.), *Handbook of Industrial and Organizational Psychology*. Chicago, IL: Rand McNally, pp. 1297–1349.

Long, R.L. (1980). Job attitudes and organizational performance under employee ownership. *Academy of Management Journal*, 23: 726–737.

Lu, H., While, A.E. and Barribal, K.I. (2007). A model of job satisfaction of nurses: a reflection of nurses' working lives in Mainland China. *JAN: Original Research*, pp. 469–479.

Luchak, A.A. and Gellatly, I.R. (2007). A comparison of linear and non-linear relations between organisational commitment and work outcomes. *Journal of Applied Psychology*, 92: 783–793.

MacDuffie, J.P. (1995). Human resource bundles and manufacturing performance; organizational logic and flexible systems in the world auto industry. *Industrial and Labour Relations Review*, 48: 197–221.

MacKenzie, S.B., Podsakoff, P.M. and Aheame, M. (1998). Some possible antecedents and consequences of in-role and extra-role salesperson performance. *Journal of Marketing*, 62: 87–98.

Macky, K. and Boxall, P. (2007). The relationship between 'high performance work practices' and employee attitudes: an investigation of additive and interaction effects. *The International Journal of Human Resource Management*, 18: 537–567.

Mael, F.A. and Ashforth, B.E. (1992). Alumni and their alma mater: a partial test of the reformulated model of organizational identification. *Journal of Organizational Behavior*, 13: 103–123.

Mahoney, T.A. (1984). Growth accounting and productivity: comments. In A.P.

Brief (ed.), *Productivity Research in the Behavioral and Social Sciences*. New York: Praeger, pp. 112–133.

March, J. and Simon, H. (1958). *Organisations*. New York: Wiley.

Marchington, M. and Wilkinson, A. (2005). Direct participation and involvement. In S. Bach (ed.), *Managing Human Resources: Personnel Management in Transition*. Oxford: Blackwell.

Markose, B. and Jayachandran, S. (2006). The impact of organisational citizenship behaviours on goal orientation and performance of salespeople: an empirical study. *International Journal of Business Insights and Transformation*, Oct.–Mar.: 17–27.

Martin, C. and Bennett, N. (1996). The role of justice judgments in explaining the relationship between job satisfaction and organizational commitment. *Group Organizational Management*, 21: 84–104.

Mathieu, J.L. (1991). A cross-level nonrecurisve model of the antecedents of organizational commitment and job satisfaction. *Journal of Applied Psychology*, 76: 607–618.

Mathieu, J.E. and Zajac, D.M. (1990). A review and meta-analysis of the antecedents, correlates, and consequences of organisational commitment. *Psychological Bulletin*, 108: 171–194.

Mayer, R.C. and Schoorman, F.D. (1992). Predicting participation and production outcomes through a two-dimensional model of organisation commitment. *The Academy of Management Journal*, 35: 671–684.

McGregor, D. (1960). *The Human Side of Enterprise*. New York: McGraw-Hill.

Meyer, J.P. and Allen, N.J. (1984). Testing the 'side-bet theory' of organizational commitment: some methodological considerations. *Journal of Applied Psychology*, 69: 372–378.

Meyer, J.P. and Allen, N.J. (1991). A three-component conceptualization of organizational commitment. *Human Resource Management Review*, 1: 64–98.

Meyer, J.P. and Allen, N.J. (1997). *Commitment in the Workplace: Theory, Research and Application*. Thousand Oaks, CA: Sage.

Meyer, J.P. and Herscovitch, L. (2001). Commitment in the workplace: toward a general model. *Human Resource Management Review*, 11: 299–326.

Meyer, J.P., Paunonen, S.V., Gellatly, I.R., Goffin, R.D. and Jackson, D.N. (1989). Organizational commitment and job performance: it's the nature of commitment that counts. *Journal of Applied Psychology*, 74: 152–156.

Meyer, J.P., Stanley, D.J., Herscovitch, L. and Topolnytsksy, L. (2002). Affective, continuance, and normative commitment to the organization: a meta-analysis of antecedents, correlates, and consequences. *Journal of Vocational Behavior*, 60: 20–52.

Meyer, J.P., Becker, T.E. and Vandenberghe, C. (2004). Employee commitment and motivation: a conceptual analysis and integrative model. *Journal of Applied Psychology*, 89: 991–1007.

Mobley, W.H. (1977). Intermediate linkage in the relationship between job satisfaction and employee turnover. *Journal of Applied Psychology*, 62: 237–240.

Mobley, W.H. (1982). *Employee Turnover: Causes, Consequences, and Control*. Reading, MA: Addison-Wesley.

Mobley, W.S.H., Horner, S.O. and Hollingsworth, A.T. (1978). An evaluation of precursors of hospital employee turnover. *Journal of Applied Psychology*, 63 (4): 408–414.

Morrell, K., Loan-Clarke, J. and Wilkinson, A. (2001). Unweaving leaving: the use of models in the management of employee turnover. *Business School Research Series*, pp. 1–65.

Mount, M., Ilies, R. and Johnson, E. (2006). Relationship of personality traits and counterproductive work behaviors: the mediating effects of job satisfaction. *Personnel Psychology*, 59: 591–622.

Mowday, R., Steers, R. and Porter, L. (1979). The measurement of organizational commitment. *Journal of Vocational Behaviour*, 14: 224–247.

Mowday, R.T., Porter, R.W. and Steers, R.M. (1982). *Employee-organization Linkage: The Psychology of Commitment, Absenteeism and Turnover.* New York: Academic Press.

Mudor, H. and Tooksoon, P. (2011). Conceptual framework on the relationship between human resource management practices, job satisfaction, and turnover. *Journal of Economics and Behavioural Studies*, 2: 41–49.

Murphy, T.E. and Zandvakili, S. (2000). Data- and metrics-driven approach to human resource practices: using customers, employees, and financial metrics. *Human Resource Management*, 39 (1): 93–105.

Nielsen, T.M., Bachrach, D.G., Sundstrom, E. and Halfhill, T.R. (2010). Utility of OCB: organizational citizenship behavior and group performance in a resource allocation framework. *Journal of Management*, Advance online publication. doi: 1177/0149206309356326.

Nijhof, W.F., De Jong, M.J. and Beukhof, G. (1998). Employee commitment in changing organizations: an exploration. *Journal of European Industrial Training*, 22: 243–248.

O'Fallon, M.J. and Butterfield, K.D. (2005). A review of the empirical ethical decision-making literature: 1996–2003. *Journal of Business Ethics*, 90: 125–141.

O'Neil, B.S. and Mone, M.A. (1998). Investigating equity sensitivity as a modera-tor of relations between self-efficacy and workplace attitudes. *Journal of Applied Psychology*, 83: 805–816.

O'Reilly, C. III, and Chatman, J. (1986). Organisational commitment and psycho-logical attachment: the effects of compliance, identification, and internalization on prosocial behaviour. *Journal of Applied Psychology*, 71: 492–499.

Oatey, M. (1970). The economics of training with respect to the firm. *British Journal of Industrial Relations*, 8: 1–21.

Organ, D.W. (1977). A reappraisal and reinterpretation of the satisfaction-causes-performance hypothesis. *Academy of Management Review*, 2: 46–53.

Organ, D.W. (1988). *Organisational Citizenship Behaviour: The Good Soldier Syndrome.* Lexington, MA: Lexington Books.

Organ, D.W. and Ryan, K. (1995). A meta-analytic review of attitudinal and dispositional predictors of organizational citizenship behavior. *Personnel Psychology*, 48: 775–802.

Organ, D.W., Podsakoff, P.M. and MacKenzie, S.B. (2006). *Organizational Citizenship Behavior: Its Nature, Antecedents and Consequences.* Thousand Oaks, CA: Sage.

Ostroff, C. (1992). The relationship between satisfaction, attitude, and perform-ance: an organizational level analysis. *Journal of Applied Psychology*, 77: 963–974.

Paauwe, J. (2009). HRM and performance: achievements, methodological issues and prospects. *Journal of Management Studies*, 46: 129–142.

Paauwe, J. and Richardson, R. (1997). Introduction. Special issue on HRM and performance. *International Journal of Human Resource Management*, 8: 257–262.

Peng, J. and Chiu, S. (2010). An integrative model linking feedback environment and organizational citizenship behavior. *The Journal of Social Psychology*, 150: 582–607.

Pepe, M. (2010). The impact of extrinsic motivational dissatisfiers on employee level of job satisfaction and commitment resulting in the intent to turnover. *EABR & ETLC Conference Proceedings*. Dublin.

Peters, L.H. and O'Connor, E.J. (1980). Situational constraints and work outcomes: the influence of a frequently overlooked construct. *Academy of Management Review*, 5: 391–397.

Pfeffer, J. (1998). *The Human Equation. Building Profits by Putting People First.* Boston: Harvard Business School Press.

Phillips, J.D. (1990). The price tag on turnover. *Personnel Journal*, 69: 58–61.

Piderit, S.K. (2000). Rethinking resistance and recognizing ambivalence: a multidimensional view of attitudes towards organisational change. *Academy of Management Review*, 25: 783–822.

Podsakoff, P.M., MacKenzie, S.B. and Bommer, W.H. (1996). Transformational leader behaviours and substitutes for leadership as determinants of employee satisfaction, commitment, trust, and organisational citizenship behaviours. *Journal of Management*, 22: 259–298.

Podsakoff, P.M., Ahearne, M. and MacKenie, S.B. (1997). Organizational citizenship behavior and the quantity and quality of work group performance. *Journal of Applied Psychology*, 82: 262–270.

Podsakoff, P.M., MacKenzie, S.B., Paine, J.B. and Bachrach, D.G. (2000). Organizational citizenship behaviors: a critical review of the theoretical and empirical literature and suggestions for future research. *Journal of Management*, 26: 513–563.

Podsakoff, P.M., MacKenzie, S.B., Lee, J.Y. and Podsakoff, N.P. (2003). Common method biases in behavioral research: a critical review of the literature and recommended remedies. *Journal of Applied Psychology*, 88: 879–903.

Porter, L.W. and Steers, R.M. (1973). Organizational work, and personal factors in employee turnover and absenteeism. *Psychological Bulletin*, 80: 151–176.

Porter, L.W., Steers, R.M., Mowday, R.T. and Boulian, P.V. (1974). Organisational commitment, job satisfaction, and turnover among psychiatric technicians. *Journal of Applied Psychology*, 59: 603–609.

Poznanski, P.J. and Bline, D.M. (1997). Using structural equation modelling to investigate the casual ordering of job satisfaction and organisational commitment among staff accountants. *Behavioural Research in Accounting*, 19: 154–165.

Price, J. (2001). Refections on the determinants of voluntary turnover. *International Journal of Manpower*, 22: 600–624.

Price, J.L. and Mueller, C.W. (1981). A causal model of turnover for nurses. *Academy of Management Journal*, 24: 543–565.

Purcell, J. and Ahlstrand, B. (1994). *Human Resource Management in the Multidivisional Company*. Oxford: OUP.

Purcell, J., Kinnie, N. and Hutchinson, S. (2003). *Understanding the People and Performance Link: Unlocking the Black Box.* London: CIPD.

Randall, D.M. and O'Driscoll, M.P. (1997). Affective versus calculative commitment: human resource implication. *The Journal of Social Psychology*, 137: 606–617.

Reisel, W.D., Probst, T.M., Chia, S., Maloles, III, C.M. and Konig, C.J. (2010). The effects of job insecurity on job satisfaction, organizational citizenship behavior, deviant behavior, and negative emotions of employees. *International Studies of Management and Organization*, 40: 74–91.

Rich, G.A. (1997). The sales manager as a role model: effects on trust, job satisfaction, and performance of salespeople. *Journal of Academy of Marketing Science*, 25: 319–328.

Richard, P.J., Devinney, T.M., Yip, G.S. and Johnson, G. (2009). Measuring organizational performance: towards methodological best practice. *Journal of Management*, 35: 718–804.

Robinson, S.R. and Morrison, E.W. (1995). Psychological contracts and OCB: the effect of unfulfilled obligations. *Journal of Organizational Behavior*, 6: 289–298.

Roethlisberger, F.J. (1959). *Management and Morale*. Cambridge, MA: Harvard University Press.

Rousseau, D.M. (1995). *Psychological Contracts in Organizations: Understanding Written and Unwritten Agreements*. Thousand Oaks, CA: Sage.

Roznowski, M. and Hulin, C. (1992). The scientific merit of valid measures of general constructs with special reference to job satisfaction and job withdrawal. In C. Cranny, P. Smith and E. Stone (eds), *Job Satisfaction: How People Feel about Their Jobs and How it Affects Their Performance*. New York: Lexington Books, pp. 123–163.

Rucci, A.J., Kirn, S.P. and Quinn, R.T. (1998). The employee-customer-profit chain at Sears. *Harvard Business Review*, 76: 82–97.

Russell, B. (1931). *The Scientific Outlook* (1st edn). London: George Allen & Unwin.

Ryan, A.M., Schmit, M.J. and Johnson, R. (1996). Attitudes and effectiveness: examining relations at an organization level. *Personnel Psychology*, 49: 853–882.

Saridakis, G., Sen-Gupta, S., Edwards, P. and Storey, D. (2008). The impact of enterprise size on employment tribunal incidence and outcomes: evidence from Britain. *British Journal of Industrial Relations*, 46: 469–499.

Saridakis, G., Munoz Torres, R. and Tracey, P. (2009). The endogeneity bias in the relationship between employee commitment and job satisfaction. Working Paper Series, Cambridge Judge Business School.

Saridakis, G., Torres, R.M. and Johnstone, S. (2012). Do human resource practices enhance organisational commitment in SMEs with low employee satisfaction? *British Journal of Management*, forthcoming.

Scherer, K. (1999). Appraisal theory. In T. Dalgleish and M. Power (ed.), *Handbook of Emotion and Cognition*. New York: Wiley, pp. 637–665.

Schneider, B. and Bowen, D.E. (1985). Employee and customer perceptions of service in banks: replication and extension. *Journal of Applied Psychology*, 70: 423–433.

Schneider, B. and Bowen, D.E. (1993). The service organisation: human resource management is crucial. *Organisational Dynamics*, 21: 39-52.

Schneider, B., Hanges, P.J., Smith, D.B. and Salvaggio, A.N. (2003). Which comes first: employee attitude or organizational financial and market performance. *Journal of Applied Psychology*, 88: 836–851.

Sethivikram, V., Meinert, D., Kingrking, R. and Seithiavsethi, V. (1996). The multi-dimensional nature of organizational commitment among information systems personnel. *Second American Conference on Information Systems*, 16–18 August, pp. 1–4.

Sheppeck, M.A. and Militello, J. (2000). Strategic HR configurations and organizational performance. *Human Resource Management*, 39: 5–16.

Shin, H.S. and Reyes, P. (1995). Teacher commitment and job satisfaction: a causal analysis. *Journal of School Leadership*, 5: 22–39.

Sims, R.L. and Keon, T.L. (1999). Determinants of ethical decision making: the relationship of the perceived organizational environment. *Journal of Business Ethics*, 19: 393–401.

Singh, P. and Loncar, N. (2010). Pay satisfaction, job satisfaction and turnover intention. *Industrial Relations*, 65: 470–490.

Sisson, K. (1990). Introducing the Human Resource Management Journal. *Human Resource Management Journal*, 1: 1–11.

Sivasubramaniam, N. and Kroeck, K.G. (1995). The concept of fit in strategic human resource management. Paper presented to the Academy of Management Conference, Vancouver, August, pp. 6–9.

Slocombe, T. and Dougherty, T. (1998). Dissecting organizational commitment and its relationship with employee behavior. *Journal of Business and Psychology*, 12: 469–491.

Smith, P.C., Kendall, L.M. and Hulin, C.L. (1969). *The Measurement of Satisfaction in Work and Retirement*. Chicago, IL: Rand McNally.

Smollan, R.K. (2006). Minds, hearts and deeds: cognitive, affective and behavioral response to change. *Journal of Change Management*, 6: 143–158.

Snape, E. and Redman, T. (2003). An evaluation of a three-component model of occupational commitment: dimensionality and consequences among United Kingdom human resource management specialists. *Journal of Applied Psychology*, 88: 152–159.

Snape, E. and Redman, T. (2010). HRM practices, organisational citizenship behaviour, and performance: a multi-level analysis. *Journal of Management Studies*, 47: 1119-1247.

Solinger, O.N., Olffen, W.V. and Roe, R.A. (2008). Beyond the three-component model of organization commitment. *Journal of Applied Psychology*, 93: 70–83.

Somers, M.J. and Birnbaum, D. (1998). Work-related commitment and job performance: it's also the nature of performance that counts. *Journal of Organisational Behaviour*, 19: 621–631.

Sousa-Poza, A. and Henneberger, F. (2002). Analysing job mobility with job turnover intentions: an international comparative study. *Research Institute for Labour Economics and Labour Law*, 82: 1–28.

Spector, P.E. (1997). *Job Satisfaction: Application, Assessment, Causes, and Consequences*. Thousand Oaks, CA: Sage.

Stallworth, L. (2004). Antecedents and consequences of organizational commitment to accounting. *Managerial Auditing Journal*, 19: 945–955.

Stanley, D.J., Meyer, J.P., Topolnytsky, L. and Herscovitch, L. (1999). Affective, continuance and normative commitment to the organization: a meta-analysis of antecedents, correlates and consequences. *Journal of Vocational Behaviour*, 61: 20–52.

Steel, R.P. (2002). Turnover theory at the empirical interface: problems of fit and function. *Academy of Management Review*, 27: 346–360.

Steijin, B. (2002). HRM and job satisfaction in the Dutch public sector. Paper presented at the EGPA Conference in Potsdam, study group on Public Personnel Policies.

Storey, J. (1992). *Developments in the Management of Human Resources.* Oxford: Blackwell.

Storey, D.J., Saridakis, G., Sen-Gupta, S., Edwards, P.K. and Blackburn, R.A. (2010). Linking HR formality with employee job quality: the role of the firm and workplace size. *Human Resource Management,* 49: 305–329.

Suliman, A.M.T. (2002). Is it really a mediating construct? The mediating role of organizational commitment in work climate-performance relationship. *Journal of Management Development,* 21: 170–183.

Suliman, A.A. and Al-Junaibi, Y. (2010). Commitment and turnover intention in the UAE oil industry. *The International Journal of Human Resource Management,* 21: 1472–1489.

Suliman, A. and Iles, P. (2000). Is continuance commitment beneficial to organizations? Commitment-performance relationship: a new look. *Journal of Managerial Psychology,* 15: 407–426.

Sun, L., Aryee, S. and Law, K.S. (2007). High-performance human resource practices, citizenship behavior, and organizational performance: a relational perspective. *Academy of Management Journal,* 50: 558–577.

Swailes, S. (2002). Organizational commitment: a critique of the construct and measures. *International Journal of Management Reviews,* 4 (2): 155–178.

Testa, M.R. (2001). Organisational commitment, job satisfaction and effort in the service environment. *The Journal of Psychology,* 135: 226–236.

Tett, R. and Meyer, J. (1993). Job satisfaction, organisational commitment, turnover intention and turnover: path analysis based on meta-analytic findings. *Personnel Psychology,* 46: 259–293.

Thorndike, R.L. (1949). *Personnel Selection: Test and Measurement Techniques.* New York: Wiley.

Ting, Y. (1997). Determinants of job satisfaction of federal government employees. *Public Personnel Management,* 26: 313–334.

Tjosvold, D., Hui, C. and Yu, Z. (2003). Conflict management and task reflexivity for team in-role and extra-role performance in China. *International Journal of Conflict Management,* 14: 141–163.

Truss, C., Gratton, L., Hope-Hailey, V., McGovern, P. and Stiles, P. (1997). Soft and hard models of human resource management: a reappraisal. *Journal of Management Studies,* 34: 54–73.

Tsai, C.T. and Su, C. (2011). Leadership, job satisfaction and service-oriented organizational citizenship behaviors in flight attendants. *African Journal of Business Management,* 5: 1915–1926.

Turnipseed, D.L. and Rassuli, A. (2005). Performance perceptions of organizational citizenship behaviors at work: a bi-level study among managers and employees. *British Journal of Management,* 16: 231–244.

Ulrich, D., Halbrook, R., Meder, D., Stuchlik, M. and Thorpe, S. (1991). Employee and customer attachment: synergies for competitive advantage. *Human Resource Planning,* 14: 89–103.

Valeau, P., Mignonac, K., Vandenberghe, C. and Gatignon-Turneau, A. (2010). The three-component model and the multiple commitments of volunteers. *Academy of Management Annual Meeting Proceedings,* August, pp. 6–10.

Valentine, S., Godkin, L., Fleischman, G.M. and Kidwell, R. (2011). Corporate ethical values, group creativity, job satisfaction and turnover intention: the impact of work context on work response. *Journal of Business Ethics*, 98: 353–372.

Van den Berg, R.J., Richardson, H.A. and Eastman, L.J. (1999). The impact of high involvement work processes on organizational effectiveness. *Group and Organization Management*, 24 (3): 300–339.

Van Dyne, L. and Pierce, J.L. (2004). Psychological ownership and feeling of possession: three field studies predicting employee attitudes and organizational citizenship behavior. *Journal of Organizational Behavior*, 25: 439–459.

Wagner, S. and Rush, M. (2000). Altruistic organizational citizenship behavior: context, disposition and age. *The Journal of Social Psychology*, 140: 379–391.

Walton, R.E. (1985). From control to commitment in the workplace. *Harvard Business Review*, 63: 77–84.

Walz, S.M. and Niehoff, B.P. (1996). Organizational citizenship behaviors and their effect on organizational effectiveness in limited-menu restaurants. *Academy of Management Best Paper Proceedings*, pp. 307–311.

Weiss, H.M. (2002). Deconstructing job satisfaction: separating evaluations, beliefs and affective experiences. *Human Resource Management Review*, 12: 173–194.

Westover, J.H., Westover, A.R., Westover, L.A. (2010). Enhancing long-term worker productivity and performance: the connection of key work domains to job satisfaction and organizational commitment. *International Journal of Productivity and Performance Management*, 59: 372–387.

Wiener, Y. (1982). Commitment in organizations: a normative view. *Academy of Management Review*, 7: 418–428.

Wiener, Y. and Vardi, Y. (1980). Relationships between job, organization, and career commitment and work outcomes: an integrative approach. *Organizational Behavior and Human Performance*, 26: 81–96.

William, L.J. and Hazer, J.T. (1986). Antecedents and consequences of satisfaction and commitment in turnover models: a reanalysis using latent variable structural equation methods. *Journal of Applied Psychology*, 71: 219–231.

Williamson, O.E., Wachter, M.L. and Harris, J.E. (1975). Understanding the employment relation: the analysis of idiosyncratic exchange. *Bell Journal of Economics*, 6: 250–278.

Wood, S. (1996). High commitment management and unionization in the UK. *International Journal of Human Resource Management*, 7: 41–58.

Wright, P.M. and Boswell, W.R. (2002). Desegregating HRM: a review and synthesis of micro and macro human resource management research. *Journal of Management*, 28: 247–276.

Wright, P.M. and Gardner, T. (2003). The human resource-firm performance relationship: methodological and theoretical challenges. In D. Holman, T.D. Wall, C.W. Clegg, P. Sparrow and A. Howard (eds), *The New Workplace: A Guide to the Human Impact of Modern Working Practices*. West Sussex: Wiley, pp. 311–328.

Wright, P.M. and Kehoe, R.R. (2007). Human resource practices and organisational commitment: a deeper examination. CAHRS Working Paper Series, Cornell University.

Wright, P.M. and Nishii, L.H. (2006). Strategic HRM and organizational behavior: integrating multiple levels of analysis. Working paper, Cornell University.

Wright, P.M., Gardner, T. and Moynihan, L. (2003). The impact of HR practice on the performance of business units. *Human Resource Management Journal*, 13 (3): 21–36.

Wright, P.M., Gardner, T.M., Moynihan, L.M. and Allen, M.R. (2005). The relationship between HR practices and firm performance: examine causal order. *Personnel Psychology*, 58: 409–446.

Yang, J. (2008). Effect of newcomer socialization on organizational commitment, job satisfaction, and turnover intention in the hotel industry. *The Service Industries Journal*, 28: 429–443.

Yang, F. and Chang, C. (2007). Emotional labour, job satisfaction and organisational commitment amongst clinical nurses: a questionnaire survey. *International Journal of Nursing Studies*, 44: 131–142.

Yao, X. and Wang, L. (2006). The predictability and normative organizational commitment for turnover in Chinese companies: a cultural perspective. *International Journal of Human Resource Management*, 17: 1058–1075.

Zaleska, K.J. and De Menezes, L.M. (2007). Human resource development practices and their association with employee attitudes: between traditional and new careers. *Human Relations*, 60: 987–1018.

Zeinabadi, H. (2010). Job satisfaction and organizational commitment as antecedents of organizational citizenship behavior (OCB) of teachers. *Procedia Social and Behavioral Science*, 5: 998–1003.

Zheng, W., Kaur, S. and Tao, Z. (2010). A critical review of employee turnover model (1938–2009) and development in perspective of performance. *African Journal of Business Management*, 4: 4146–4158.

10. Creating and sustaining economic growth through HR

Hai-Ming Chen, Ku-Jun Lin and Yen-Lin Huang

1. INTRODUCTION

With the rise of the knowledge economy, the importance of intellectual capital has grown. The concept of intellectual capital was raised by Galbraith in 1969, since when the market to book value of corporations around the world has increased dramatically. The implication of this phenomenon is that value creating factors have shifted from tangible assets to intangible ones. Thus, in order to create and sustain economic growth, there is a need for both scholars and practitioners to break down the value creating process and identify the crucial intellectual capital that creates value.

However, there is no consistent definition of intellectual capital. For example, Chen et al. (2004) argue that intellectual capital includes human capital, structural capital, innovation capital and customer capital. Human capital is the source of all intellectual capital, and through structural capital and innovation capital, human capital can enhance customer capital. Wang and Chang (2005) use the Taiwanese information technology industry as an example and conclude that by using the human capital, performance can be increased through the enhancement of innovation capital and process capital. Sveiby (1997) suggested that market value is created by tangible net book value and intangible value, which includes external structure, internal structure and individual competence. Edvinsson and Malone (1997), using a similar structure, argue that market value is composed of financial capital and intellectual capital, including human capital, structure capital and customer capital.

Edvinsson (1997) also mentioned a 'Skandia navigator framework', arguing that in the past, 'human capital' is provided only in the form of 'labor' in corporations, and tangible assets such as machines are the source of value, so a historically based financial analysis is enough to modify the efficiency of material input, labor and machine usage. However, since the modern business focus on service and value created by intangible assets, human capital becomes the source of customer capital, process capital and innovation capital. All those intellectual capitals are future oriented and focus on the leading input instead of lagging result.

Based on the previous analysis, human resource management is a critical issue in management. Unlike the traditional resources, such as accounting assets, human capital is not a simple physical substance. Roos et al. (2005) define human capital as all people-related characteristics that cannot be replaced by machine or recorded by words, including capability, skills, tacit knowledge and human networks. Human capital triggers the value creation process of business, so it becomes important to retain human capital in the business.

Based on the resource based view theory, to optimize corporation profit, investment in human capital must be valid and efficient. However, based on our previous research, investment in human capital alone has little effect on firm performance. This is because the current accounting system is not designed for collecting human capital information, so the data collected from this system may not be an adequate measurement. The system may mislead organizations to invest in so called 'human capital' items but produce an irrelevant financial result. Thus, focus on the behavior perspective of employees can be a more efficient way to observe the influence of human capital investment.

Employee attitude is a critical issue for retaining talent within organization. This study investigates the relationship between employee participation, trust and affective commitment. We use path analysis and find out that both perceptions of financial participation and degree of non financial participation are positively associated with affective commitment. Also, the relationship between financial participation and affective commitment is mediated by trust. However, trust doesn't have complete mediation effects on the relationship between non financial participation and affective commitment. This result is of interest to decision makers concerned with human capital retention.

2. HUMAN RESOURCE ACCOUNTING

What is the component of human capital? Chen and Lin (2004) suggested that unique employees who can contribute high value to business are human capital. The investment in employees with these characteristics is an investment in human capital. Flamholtz (1999) classified the investment in human capital into three categories:

1. *Acquisition cost*   e.g. recruitment and selection costs, cost of promotion within organizations.
2. *Development cost*   e.g. cost of orientation, formal workshop training, formal and informal on-the-job training, and other development (such as formal outside training).
3. *Replacement cost*   For example, separation costs and pension.

If human capital is the source of other intellectual capital and critical to the creation and sustaining of value, should performance be in better shape once we invest more in human capital? The answer is not necessarily. We carried out several empirical tests on different intellectually oriented industries since 2005, such as high technology electronics, software and pharmaceuticals. The results suggest that investment in human capital alone does not significantly influence firm performance. However, if we included the investment in other intellectual capital, such as structure capital or customer capital, it would create synergy and improve performance.

The disadvantage of using the accounting system to calculate investment in intellectual capital is that it is hard to collect the data. The traditional accounting system does a great job in recording hard assets but is not designed for collecting intellectual capital data. The lack of physical substance of intellectual capital makes it difficult to present the fair market value in monetary units. Even if we use formulae to calculate ratios that may represent intellectual capital, it is still unsatisfactory. To sum up, an incorrect measurement of human capital may mislead decision making and show no result from the current accounting system.

3.   THE MEASUREMENT OF INTANGIBLES

Monetary investment is not an efficient tool to measure human capital. Instead, we argue that it is better to measure intellectual capital by using 'connections' between people and organizations. To involve human capital in the organization process, the most important thing is to 'keep' the high value and unique employee in the organization. Thus, we suggest that employee participation, trust and affective commitment are the three critical functions.

Kaler (1999) defined participating as a form of sharing among employees of business. Organizations may choose to share power and benefits with employees, which may increase employee trust in managers and the organization. Trust involves willing to increase one's resource investment in another entity, based on positive interaction between the two parties

(Tzafrir and Dolan, 2004). There is relatively little research discussing the relationship between participating and trust. For example, Coyle-Shapiro et al. (2002) considered financial participation and the trust between employee and manager. We will expand the aspects of participation, including non-financial participation, in this research.

Lastly, Meyer and Herscovitch (2001) defined commitment as a power that glues the related action guidelines between one entity and others. Employee commitment makes organizations retain valuable employees. When employee commitment exists, it means that an employee would like to contribute his or her efforts to the organization. A business devoted to gaining commitment from valuable employees may get better performance.

This research is developed on accounting firms. The reason we look to accounting firms as our sample is because they are in a human capital oriented service industry, and the high turnover rate is a common issue and constant problem in the industry. A high turnover rate means that every year, the employer loses huge training and development cost and has to go through the recruitment procedure again and again. Professional skills that can contribute high value can be viewed as human capital (Chen and Lin, 2004), which can help accounting firms to make profit and create value. Investment in retaining human capital in accounting firms will lower the separation cost and create value. After several conversations with the partners in the industry, we decide to discuss the relations among employee participation, trust and commitment in the accounting firms.

3.1 Employee Participation

Researchers classify employee participation as financial participation and participation in decision making (Bakan et al., 2004; Wilson and Peel, 1991). Kaler (1999) classified participating into two sorts: financial participation and operational participation. Operational participation includes delegatory, informatory and consultative. For delegatory participation, managers hand over the running of certain areas to the workforce, such as quality circles. Informatory is employee sharing in business information, which is essential to the process of running the organization. It is not just participation, but a specifically operational form of it. Consultative is not joint decision making in any straightforward sense. It is an opportunity for employees to influence decision making through persuasion. Combining the three characteristics gives the so called co-determinatory. The co-determinatory can be identified by degree (partial or full), level (procedure or strategic), mode (direct or indirect), and weighting (Kaler, 1999).

3.2 Financial Participation

Vaughan-Whitehead (1995) defined financial participation as employee incentives from all plans that are proportional to business performance, excluding salary. It can be classified as 'gain sharing', 'profit sharing' and 'workers' share-ownership'. In 'gain sharing', a gain is calculated by a pre-determined formula and the purpose is to encourage individual employees to make an improvement on corporate performance. 'Profit sharing' considers the contribution from all employees and can be deferred or paid in cash. 'Workers' share-ownership' is an incentive plan for an organization to offer its own capital stocks to employees at a bargain price or at no cost. Because of the capital structure of accounting firms, the financial participation in the research refers to 'gain sharing' and 'profit sharing'.

3.3 Non Financial Participation

Non financial participation is defined as people contributing to decision making, not because of their position but according to their ability. More precise information is communicated through an open channel (Mitchell, 1973).

Based on previous research (Dachler and Wilpert, 1978), Cotton et al. (1988) illustrate that employee non-financial participation includes (1) participation in work decisions; (2) consultative participation; (3) short-term participation; (4) informal participation; and (5) representative participation. This research will reference the classification by Cotton et al. (1988) to define non financial participation.

3.4 Trust

Trust is considered as the result of judgement about different character-istics of the trustee (Dietz and Hartog, 2006). Trust behavior is formed after the trustee has satisfied specific requirements (Tzafrir and Dolan, 2004). Considering these characteristics of trustee, we can know why trust occurred and measure the level of trust (Mayer et al., 1995), or understand which characteristics trigger the trust (Burke et al., 2007).

Mayer et al. (1995) summarized those characteristics as three cri-teria: ability, benevolence and integrity. Dietz and Hartog (2006) extended Mayer's research and add predictability as the forth criterion. In our research, we consider the manager as the trustee and the whole organization.

3.5   Commitment

Brown (1996) defines commitment as a force obliging the keeping of the promise. For years, researchers have developed ways to conceptualize and measure organization commitment (Meyer et al., 1990). Organization commitment can be divided into affective commitment, continuance commitment and normative commitment (Allen and Meyer, 1990; Meyer and Allen, 1984, 1991). Affective commitment is the employee's feeling of attachment to the organization. The employee 'wants to' stay in the organization. Continuance commitment means that the employee 'needs to' stay in the organization because of the separation cost. Normative commitment is the employee's feeling of obligation to stay in the organization and means that the employee feels they 'ought to' stay in the organization. However, based on empirical study (Meyer et al., 2002), only affective commitment has positive correlation to organization performance. So we adopt affective commitment only as a variable in our research.

3.6   The Relationship Among Employee Participation, Trust and Commitment

3.6.1   Employee participation and affective commitment

According to the expectation theory (Vroom, 1964), people take actions because they expect that such actions will lead to a desirable result. So the employee would expect there to be some kind of connection between hard work, performance and reward. The level of support for that connection by the organization would have a connection to the employee attitude (Coyle-Shapiro et al., 2002).

Blau (1964) uses the basic assumption of social exchange theory and points out that if one side offers tangible or intangible benefits to the other side, there is a moral obligation for the other side to provide feedback to the benefit provider. Based on social exchange theory, Eisenberger et al. (1986) suggest the theory of 'perceptions of organizational support' (POS). The meaning of POS is the employees' beliefs about how much the organization cares about their contribution and welfare. Rhoades and Eisenberger (2002) clarify the cause and influence of POS. The cause of POS includes fairness, support of supervisor, organizational reward and fair working environment. The influence would be job satisfaction, affective commitment, performance and lower separation rate. The financial and non-financial participation can be seen as a cause of POS and in some cases the financial participation can be viewed as the reward from organization to employee. The implementation of employee participation is a signal that the corporation cares about the employee's welfare. So the employee may use affective commitment as the repayment to the organization.

Klein (1987) constructed a model arguing that there are three kinds of employee share option plan that can increase the satisfaction of the employee with the organization and cause employee commitment.

1. Intrinsic, or direct effect. The benefit of this plan is that the employees acquire the ownership rather than the plan itself.
2. Instrumental satisfaction model, or indirect effect in which employees' influence and control over organizational decisions is increased.
3. extrinsic model, whereby participation brings financial reward to employees and it is a system reward.

Bakan et al. (2004) performed an empirical study and found that when employees participate in the organization decision making process, it has a stronger positive influence on employees' attitude and organization commitmment. Thus, this research proposes the following hypothesis:

H1: Employee participation positively affects affective commitment;
H1a: Financial participation positively affects affective commitment;
H1b: Non financial participation positively affects affective commitment.

3.6.2   Employee participation and trust
Based on the exchange theory, we will help and give feedback to those who gave us favor. Lewis and Weigert (1985) argue that when we receive 'trust' from others, we become more willing to trust others. Singh (2009) took an empirical study showing that non-financial participation related to trust. Scholars also found the perception of profit sharing positively related to the trust in the employer (Coyle-Shapiro et al., 2002). Based on the literature review, we propose that:

H2: Employee participation positively affects trust in managers;
H2a: Financial participation positively affects trust in managers;
H2b: Non financial participation positively affects trust in managers.

3.6.3   Trust and affective commitment
Nyhan (1999) found that in public organizations, interpersonal trust can increase the affective commitment in the organization. He also found that if employees can participate in the decision making process, have feedback from the organization and have the chance to complete work autonomously, it will help productivity and organizational commitment (Nyhan,

2000). Perry (2004) also believed that trust in the employer will increase the level of organization commitment.

Coyle-Shapiro et al. (2002) argued that personal ability in contribution to the organization and the perception of relation with the organization are positively related to organization commitment. Trust in the manager can be an intermediate variable between personal ability in contribution to the organization and organization commitment.

Based on the literature review, this research suggests that the trust in the manager can increase employees' affective commitment. Once the employee builds up trust in the manager, it may mean that the employee has attached to the organization and has positive expectations of the employer. Human capital may be retained in this way. Thus we propose that:

H3: Trust in managers positively affects affective commitment;
H4: Trust has a mediation effect between employee participation and affective commitment;
H4a: Trust has a mediation effect between financial participation and affective commitment;
H4b: Trust has a mediation effect between non financial participation and affective commitment.

4. METHODOLOGY

4.1 Research Structure and Propositions

Based on the literature, we present our conceptual framework in Figure 10.1

4.2 Questionnaire and Sample

In our research, we use the questionnaire developed by Pendleton et al. (1998) for financial participation, and the questionnaire developed by Cotton et al. (1988) for non financial participation. We also modify the questionnaire developed by Dietz and Hartog (2006) and Mayer and Davis (1999) for the test of trust between employee and managers. Finally, the affective commitment questionnaire is adapted from the Allen and Meyer (1990) questionnaire. We use a Likert 5-point scale for research questions to investigate the response.

Pretesting was done to adjust the questions. After that, we distributed 370 copies of the questionnaire to the accounting firm employees, and

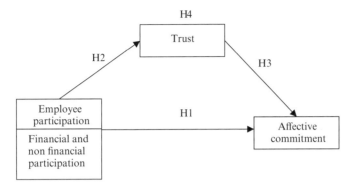

Figure 10.1   Conceptual framework

330 copies were collected back. After elimination of 49 invalid question-naires, 281 valid copies remained for analysis. The KMO values for employee financial participation, non-financial participation, trust and affective commitment are 0.860, 0.835, 0.955 and 0.769 respectively. The Cronbach's α for each perspective is 0.807, 0.925, 0.956 and 0.807.

5.   RESEARCH METHOD AND RESULT

We adopted the questionnaire investigation method and used statistical software SPSS 12.0 in the research. Regression and path analysis are performed to examine the relationship between perspectives. The results are showing in Figure 10.2 and Figure 10.3.

In Figure 10.2, we can observe that both financial and non financial participation has a positive and significant influence on affective commitment, which supports proposition 1. We also find that non financial participation has greater influence on affective commitment compared to financial participation.

In Figure 10.3, we add trust as a mediator variable to test the relationship between participation and affective commitment. Figure 10.3 shows that both financial participation and non financial participation have significant influence (0.101^* and 0.31^{***}) on trust; the empirical result supports propositions 2, 2a and 2b. The significant influence from trust to affective commitment (0.305^{***}) also supports proposition 3. Finally, after we add trust as the mediator variable, the direct effect of financial participation to affective commitment becomes 0.071 and is not significant. Thus proposition 4a is supported. However, although the

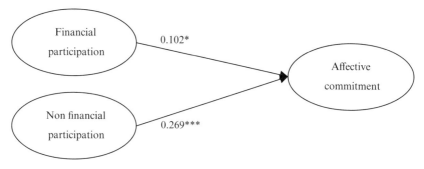

Note: P< 0.01***, P<0.05**, P<0.1*.

Figure 10.2   Path analysis for participation and affective commitment

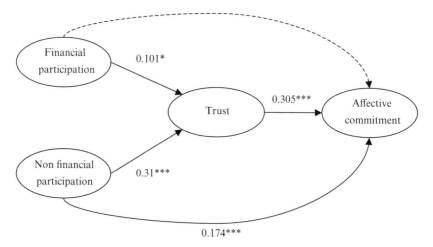

Note: P< 0.01***, P<0.05**, P<0.1*

Figure 10.3   Path analysis for participation, trust and affective commitment

direct effect of non financial participation to affective commitment is significant, it is lower (0.174***<0.269***) after we put trust as a mediator variable in the framework. The result suggests that trust has only a partial mediation effect to non financial participation and affective commitment. Proposition 4b is partially supported as well as proposition 4.

6.   DISCUSSION AND CONCLUSIONS

Based on the empirical evidence, we found trust is a mediator variable to financial participation and affective commitment, but does not have full mediation effect for non financial participation and affective commitment. To maintain human capital in the accounting firm, we suggest that:

1.   Although financial participation is adopted in the sample accounting firms, trust should be cultivated between employee and manager to gain affective commitment.
2.   We suggest the accounting firms design activities or create an atmosphere that helps the construction of trust between employee and manager. It also helps to enhance the connection between non financial participation and affective commitment. Trust may also reduce turnover rate and maintain human capital in the accounting firm.

The result told us again that for investment in human capital such as giving incentives, the influence on firm performance may not be significant. Based on the resource-based view theory, the limited firm resources should be invested in the place that can improve the performance most. In this case, the accounting firm should first use resources in activities that can improve 'trust', and use non financial participation as a powerful way to improve affective commitment. Implementation of the two human resource strategies may cause the turnover rate to decrease and the performance to increase at the same time, thus creating and sustaining the accounting firms' economic growth through HR.

REFERENCES

Allen, N.J., and Meyer, J.P. 1990. The measurement and antecedents of affective, continuance and normative commitment to the organization. *Journal of Occupational Psychology*, 63 (1), 1–18.
Bakan, I., Suseno, Y., Pinnington, A., and Money, A. 2004. The influence of financial participation and participation in decision-making on employee job attitudes. *The International Journal of Human Resource Management*, 15 (3), 587–616.
Blau, P.M. 1964. *Exchange and Power in Social Life*. New York: Wiley.
Brown, R.B. 1996. Organizational commitment: clarifying the concept and simplifying the existing construct typology. *Journal of Vocational Behavior*, 49 (3), 230–251.
Burke, C.S., Sims, D.E., Lazzara, E.H., and Salas, E. 2007. Trust in leadership: a multi-level review and integration. *The Leadership Quarterly*, 18 (6), 606–632.
Chen, H.M. and Lin, K.J. 2004. The role of human capital in accounting. *Journal of Intellectual Capital*, 5 (1), 116–130.

Chen, J., Zhu, Z. and Xie, H.Y. 2004. Measuring intellectual capital: a new model and empirical study. *Journal of Intellectual Capital*, 5 (1), 195–212.

Cotton, J.L., Vollrath, D.A., Froggatt, K.L., Lengnick-Hall, M.L., and Jennings, K.R. 1988. Employee participation: diverse forms and different outcomes. *The Academy of Management Review*, 13 (1), 8–22.

Coyle-Shapiro, J.A.-M., Morrow, P.C., Richardson, R., and Dunn, S.R. 2002. Using profit sharing to enhance employee attitudes: a longitudinal examination of the effects on trust and commitment. *Human Resource Management*, 41 (4), 423–439.

Dachler, H.P., and Wilpert, B. 1978. Conceptual dimensions and boundaries of participation in organizations: a critical evaluation. *Administrative Science Quarterly*, 23 (1), 1–39.

Dietz, G., and Hartog, D.N.D. 2006. Measuring trust inside organisations. *Personnel Review*, 33 (5), 557–588.

Edvinsson, L. 1997. Developing intellectual capital at Skandia. *Long Range Planning*, 30 (3), 366–373.

Edvinsson, L. and Malone, M.A. 1997. *Intellectual Capital: Realizing Your Company's True Value By Finding Its Hidden Brainpower*, Harper Business.

Eisenberger, R., Huntington, R., Hutchison, S., and Sowa, D. 1986. Perceived organizational support. *Journal of Applied Psychology*, 71 (3), 500–507.

Flamholtz, E.G. 1999. *Human Resource Accounting: Advances In Concepts, Methods, and Applications*, 3rd edn. Kluwer Academic.

Kaler, J. 1999. Understanding participation. *Journal of Business Ethics*, 21 (2), 125–135.

Klein, K.J. 1987. Employee stock ownership and employee attitudes: a test of three models. *Journal of Applied Psychology*, 72 (2), 319–332.

Lewis, J.D., and Weigert, A. 1985. Trust as a social reality. *Social Forces*, 63 (4), 967–985.

Mayer, R.C., and Davis, J.H. 1999. The effect of the performance appraisal system on trust for management: a field quasi-experiment. *Journal of Applied Psychology*, 84 (1), 123–136.

Mayer, R.C., Davis, J.H., and Schoorman, F.D. 1995. An integrative model of organizational trust. *The Academy of Management Review*, 20 (3), 709–734.

Meyer, J.P., and Allen, N.J. 1984. Testing the 'side-bet theory' of organizational commitment: some methodological considerations. *Journal of Applied Psychology*, 69 (3), 372–378.

Meyer, J.P., and Allen, N.J. 1991. A three-component conceptualization of organizational commitment. *Human Resource Management Review*, 1 (1), 61–89.

Meyer, J.P., and Herscovitch, L. 2001. Commitment in the workplace: toward a general model. *Human Resource Management Review*, 11 (3), 299–326.

Meyer, J.P., Allen, N.J., and Gellatly, I.R. 1990. Affective and continuance commitment to the organization: evaluation of measures and analysis of concurrent and time-lagged relations. *Journal of Applied Psychology*, 75 (6), 710–720.

Meyer, J.P., Stanley, D.J., Herscovitch, L., and Topolnytsky, L. 2002. Affective, continuance, and normative commitment to the organization: a meta-analysis of antecedents, correlates, and consequences. *Journal of Vocational Behavior*, 61 (1), 20–52.

Mitchell, T.R. 1973. Motivation and participation: an integration. *The Academy of Management Journal*, 16 (4), 670–679.

Nyhan, R.C. 1999. Increasing affective organizational commitment in public organizations. *Review of Public Personnel Administration*, 19 (3), 58–70.

Nyhan, R.C. 2000. Changing the paradigm. *The American Review of Public Administration*, 30 (1), 87–109.

Pendleton, A., Wilson, N., and Wright, M. 1998. The perception and effects of share ownership: empirical evidence from employee buy-outs. *British Journal of Industrial Relations*, 36 (1), 99–123.

Perry, R.W. 2004. The relationship of affective organizational commitment with supervisory trust. *Review of Public Personnel Administration*, 24 (2), 133–149.

Rhoades, L., and Eisenberger, R. 2002. Perceived organizational support: a review of the literature. *Journal of Applied Psychology*, 87 (4), 698–714.

Roos, G., Pike, S., and Fernström, L. 2005. *Managing Intellectual Capital In Practice*. Burlington, MA: Elesevier.

Singh, S.K.G. 2009. A study on employee participation in decision making. *Unitar E-Journal*, 5 (1), 20–38.

Sveiby, K.E. 2000., *The New Organizational Wealth: Managing and Measuring Knowledge Based Assets into Market Value*. John Wiley.

Tzafrir, S.S., and Dolan, S.L. 2004. Trust me: a scale for measuring manager-employee trust. *Management Research: The Journal of the Iberoamerican Academy of Management*, 2 (2), 115–132.

Vaughan-Whitehead, D. 1995. Introduction: an international overview. In *Workers' Financial Participation: East-West Experiences*. Geneva: International Labour Office.

Vroom, V.H. 1964. *Work and Motivation*. New York: Wiley.

Wang, W.Y. and Chang, C. 2005. Intellectual capital and performance in causal models: evidence from the information technology industry in Taiwan, *Journal of Intellectual Capital*, 6 (2), 222–236.

Wilson, N., and Peel, M.J. 1991. The impact on absenteeism and quits of profit-sharing and other forms of employee participation. *Industrial and Labor Relations Review*, 44 (3), 454–468.

11. Using HPWP to drive towards growth: the impact of occupational health and safety leadership

Chidiebere Ogbonnaya, Kevin Daniels, Olga Tregaskis and Marc van Veldhoven

1. INTRODUCTION

In recent years, investigations into several major industrial accidents, for example the Three Mile Island nuclear accident, the Chernobyl disaster, and the King's Cross fire, have prompted a growing concern among scholars to derive new models and approaches to the management of occupational risks to health and safety (Nunez and Villanueva, 2011; O'Dea and Flin, 2003). Occupational accidents and injuries are generally known to provoke a broad range of negative consequences on the performance of an organization. They can cause significant losses to an organization's human capital, generate huge costs due to losses in labour productivity, damage workplace equipment and decrease the organization's corporate reputation (O'Dea and Flin, 2003; Fernández-Muñiz et al., 2007; Ring, 2011). Moreover, unsafe working conditions may undermine employees' commitment to the organization, increase the likelihood for workplace conflicts and stifle the organization's potential for growth and competitiveness (Fernández-Muñiz et al., 2009). As a result, occupational health and safety (OHS) matters are given high priority among scholars, managers and regulators.

Research in OHS has shown that human resource management (HRM) is important for achieving acceptable levels of safety performance (Barling et al., 2003; Zacharatos et al., 2005; Griffin and Neal, 2000). According to Fernández-Muñiz et al. (2007), the human factor accounts for a high percentage of accidents occurring in complex process industries, and thus places an obligation on employers to adopt advanced HRM strategies to promote better safety-related work behaviours. Indeed, OHS scholars have argued that occupational risks and hazards are better managed where firms adopt the commitment-based approach to HRM that allows employees to participate actively in workplace decision-making activities, rather than management practices that focus on rule enforcement and increased supervisory control (Zacharatos et al., 2005; Ring, 2011). The commitment-based approach to HRM, also known as high-performance work practices (HPWP), creates opportunities for employees to develop useful skills for enhancing the safety performance of the organization (Askenazy, 2001; Barling et al., 2003; Tregaskis et al., 2012). Thus, whereas managers are exposed to a range of 'competing' business priorities (Buenger et al., 1996; Michael et al., 2005), they also need to devise more innovative ways of managing OHS concerns in order to achieve better organizational growth.

The primary aim of this chapter is to highlight the fundamental role of HPWP in promoting improved OHS outcomes, as a way to drive organizational growth and effectiveness. Accordingly, the main objectives of this chapter are:

- To describe the concept of HPWP and review some of the main constituents;
- To describe the nature of the relationship between HPWP and the realization of better OHS outcomes. Three perspectives on this relationship will be presented: the mainstream approach, the approach based on employee attitudes, and the critical perspective;
- To highlight the role of leadership in strengthening the links between HPWP and OHS;
- To examine the underlying mechanisms via which the relationship between HPWP and OHS may engender organizational growth.

2. THE HPWP FRAMEWORK

Research into HRM has progressively shifted from the traditional, Tayloristic forms of work (characterized mainly by hierarchical decision-making structures and high levels of supervisory control) to a more flexible, commitment-based form of management (Edwards and Wright, 2001; Dell'Aringa et al., 2003). This new approach to HRM, which forms the bedrock for the concept of HPWP, is largely claimed to have strong beneficial effects on organizational success (Huselid, 1995; MacDuffie, 1995; Appelbaum et al., 2000; Combs et al., 2006). Although the term 'HPWP' does not have a single binding meaning among HRM researchers, the dominant view suggests a system that embodies bundles of HRM practices aimed at developing a committed workforce who can be empowered to use their discretion in conducting their job roles in ways that are valuable to the organization (Arthur, 1994; Ichniowski et al., 1997; Wood, 1999; Dell'Aringa et al., 2003; Gould-Williams and Davies, 2005).

The HPWP literature has often underscored the need to analyse HRM practices in certain coherent combinations or groups, rather than in isolation, to exploit their existing complementarities and accrue the largest organizational gains (Schulte et al., 2006; Guest et al., 2004; Huselid, 1995; Arthur, 1994). This idea is premised on the assumption that single HRM practices are driven from a common philosophy (Beltrán-Martín et al., 2008) and are more likely to mutually strengthen one another when taken together as a group (MacDuffie, 1995; Ichniowski et al., 1997; Delery, 1998; Wood, 1999; Schulte et al., 2006). In contrast, however, some sceptics believe that the idea of 'grouping' individual HRM practices may substantially undercut their valuable, unique effects; not least because each practice presents a varying and/or opposing degree of association with various outcome variables (Kalmi and Kauhanen, 2008; Bryson and White, 2008). In other words, when a single HRM practice is analysed in combination with others, its unique, independent effects may be underplayed, leading to only a partial estimation of its actual influences. To fully understand the intricacies of the HPWP framework, it is worthwhile to examine the various HRM practices thought to constitute an innovative HRM system.

The consensus among many scholars regarding the main constituents of the HPWP concept is the assumption that it embodies four overlapping dimensions including: (1) the selective hiring of potentially skilled job candidates; (2) the provision of extensive training to reinforce their skills; (3) the adoption of workplace practices that increase job discretion and employee involvement; and (4) the establishment of a climate of care and support at work (Huselid, 1995; Guest et al., 2004; Combs et al., 2006; Wood and De Menezes, 2011; Lawler et al., 2011).

The selective recruitment of qualified job candidates is arguably a very crucial, preliminary step in the process of implementing HPWP, considering its usefulness in strengthening the nature of the organization's workforce (Beltrán-Martín et al., 2008; Whitener, 2001; Batt et al., 2010). Extensive recruitment procedures, incorporating various personality and competency tests, may afford a large pool of qualified employees and allow employers to achieve better person-job fit (Carless, 2005; Beltrán-Martín et al., 2008). Consequent to an effective recruitment exercise, it is also important to enhance the skills and abilities of employees through various staff development programs such as on-the-job training and career development workshops (Huselid, 1995; MacDuffie, 1995; Lawler et al., 2011). Owing to the significance of the 'rareness' element of employees' competencies in attaining sustainable competitive advantage for an organization, the proper training of employees in modern workplaces remains of key value (Paré and Tremblay, 2007).

Another crucial aspect of HPWP has to do with creating job designs that afford employees a degree of discretion in the way they conduct their job tasks (Appelbaum et al., 2000; Beltrán-Martín et al., 2008; Wood and De Menezes, 2011). As often reported in HRM studies, such practices allow employees to autonomously apply their knowledge in addressing workplace issues more efficiently and/or more innovatively, rather than being overly restricted to managerial dictates (Paré et al., 2007; Kalmi and Kauhanen, 2008; Cañibano, 2011). Similarly, practices such as compressed working weeks, flexi-time schemes, work shifts, job sharing and career breaks, which afford employees some freedom as to how they maximize their working hours and balance the work-family interface, have also been identified as being integral to the HPWP framework (Kelliher and Anderson, 2010; Atkinson and Hall, 2011).

Increasingly prominent in the HPWP literature is the need to actively involve employees in both workplace activities and in decision-making processes, in order to fully engage employees' potentials (Huselid, 1995; Ichniowski et al., 1997; Appelbaum et al., 2000; Barling et al., 2003; Kalmi and Kauhanen, 2008). This body of literature has advocated the adoption of team-based work systems (such as self-directed teams and quality circles) and various participative decision-making activities within the HPWP regime, to foster a sense of responsibility among employees, and create opportunities for them to make innovative contributions to the work process (Appelbaum et al. 2000; Wood and De Menezes, 2011).

Some researchers have also advocated, as part of the HPWP framework, the need to actively involve employees through formal employee representation structures like trade unions and consultative committees (Kalmi and Kauhanen, 2008; Godard, 2009; Wood and De Menezes, 2011). Often theorized as the concept of 'voice', these mechanisms can be important ways in which employees or their representatives have the opportunity to express their dissatisfactions and reactions to new organizational policies and initiatives. Employee voice mechanisms are thought to be important contextual factors surrounding the effects of organizational processes on performance outcomes (Edwards and Wright, 2001; Godard, 2009; Wood and De Menezes, 2011). Relevant studies have illustrated the value of union-management partnerships in building the trust relationship and in defining and reinforcing a shift in safety behaviour as part of a HPWP program (Walters, 2011; Tregaskis et al 2012).

The HPWP literature has also highlighted the importance of adopting mechanisms for enhancing employee motivation through adequate levels of managerial support (Lawler et al., 2011; Schulte et al., 2006). In this regard, commentators have emphasized the adoption of family-friendly work practices such as parental-care and child-care support services (Ngo et al., 2009; Lobel, 1999), information sharing activities, as well as the provision of equitable monetary and non-monetary rewards like performance-related pay, promotion, and profit-sharing schemes (Applebaum et al., 2000; Beltrán-Martín et al., 2008; Wood and De Menezes, 2011). Employees may perceive the provision of such services as a sign of care and support from the organization, and therefore feel obligated to reciprocate through desirable work-related attitudes and safety compliant behaviours.

3. LINKS BETWEEN HPWP AND OHS (THE MAINSTREAM PERSPECTIVE)

Research evidence indicates that adequate investments in HPWP may enhance various organizational performance outcomes such as financial profits (Huselid, 1995) and productivity (MacDuffie, 1995; Ichniowski et al., 1997; Askenazy, 2001). Zacharatos et al. (2005) further noted that the impacts of HPWP may actually surpass these traditional performance outcomes to enhance the safety-related aspects of work. Indeed, safety performance is arguably a subset of overall organizational performance and should be analyzed in a similar way as other organizational performance outcomes (Zacharatos et al., 2005; Wu et al., 2008; Tregaskis et al., 2012).

Safety performance has been described as a measure of the quantity and quality of those workplace activities geared towards assessing the nature and consequences of occupational risks and injuries. It is measured through 'pre-incident' data collection practices such as safety inspections or audits, as well as 'post-incident' practices like measuring incident frequency and severity or estimating lost time costs (Lin and Mills, 2001; Fernández-Muñiz et al., 2009; Giovanis, 2010). The literature has also underlined a range of behaviours as relevant indicators of positive safety performance (see Hofmann et al., 1995; Simard and Marchand, 1995; Griffin and Neal, 2000; O'Dea and Flin, 2001, 2003; Barling et al., 2003). The first, 'safety compliance' (e.g. adhering to lockout procedures or wearing protective gear at construction sites), refers to those activities that predict an employee's propensity to follow OHS rules and procedures. The second, 'safety knowledge', is often demonstrated in the employees' ability to show sufficient knowledge of the general working environment and in conducting the complex aspects of their jobs in a safe manner. The third, 'safety motivation', puts more emphasis on employees' propensity to take proactive actions towards OHS rather than their mere willingness to abide by safety-related rules and procedures.

Scholars have typically discussed OHS matters in the light of two basic HRM perspectives: the control-based and the commitment-based approach (Arthur, 1994; Barling and Hutchinson, 2000; Barling et al., 2003; Ring, 2011). The control-based approach to OHS management emphasizes the enforcement of safety rules, and encourages the use of reward and punishment structures in achieving predetermined OHS goals. In contrast, the commitment-based approach is aimed at encouraging higher levels of employee trust and commitment by allowing employees some decision-making authority instead of simply compelling them to comply with safety rules and regulations. The latter approach is believed to produce stronger effects on enhanced safety performance and consequently, organizational growth (Zacharatos et al., 2005; Ring, 2011).

Some studies have revealed useful links between the various components of HPWP and the safety performance of a firm. Zacharatos et al. (2005), for instance, suggested that employers who adopted a more extensive selection procedure such as using personality tests to exclude high-risk job candidates such as those with drug or alcohol dependence, may realize lower incidence of occupational accidents and injuries. Some scholars (Carless, 2005; Sekiguchi, 2004) have offered useful insights into explaining this relationship, based on Person–Environment (P-E) fit theories. Paying particular attention on two generic forms of the theory (Person-Organization fit and Person-Job fit), it is argued that an individual's attraction to and intent to remain in an organization depends on the level of compatibility between their individual characteristics and various aspects of the job. By interpretation, employees who are hired such that there is some congruence between their career-relevant personalities and the requirements of their job will demonstrate better work-related attitudes (Sekiguchi, 2004; Green and Tsitsianis, 2005; Carless, 2005) and display less vulnerability to occupational accidents and injuries (Zacharatos et al., 2005).

The implementation of discretionary work practices within the HPWP regime has also been associated with enhanced safety performance. As much as increased levels of job autonomy allow employees to exercise a degree of freedom in the way they conduct their jobs, such practices may also broaden their capacity to minimize the occurrence of occupational injuries over time (De Jonge et al., 2000; Barling et al., 2003). Echoing this, Simard and Marchand (1995), in their study of manufacturing plants, noted that the provision of greater job autonomy to employees might increase their scope for initiatives and enable them to deal with occupational risks and hazards more efficiently. The rationale for this relationship, as indicated in the Job Demand-Control (JD-C) Model of stress, rests on the claim that greater levels of freedom to decide how, when and where to meet one's job demands may abate high levels of work-related stress (Bakker and Demerouti, 2007). Work-related stress in this context is seen to be a condition that may impair one's cognitive abilities, leading to the display of non-safety compliant behaviours (Daniels et al., 2008). As such, jobs with higher demands and time constraints combined with low employee autonomy are those that may give rise to increased work-related stress and consequently affect the firm's safety performance and growth (De Jonge et al., 2000; Boisard et al., 2003; Macky and Boxall, 2008).

Relying further on this theoretical backdrop, some authors have suggested that the adoption of flexible working arrangements may remediate the undesirable consequences of work-related stress and other occupational injuries; not least because such practices optimize the worker's choice over where and when to carry out their job tasks (Atkinson and Hall, 2011; Judge and Colquitt, 2004; Kelliher and Anderson, 2010). More so, considering that flexible work patterns allow workers to achieve a more suitable work–life balance, employees enjoy greater freedom to cope with and recover from high work demands, such that they are able to concentrate better at work and display desirable safety-related behaviours (Kelliher and Anderson, 2010). Along similar lines, it has also been suggested that the implementation of family-friendly work practices like dependent-care support programs, within the HPWP framework, could attenuate feelings of distress at work by allowing employees to satisfactorily balance their work and family lives (Lobel, 1999). Reiterating this claim, Ngo et al. (2009) noted that the adoption of such practices provides the right resources for employees to manage the likely debilitating work-life interferences that could otherwise constitute a source of emotional distraction at work and lead to a weaker disposition towards OHS.

Furthermore, the OHS literature has indicated that a more decentralized managerial approach (involving the adoption of participative decision-making activities) to OHS would motivate employees to take ownership and responsibility for their safety-related work behaviours and give them the opportunity to change practices (Hofmann et al., 1995; Lin and Mills, 2001; O'Dea and Flin, 2001, 2003). This argument has been reinforced in studies that have demonstrated associations between participative management style and the extent to which employees proactively engage in OHS activities, rather than merely complying with safety rules and regulations (Simard and Marchand, 1997; Barling et al., 2003; Zohar and Luria, 2005). Active employee involvement through team-based work systems is also believed to play a prominent role in accruing better OHS outcomes for an organization. Teamwork activities amplify the potential for social interaction among employees, increase their level of cooperation, and prompt them to take responsibility for each other's safety-related behaviours at work (Simard and Marchand, 1997; Ring, 2011). In support of this, Tregaskis et al. (2012) noted that greater cohesion within problem solving teams may instigate team members to show stronger commitment towards safeguarding each other's safety as a way to stimulate better safety performance and organizational growth.

Enhanced safety performance has also been linked to the adoption of an open, two-way communication path to information sharing in innovative workplaces (Hofmann et al., 1995; Clarke, 1999; Lin and Mills, 2001). More specifically, the plausibility for employees to work more safely depends largely on the availability of information as to the safety aspects of their jobs (Tervonen et al., 2009). In fact, it is argued that managers who implemented effective feedback systems, characterized by greater levels of employer-employee interaction, were able to realize lower accident rates compared to those who avoided direct contacts with employees (O'Dea and Flin, 2003). Similarly, evidence is also growing to suggest a positive relationship between the adoption of formal employee representation structures and improvements in the safety performance of a firm (O'Dea and Flin, 2003; Zacharatos et al., 2005; Michael et al., 2005; Walters, 2011). It is argued that active trade union activities at work, for instance, could provide the useful two-way communication path to quality employer-employee relations that help employees to identify and channel their work-related concerns, including matters pertaining to OHS, to the appropriate managers (Walters, 2011). As such, these mechanisms could serve as a platform for reducing feelings of dissatisfaction and distrust among workers (especially if management demonstrates appreciable levels of responsiveness to employees' contributions), prompting them to display favourable work-related behaviours that could translate into better OHS outcomes (Edwards and Wright, 2001; O'Dea and Flin, 2003; Walters, 2011). Research in organizational psychology has indicated that the level of care and support offered to employees could enhance their psychological well-being (Daniels et al., 2008; Newman et al., 2011) and promote better safety-related behaviours (Hofmann et al., 1995; O'Dea and Flin, 2003; Ring, 2011). This assertion is often explained based on the Job Demands–Resource (JD-R) Model of stress. According to the JD-R model, the adverse effects of high work demands and other occupational risks to health and safety can be minimized through the provision of valuable resources like training and coaching, counselling services, promotion prospects and rewards (De Jonge et al., 2000; Balducci et al., 2011).

Drawing on this model, some scholars have argued that extensive safety training could create opportunities for employees to acquire greater competencies for conducting their jobs more safely, and therefore engender improved safety performance (Barling et al., 2003; Fernández-Muñiz et al., 2007; Ring, 2011). This positive relationship is also linked to the assumption that well-trained employees are potentially aware of the inherent risks at work and are better informed about the procedures available for the prevention of such risks (Fernández-Muñiz et al., 2007). Accordingly, employees who receive better safety training may suffer reduced occupational risks and injuries compared to those who are untrained. On a related note, a number of studies have proposed that the provision of monetary and non-monetary incentives to employees, based on their performance in safety-related matters, might reduce the occurrence of occupational accidents and injuries (O'Dea and Flin, 2003; Zacharatos et al., 2005). This assumption is contingent on the idea that rewards are a means by which employees recognize what their employer values; hence, by expressly linking rewards with specific work behaviours, performance expectations become clearer and less ambiguous for employees. As such, if OHS issues are constantly overlooked by the employer, such that rewards are offered mostly for meeting production targets rather than for appropriate safety behaviours, then employees might assume a low managerial priority for OHS, and consequently display poor safety-related behaviours (Hofmann et al., 1995; Zohar and Luria, 2005).

Another prominent theme in the HPWP literature is the assumption that individual HRM practices may accrue larger organizational benefits when they are used together in concert (MacDuffie, 1995; Combs et al., 2006; Beltrán-Martín et al., 2008). The key tenet here is that individual HRM practices interact in mutually supportive ways to produce stronger effects on organizational performance outcomes. This perspective has also been supported in the OHS literature where several authors have demonstrated useful links between bundles of HRM practices and safety performance (Barling and Hutchinson, 2000; Barling et al., 2003; Tregaskis et al., 2012). Barling et al. (2003), for example, showed how one such bundle, high-quality work (comprising employee autonomy, task variety and extensive training), was inversely associated with occupational injuries. Likewise, Zacharatos et al. (2005) found useful links between a single index of HPWP, consisting of ten different HRM practices, and various safety performance indicators. These studies demonstrate that complementarities exist between individual HRM practices, and in combination, these practices produce greater influences on OHS and promote organizational growth.

HPWP – Employee Attitudes – OHS

The non-safety work attitudes and behaviours of employees (e.g. job satisfaction, trust, commitment, and citizenship behaviours) are equally important in improving OHS (Barling and Hutchinson, 2000; Griffin and

Neal, 2000; O'Dea and Flin, 2003; Tervonen et al., 2009; Ring, 2011). From this standpoint, commentators presume that worker behaviours and attitudes mediate the relationship between HPWP and safety perform- ance. In other words, the adoption of HPWP may accrue positive safety- related outcomes and drive organizational growth by increasing levels of employee satisfaction, commitment or trust in management (Michael et al., 2005; Fernández-Muñiz et al., 2007). Drawing on Kanfer and Ackerman's (1989) cognitive resources framework, Barling et al. (2003) gave an explanation for the mediating role of positive employee attitudes in the HPWP-OHS relationship. On the one hand, when the quality of work is low (perhaps due to poor work design), employees become more disconnected from on-task activities (such as productivity, quality, and safety compliance) and channel their cognitive resources (e.g. creative reasoning or attention) toward less productive workplace activities like taking long breaks or intentionally working sluggishly. Conversely, when the quality of work is high, as presumed in the case of HPWP, employees deploy these cognitive resources to on-task activities, leading to better organizational and safety performance outcomes.

Consistent with this line of reasoning is the norm of reciprocity or social exchange theory. Accordingly, employee perceptions regarding the extent to which their employer values and cares about their well-being may instigate them to respond through positive work-related behaviours and attitudes (Whitener, 2001; Gould-Williams and Davies, 2005; Bakker and Demerouti, 2007; Newman et al., 2011). These theories have also been successfully applied in various OHS studies where it has been stated that perceptions of favourable managerial treatment, perhaps emanat- ing from the adoption of a commitment-based approach to HRM and OHS management, could motivate employees to respond through better safety-related behaviours (O'Dea and Flin, 2003; Michael et al., 2005; Zacharatos et al., 2005; Ring, 2011). In other words, if employees per- ceive the OHS management strategy of the employer as being driven by a sincere concern for their well-being, then their safety-related behaviours may become considerably stronger than if they felt such practices were inspired by the employer's propensity just to enforce safety compliance (Barling and Hutchinson, 2000).

4. LINKS BETWEEN HPWP AND OHS (THE CRITICAL PERSPECTIVE)

Insofar as the foregoing review may have implied a positive relationship between HPWP and employee-level outcomes (including safety-related behaviours), there is also an emerging stream of research suggesting otherwise (Ramsay et al., 2000; Askenazy, 2001; Sparham and Sung, 2007; Kalmi and Kauhanen, 2008; Macky and Boxall, 2008). Generally, scholarly debates in this respect have been fashioned around a critical perspective, counter-positioned against treating HPWP as mutually beneficial for employers and employees (Harley et al., 2007; Van De Voorde et al., 2011). Mutual gains, as has been illustrated so far in this chapter, suggests that employers gain through improved productivity and reduced turnover rates, whereas employees benefit through higher levels of support and job satisfaction (Ichniowski et al., 1997; Macky and Boxall, 2008; Kalmi and Kauhanen, 2008). In contrast, an alternative view, the critical perspective, suggests that HPWP may actually accrue far-reaching gains for both the organization and its employees, but these benefits are not without associated increases in work intensification (Ramsay et al., 2000; White et al., 2003; Harley et al., 2007; Sparham and Sung, 2007). Work intensification has been defined as a measure of the amount of effort expended at work in relation to the amount of hours invested therein (White et al., 2003; Kelliher and Anderson, 2010). It is usually reported as emanating from an exposure to high working speeds, tight deadlines, and poor interpersonal working relationships, all of which may lead to poor safety performance outcomes (Boisard et al., 2003; Cañibano, 2011).

With regards to the mechanisms by which safety performance is adversely affected through work intensification, studies have revealed various processes that may explain the likely negative consequences of HPWP. It is argued, for instance, that the implementation of discretionary work activities may not always accrue desirable outcomes in the 'real' workplace scenario (Appelbaum et al., 2000; Askenazy, 2001). According to Kalmi and Kauhanen (2008), employers may relinquish their operational control only as far as is essential to achieve the loyalty of their employees. That means, while employees may be allowed a degree of autonomy in certain work activities, they do not necessarily have full control over their work pace and workloads, and therefore remain quite susceptible to increased levels of occupational strain and burnout. In a similar way, the adoption of flexible work arrangements may also lead to increased work intensification, despite offering higher work time flexibility (Kelliher and Anderson, 2010). Accordingly, flexible work arrangements may alter the traditional conceptualization of 'a typical working day' by creating a degree of irregularity in the work schedules of employees, forcing them to work at times when they would otherwise prefer not to. Moreover, Askenazy (2001) has noted that time flexibility may adversely impact on safety performance since the frequency of occupational accidents is significantly related to the frequency of alterations in the number of hours expended at work.

Although a number of empirical studies (see Appelbaum et al., 2000; Scott-Ladd et al., 2006; Paré and Tremblay, 2007; Wood and De Menezes, 2011) have acknowledged the value of high-involvement practices such as teamwork activities, participative decision-making and employee representation structures in reducing feelings of alienation and dissatisfaction at work, there is also some support for the claim that such practices may increase work intensity (White et al., 2003; Kalmi and Kauhanen, 2008; Mohr and Zoghi, 2008; Macky and Boxall, 2008). Attempts to explain this relationship have often relied on the linkages between the level of formalization at work and the concept of 'role stress' (Adler and Borys, 1996; Bainbridge, 1998; Tubre and Collins, 2000; Nygaard and Dahlstrom, 2002). It is assumed that workplace activities that afford employees some decision-making latitude may degrade hierarchical structures at work, thereby increasing perceived levels of role ambiguity, role conflict and role overload. For example, some authors (Kalmi and Kauhanen, 2008; Mohr and Zoghi, 2008) have noted that the adoption of team-based systems may reduce the level of formalization of workplace activities, and induce workers to monitor one another, leading to more stressful work conditions. Similarly, other authors have suggested that active employee involvement through participative decision-making activities (Adler and Borys, 1996; Nygaard and Dahlstrom, 2002), and perhaps through employee representation structures (Bainbridge, 1998; Tubre and Collins, 2000), may prompt workers to overly exert their authority as a way of making their voices heard. This could trigger an increased sense of disorderliness in the delegation of authority at work; the ultimate consequence of which could be occupational distress (Nygaard and Dahlstrom, 2002).

The case is also quite similar for the provision of performance-linked rewards and incentives as part of HPWP. Although the offering of performance-linked rewards may improve staff morale and satisfaction, such practices are also believed to instigate employees to expend more effort at work, driven largely by their desire to obtain these rewards (Macky and Boxall, 2008; White et al., 2003). As such, employees could become unduly motivated to work extra shifts, or take up more job tasks, leading to increased work intensification, and consequently, to increased rates of occupational accidents.

5. THE ROLE OF LEADERSHIP IN THE HPWP–OHS RELATIONSHIP

To gain better insights into the role of leadership in the linkages between HPWP and OHS, it is worth recognizing the 'competing' nature of business goals and the complexity of choices facing managers. Based on Quinn and Rohrbaugh's (1983) competing values model, Buenger et al. (1996) explained that the business challenges facing managers ensue mainly from the inherent competition among various business values and the likely adverse consequences that may result when managers pay more attention to certain values and neglect others. In other words, managers are exposed to a range of conflicting business priorities, and may need to create a balance by focusing more on business aspects which they consider useful for organizational success, while overlooking others (Michael et al., 2005). In a similar vein, OHS concerns in an organization compete daily with other business values like ensuring product quality or providing better customer services, and managers have to balance the need to promote better OHS with these other responsibilities (Lin and Mills, 2001; Michael et al., 2005; Zohar and Luria, 2005). Drawing on this, it makes sense to argue that the path towards achieving enhanced safety performance lies around the corporate decisions and choices (including the prioritizing of OHS matters) made at the top management level. In many ways, the decisions made at the top management level of an enterprise could affect those at lower managerial levels, and consequently, the safety-related behaviours of employees (Simard and Marchand, 1995; Reason, 1997; O'Dea and Flin, 2001; Alli, 2001). Thus, if the top management exhibits a high degree of commitment to OHS matters, supervisors and employees alike would most probably respond favourably to OHS concerns.

A stream of research evidence has indicated that board-level management's commitment to OHS is reflected in the prevalence of a positive safety culture in the workplace (Griffin and Neal, 2000; O'Dea and Flin, 2001; Tervonen et al., 2009; Wu, Chang, Shu, Chen and Wang, 2011). A company's safety culture entails a range of safety-related policies, procedures and attitudes that reflect a high degree of concern and commitment to the reduction of occupational accidents and injuries (Clarke, 1999; Tervonen et al., 2009). It may be considered as a subset of a firm's overall culture where formal and informal organizational structures are dedicated solely to OHS matters, such that employees are encouraged to take responsibility for their own and each other's safety (Clarke, 1999; OECD, 2003; O'Dea and Flin, 2003). A positive safety culture is generally argued as comprising two broad components – a well-defined safety management system and a suitable safety climate (Clarke, 1999; Tervonen et al., 2009; Ring, 2011).

Safety Management System

A safety management system is conceived as encompassing the more tangible elements of a firm's safety culture such as OHS policies, strategies and procedures, which serve as a platform for achieving good safety performance within the firm (OECD, 2003; Fernández-Muñiz et al., 2007; Tervonen et al., 2009). Based on a review of relevant OHS studies, a good safety management system is thought to include the following key dimensions:

- A clear and implementable OHS policy statement that adequately defines the main objectives, principles, strategies and guidelines to follow as regards OHS (Alli, 2001; O'Dea and Flin, 2003; Fernández-Muñiz et al., 2007; Tervonen et al., 2009). This is essential as without such policies, the OHS function of the firm may be marred by infinite safety management models, which could make the OHS system rather difficult to assess (Nunez and Villanueva, 2011). Moreover, the policy statement should not only fulfil the basic requirements of relevant OHS legislation, but should also specify OHS functions in terms of the precise responsibilities of both management and employees (Lin and Mills, 2001; OECD, 2003).

- A well-defined mechanism for allocating sufficient resources (both financial and otherwise) to ensure a smooth and efficient running of OHS concerns (Alli, 2001; Tervonen et al., 2009). Just like every other aspect of an organization's business operation, better safety performance cannot be realistically achieved in the absence of adequate resources. In support of this, O'Dea and Flin (2003) noted that managers who demonstrated their commitment to OHS by providing resources such as time and money, among other things, reported lower levels of industrial accidents.

- A system of continuous re-education of employees to update their knowledge on critical safety-related matters. Safety training is allegedly quite central to achieving better safety performance (Fernández-Muñiz et al., 2007; Ring, 2011). Managers have the core responsibility of ensuring that their employees are suitably informed about all aspects of OHS and are empowered with requisite skills to take care of their own safety, as well as the safety of others who might be affected by their activities at work (Lin and Mills, 2001; Alli, 2001; Fernández-Muñiz et al., 2009).

- A communication system that encourages an open, two-way exchange of information regarding the potential risks and hazards within the workplace (O'Dea and Flin, 2003; Tervonen et al., 2009; Fernández-Muñiz et al., 2009). This communication system should incorporate both formal and informal elements that promote better employer-employee interaction with respect to the dissemination of

OHS information. Such a system would possibly stimulate the active involvement of all members of the organization in OHS activities (Hofmann et al., 1995; Fernández-Muñiz et al., 2007).

- A system for controlling and monitoring the safety-related behaviours of employees, perhaps through regular OHS inspections and the enforcement of OHS rules and regulations (Wu et al., 2008; Giovanis, 2010). Evidence suggests that safety compliance can be encouraged through appropriate incentives such as easy access to safety equipment and safety guidelines (Lin and Mills, 2001). Where necessary, non-compliance may need to be attended to through disciplinary procedures. However, a fundamental dimension to achieving compliance appears to be identifying and establishing safety rules and procedures that employees can relate to, understand and use.

- A well-defined mechanism for keeping records of information pertaining to OHS and the overall working environment (Alli, 2001). Such information might include records of all occurrences of occupational accidents and injuries, records of cases of near misses and records of harmful substances in the workplace (O'Dea and Flin, 2003; Zacharatos et al., 2005). Records of this nature can be used to estimate the level of success achieved with regards to the firm's safety performance and progress over time (Alli, 2001).

- A structured system for undertaking regular reviews of the safety policies, procedures and performance of the organization. The organization's commitment to safety can be reviewed by conducting a detailed audit of the entire OHS system to estimate the level of success achieved, and identify areas for possible improvements (OECD, 2003; Giovanis, 2010). Given the likelihood for the OHS function of a firm to change over time, relevant safety policies and procedures require periodic review (Alli, 2001).

Safety Climate

The safety climate of an organization incorporates the more intangible (e.g. psychological and behavioural) elements of an organization's safety culture (Griffin and Neal, 2000; Giovanis, 2010). It is concerned with the attitudes and perceptions of employees as to those workplace characteristics that reflect the degree of managerial commitment to OHS (Alli, 2001; O'Dea and Flin, 2003; Wu et al., 2008; Ring, 2011). Accordingly, an atmosphere where both the employer and employees express similar perceptions of care and concern for OHS matters can be deemed as constituting a good safety climate (Clarke, 1999; Zohar and Luria, 2005).

Although scholars may have varying opinions regarding the specific features of a good safety climate, there is consensus that it encompasses three key facets – the degree of managerial commitment to OHS, the nature of managerial actions (either actual or spoken) directed towards OHS, and perceptions of the level of risk in the work environment (Griffin and Neal, 2000; O'Dea and Flin, 2001, 2003; Zohar and Luria, 2005; Ring, 2011).

To a large extent, managers are believed to influence the safety climate of their organization through their various attitudes, behaviours and leadership actions (O'Dea and Flin, 2003). Some studies have highlighted a range of managerial behaviours, classified under the broad term 'participative management', as being connected to better safety performance (Hofmann et al., 1995; Clarke, 1999; O'Dea and Flin, 2001). From this perspective, it is often advocated that managers should adopt a more decentralized approach to safety management where status distinctions between managers and employees are underplayed to allow more effective open and honest dialogue around achieving better safety performance. This decentralization contrasts with traditional centralized and bureaucratic models where safety rules and procedures are driven from the top and often removed from everyday practice (Simard and Marchand, 1995; Zacharatos et al., 2005). As such, when managers seek a more cooperative relationship with their employees, both parties are more likely to feel an increased responsibility towards safeguarding each other's health and safety.

Research has also shown that success in establishing a good safety climate through progressive HRM practices may promote better safety performance in much the same way as effective management systems may impact on organizational performance through an influence on the organizational climate (Wu et al., 2008). This proposition is strengthened by the claim that safety climate and safety performance are subcomponents of organizational climate and organizational performance respectively (Griffin and Neal, 2000; Wu et al., 2008). Several authors have suggested that managers may achieve enhanced safety performance where their efforts are geared towards establishing a strong safety climate (Fernández-Muñiz et al., 2007; Ring, 2011; Wu et al., 2011; Tregaskis et al., 2012). In particular, Wu et al. (2008) found that safety climate mediates the relationship between quality management of OHS and the achievement of greater safety performance. As such, a leader's display of safety leadership through creating a positive safety climate, may improve workers' ability to take proactive steps towards OHS matters and promote better safety and organizational performance.

6. THE ROLE OF HPWP AND OHS IN DRIVING ORGANIZATIONAL GROWTH

Having so far explored the nature of the links between innovative workplace practices and the safety performance of an enterprise, it is equally useful to examine the precise mechanisms via which such relationships might engender organizational growth and effectiveness. Owing to the claim that occupational accidents may disrupt the production process and diminish the quantity and quality of production achieved, commentators have often stressed the usefulness of a well-structured OHS system in enhancing the productivity of a firm, as a way to attain improved organizational growth (Fernández-Muñiz et al., 2009; Nunez and Villanueva, 2011). In fact, some studies have reported that managers who prioritize OHS matters and integrate them into production processes may experience appreciable levels of organizational success (OECD, 2003; O'Dea and Flin, 2003; Zohar and Luria, 2005). This argument seems quite reasonable given that healthier workers are more likely to contribute to better-quality products and services (Alli, 2001). In recognition of this, HRM systems should therefore be designed such that they are akin to achieving better safety performance and greater productivity gains for the organization (Fernández-Muñiz et al., 2009; Alli, 2001).

Moreover, firms are normally exposed to a high degree of both financial and opportunity costs in the face of recurrent occupational accidents and injuries (Fernández-Muñiz et al., 2009; Ring, 2011). To an extent, these costs may stem from the need to pay compensation and insurance claims, medical expenditures, or costs due to disruptions in production processes (Fernández-Muñiz et al., 2007, 2009; Giovanis, 2010). The huge negative effects of these costs on a firm's potential to achieve organizational growth therefore accentuates the need for firms to adopt better OHS strategies (Fernández-Muñiz et al., 2009; Ring, 2011). On explaining the significance of enhanced safety performance on a firm's financial growth, Reason (1997) argued that companies are naturally susceptible to various forms of risks and hazards which may instil an inherent obligation, on the part of the employer, to invest in safeguarding the well-being of the workforce. Hence, if the company, right from the start, does not cater for these hazards by establishing an effective safety management system, the company could (in the long run) be forced to divert valuable resources which were originally mapped for other business operations, thereby jeopardizing their financial prospects. Such arguments suggest therefore that OHS is a salient ingredient for achieving sustainable economic growth.

Going by the positive links established in the literature between OHS and higher levels of employee satisfaction, commitment and trust in management (see Barling et al., 2003; O'Dea and Flin, 2003; Barling and Hutchinson, 2000; Michael et al., 2005), it seems fair to argue that a good safety management system would minimize cases of absenteeism, reduce the likelihood for employees to leave the firm, and thus promote better organizational growth. Over the years, HRM scholars have established a negative relationship between increased staff turnover rates and the performance of a firm, owing to the costs associated with recruiting and training new employees (Fernández-Muñiz et al., 2007, 2009; Ring, 2011). Indeed, Fernández-Muñiz et al. (2007) argued that when employees are either partially or entirely disengaged from the productive process due to occupational accidents, the firm could experience deterioration in their growth prospects since workers' knowledge is inevitably tied to operation of production processes. Thus, employee management strategies that incorporate the effective management of OHS matters would, in addition to reducing the incidence of occupational injuries, drive organizational growth by reducing labour absenteeism (Fernández-Muñiz et al., 2009).

Furthermore, organizations which have fared significantly well in achieving enhanced OHS records through the implementation of advanced HRM practices could ultimately build a good reputation and attain stronger relations both internally (within the workforce) and externally (among stakeholders, customers, the media and other firms) (OECD, 2003). In fact, other researchers have reinforced this claim by arguing that the corporate reputation of an organization could serve as a critical ingredient for their socio-economic growth and competitiveness (O'Dea and Flin, 2003; Tervonen et al., 2009; Ring, 2011). As an illustration, it is quite generally believed that high rates of occupational injuries may adversely affect the public image of an enterprise. Hence, if the firm fails to properly manage its OHS affairs, it could have a negative consequence on publicity and consumer loyalty to their products, ultimately impacting on the firm's commercial performance (Barling and Hutchinson, 2000; Fernández-Muñiz et al., 2009). On account of this, it can be presumed that a well-managed OHS system would not only have a positive impact on the firm's public image, but will also enhance its attractiveness to prospective job applicants and increase its market position and profit-making potential.

Factors to Consider on Implementing OHS Management Systems

Despite recent acknowledgements in the HRM literature as to the widespread gains associated with the effective management of OHS matters, it is purported that several managers are yet to adequately translate this knowledge into practice (Alli, 2001; Lin and Mills, 2001; O'Dea and Flin,

2003). As earlier stated, managers are often faced with the intricate task of choosing between a range of competing business priorities. Sadly, however, several authors have alleged that OHS concerns are normally the first items to be traded off in this regard (Lin and Mills, 2001; O'Dea and Flin, 2003; Zohar and Luria, 2005). In fact, it seems as though companies are progressively placing more value on production processes, while dedicating fewer resources to human capital and OHS expenditures, which, perhaps, they consider as costs rather than investments (Fernández-Muñiz et al., 2009). This orientation may have ensued from the assumption that investments into HRM and OHS systems do not necessarily yield any visible effects on production gains in the short term. Hence, to the extent that firms remain quite constrained by increasing levels of global competition, managers tend more towards shifting their attention away from the long-term economic benefits of achieving a safe and healthy workplace, leading to reduced investments in OHS affairs (Alli, 2001).

Another factor that should be considered as regards the proper integration of OHS matters into strategic HRM is the relative size of the firm. In general, it is believed that smaller workplaces (defined as having less than 50 employees) would attain poorer safety records compared to the much larger workplaces, owing to (but not limited to) the huge costs associated with establishing a good OHS framework (Alli, 2001). In support of this, Lin and Mills (2001), making reference to Holmes's (1999) study on Australian companies, noted that small construction firms were unable to manage their OHS risks as effectively as the much larger firms. This assertion, as indicated in Holmes's study, was tied mainly to the claim that managers in the small firms did not deem it necessary to promote better OHS because they felt such issues were the responsibility of employees. In contrast, however, managers in the larger firms were more aware of the importance of OHS and therefore integrated such matters into their overall management strategy. Arguably, managers in larger firms may also have access to experience and resources to make OHS systems more effective. In this light, it is suggested that managers in smaller companies, unlike their counterparts in larger firms, may not necessarily see the benefits associated with prioritizing OHS matters (Lin and Mills, 2001).

Finally, it has been argued that the prospects for incorporating OHS matters into innovative management systems depend on the geographical location of the company, as well as the economic sector or industry to which the company belongs (OECD, 2003). Some studies have shown that the implementation of HPWP may vary across national borders, owing to factors such as government regulations, differences in national culture and educational institutions (Green and Tsitsianis, 2005; Godard, 2009; Batt et al., 2010). As such, existing OHS laws and procedures may differ considerably from one country to another, narrowing the scope for developing more flexible and innovative ways of integrating OHS matters into HRM systems. Moreover, the economic sector to which the firm belongs could greatly influence managerial decisions with respect to OHS (Hofmann et al., 1995; Alli, 2001; Lin and Mills, 2001). As reported in Alli's (2001) paper, industrial sectors like agriculture, forestry, mining and construction take the lead in the incidence of occupational accidents worldwide, while other sectors may feature at the lower end of the spectrum. Accordingly, it appears reasonable to assert that companies which fall within the lower end of the spectrum might not feel the need to prioritize OHS matters. In some ways, this flaw may consequently produce adverse effects on the likelihood of companies in low hazard sectors to apply innovative HRM systems to OHS management.

7. CONCLUSION

This chapter has illustrated the links between HPWP and OHS, and how such associations may engender organizational growth. HRM approaches which aim at enforcing compliance with OHS procedures have been shown to be less effective compared to practices aimed at instilling higher levels of employee trust and commitment through participative decision-making activities. Whereas this commitment-based approach to OHS management is believed to produce a wide range of benefits for employers and their employees, such practices may also lead to increases in work intensification and consequently, reduced employee well-being. The acknowledgement of this useful relationship has been shown to be vital in stimulating the top management of an enterprise to proactively demonstrate their commitment to matters pertaining to safeguarding the health and well-being of employees. It has also been recognized that the managerial responsibility of promoting better OHS competes daily with other key business priorities, and managers need to make sound choices in favour of those priorities associated with enhanced organizational growth. Accordingly, the evidence presented in this chapter has shown that an effective safety leadership system coupled with innovative HRM practices, such as those embodied in HPWP, may significantly increase the growth and socio-economic performance of the firm by optimizing the firm's potential for better productivity, profitability and corporate reputation, while encouraging favourable work-related behaviours.

REFERENCES

Adler, P. and Borys, B. (1996) Two types of bureaucracy: enabling and coercive. *Administrative Science Quarterly*, 41 (1), 61.

Alli, B. (2001) Fundamental principles of occupational health and safety. Geneva: International Labour Organization (ILO).

Appelbaum, E., Bailey, T., Berg, P. and Kalleberg, A. (2000) *Manufacturing Advantage: Why High-Performance Work Systems Pay Off*. Ithaca, NY: ILR Press.

Arthur, J. (1994) Effects of human resource systems on manufacturing performance and turnover. *Academy of Management Journal*, 37, 670–687.

Askenazy, P. (2001) Innovative workplace practices and occupational injuries and illnesses in the United States. *Economic and Industrial Democracy*, 22 (3), 485–516.

Atkinson, C. and Hall, L. (2011) Flexible working and happiness in the NHS. *Employee Relations*, 33 (2), 88–105.

Bakker, A. and Demerouti, E. (2007) The job demands-resources model: state of the art. *Journal of Managerial Psychology*, 22 (3), 309–328.

Balducci, C., Schaufeli, W. and Fraccaroli, F. (2011) The job demands–resources model and counterproductive work behaviour: the role of job-related affect. *European Journal of Work and Organizational Psychology*, 20 (4), pp. 467–496.

Bainbridge, S. (1998) Privately ordered participatory management: an organizational failures analysis. *Delaware Journal of Corporate Law*, 23 (3), 979–1076.

Barling, J. and Hutchinson, I. (2000) Commitment vs. control-based safety practices, safety reputation, and perceived safety climate. *Canadian Journal of Administrative Sciences*, 17 (1), 76–84.

Barling, J., Iverson, R. and Kelloway, K. (2003) High-quality work, job satisfaction, and occupational injuries. *Journal of Applied Psychology*, 88 (2), 276–283.

Batt, R., Nohara, H. and Kwon, H. (2010) Employer strategies and wages in new service activities: a comparison of coordinated and liberal market economies. *British Journal of Industrial Relations*, 48 (2), 400–35.

Beltrán-Martín, I., Roca-Puig, V., Escrig-Tena, A. and Bou-Llusar, J. (2008) Human resource flexibility as a mediating variable between high performance work systems and performance. *Journal of Management*, 34 (5), 1009–1044.

Boisard, P., Gollac, M., Valeyre, A. and Cartron, D. (2003) Time and work: work intensity. Dublin: European Foundation for the Improvement of Living and Working Conditions.

Buenger, V., Daft, R., Conlon, E. and Austin, J. (1996) Competing values in organizations: contextual influences and structural consequences. *Organization Science*, 7 (5), 557–576.

Bryson, A. and White, M. (2008) Organizational commitment: do workplace practices matter? Centre for Economic Performance, Discussion Paper No. 881.

Cañibano, A. (2011) Exploring the negative outcomes of flexible work arrangements. The case of a consultancy firm in Spain. Paper presented at the British Academy of Management, HRM conference, London.

Carless, S. (2005) Person–job fit versus person–organization fit as predictors of organizational attraction and job acceptance intentions: a longitudinal study. *Journal of Occupational and Organizational Psychology*, 78, 411–429.

Clarke, S. (1999) Perceptions of organizational safety: implications for the development of safety culture. *Journal of Organizational Behavior*, 20, 185–198.

Combs, J., Liu, Y., Hall, A. and Ketchen, D. (2006) How much do high-performance work practices matter? A meta-analysis of their effects on organizational performance. *Personnel Psychology*, 59, 501–528.

Daniels, K., Beesley, N., Cheyne, A. and Wimalasiri, V. (2008) Coping processes linking the Demands-Control-Support model, affect and risky decisions at work. *Human Relations*, 61, 845–874.

De Jonge, J., Bosma, H., Peter, R. and Siegrist, J. (2000) Job strain, effort-reward imbalance and employee well-being: a large-scale cross-sectional study. *Social Science & Medicine*, 50, 1317–1327.

Delery, J. (1998) Issues of fit in strategic human resource management: implications for research. *Human Resource Management Review*, 8, 289–309.

Dell'Aringa, C., Ghinetti, P. and Lucifora, C. (2003) *High Performance Work Systems, Industrial Relations and Pay Settings in Europe*. Institute of the Economics of Enterprise and of Work, Catholic Sacred Heart University: Milan.

Edwards, P. and Wright, M. (2001) High-involvement work systems and performance outcomes: the strength of variable, contingent and context-bound relationships. *The International Journal of Human Resource Management*, 12 (4), 568–585.

Fernández-Muñiz, B., Montes-Peon, J. and Vazquez-Ordas, C. (2007) Safety management system: development and validation of multidimensional scale. *Journal of Loss Prevention in the Process Industries*, 20, 52–68.

Fernández-Muñiz, B., Montes-Peón, J. and Vázquez-Ordás, C. (2009) Relation between occupational safety management and firm performance. *Safety Science*, 47, 980–991.

Giovanis, N. (2010) The measurement of health and safety conditions at work, theoretical approaches, tools and techniques: a literature review. *International Research Journal of Finance and Economics*, (36).

Gould-Williams, J. and Davies, F. (2005) Using social exchange theory to predict the effects of HRM practice on employee outcomes. *Public Management Review*, 7 (1), 1–24.

Godard, J. (2009) Institutional environments, work and human resource practices, and unions: Canada vs. England. *Industrial & Labor Relations Review*, 62 (2).

Green, F. and Tsitsianis, N. (2005) An investigation of national trends in job satisfaction in Britain and Germany. *British Journal of Industrial Relations*, 43 (3), 401–429.

Griffin, M. and Neal, A. (2000) Perceptions of safety at work: a framework for linking safety climate to safety performance, knowledge, and motivation. *Journal of Occupational Health Psychology*, 5, 347–358.

Guest, D., Conway, N. and Dewe, P. (2004) Using sequential tree analysis to search for 'bundles' of HR practices. *Human Resource Management Journal*, 14 (1), 79–96.

Harley, B., Allen, B. and Sargent, L. (2007) High performance work systems and employee experience of work in the service sector: the case of aged care. *British Journal of Industrial Relations*, 45 (3), 607–633.

Hofmann, D., Jacobs, R. and Landy, F. (1995) High reliability process industries: individual, micro, and macro organizational influences on safety performance. *Journal of Safety Research*, 26 (3), 131–149.

Holmes, N. (1999) An exploratory study of meaings of risk control for long term and acute effect occupational health and safety risk in small business construction firms. *Journal of Safety Research*, 30 (4), 61–71.

Huselid, M. (1995) The impact of human resource management practices on turnover, productivity, and corporate financial performance. *Academy of Management Journal*, 38 (3), 635–872.

Ichniowski, C., Shaw, K. and Prennushi, G. (1997) The effects of human resource management practices on productivity: a study of steel finishing lines. *The American Economic Review*, 87 (3), 291–313.

Judge, T. and Colquitt, J. (2004) Organizational justice and stress: the mediating role of work–family conflict. *Journal of Applied Psychology*, 89 (3), 395–404.

Kalmi, P. and Kauhanen, A. (2008) Workplace innovations and employee outcomes: evidence from Finland. *Industrial Relations*, 35 (3), 430–459.

Kanfer, R. and Ackerman, P. (1989) Motivation and cognitive abilities: an integrative/aptitude-treatment interaction approach to skill acquisition. *Journal of Applied Psychology*, 74, 657–690.

Kelliher, C., and Anderson, D. (2010) Doing more with less? Flexible working practices and the intensification of work. *Human Relations*, 63 (1), 83–106.

Lawler, J., Chen, S., Wu, P., Bae, J. and Bai, B. (2011) High-performance work systems in foreign subsidiaries of American multinationals: an institutional model. *Journal of International Business Studies*, 42, 202–220.

Lobel, S. (1999) *Impacts of Diversity and Work-Life Initiatives in Organizations*. Newbury Park, CA: Sage.

Lin, J. and Mills, A. (2001) Measuring the occupational health and safety performance of construction companies in Australia. *Facilities*, 19 (3/4), 131–138.

MacDuffie, J. (1995) Human resource bundles and manufacturing performance: organizational logic and flexible production systems in the world auto industry. *Industrial and Labor Relations Review*, 48 (2), 197–221.

Macky, K. and Boxall, P. (2008) High-performance work systems and employee well-being: does employee involvement really intensify work? *Asia Pacific Journal of Human Resources*, 46 (1), 38–55.

Michael, J., Evans, D., Jansen, K. and Haight, J. (2005) Management commitment to safety as organizational support: relationships with non-safety outcomes in wood manufacturing employees. *Journal of Safety Research*, 36, 171–179.

Mohr, R. and Zoghi, C. (2008) High-involvement work design and job satisfaction. *Industrial and Labor Relations Review*, 61 (3), article 1.

Newman, A., Thanacoody, R. and Hui, W. (2011) The impact of employee perceptions of training on organisational commitment and turnover intentions: a study of multinationals in the Chinese service sector. *International Journal of Human Resource Management*, 22 (8), 1765–1787.

Ngo, H., Folcy, S. and Loi, R. (2009) Family friendly work practices, organizational climate, and firm performance: a study of multinational corporations in Hong Kong. *Journal of Organizational Behavior*, 30, 665–680.

Nunez, I. and Villanueva, M. (2011) Safety capital: the management of organizational knowledge on occupational health and safety. *Journal of Workplace Learning*, 23 (1), 56–71.

Nygaard, A. and Dahlstrom, R. (2002) Role stress and effectiveness in horizontal alliances. *The Journal of Marketing*, 66 (2), 61–82.

O'Dea, A. and Flin, R. (2001) Site managers and safety leadership in the offshore oil and gas industry. *Safety Science*, 37, 39–57.

O'Dea, A. and Flin, R. (2003) *The Role of Managerial Leadership in Determining Workplace Safety Outcomes*. Suffolk: Health and Safety Executive (HSE).

Organisation for Economic Co-Operation and Development (OECD) (2003) *Guidance on Safety Performance Indicators: A Companion to the OECD Guiding Principles for Chemical Accident Prevention, Preparedness and Response*. Paris: OECD Publications.

Paré, G. and Tremblay, M. (2007) The influence of high-involvement human resources practices, procedural justice, organizational commitment, and citizenship behaviours on information technology professionals' turnover intentions. *Group & Organization Management*, 32 (3), 326–357.

Quinn, R. and Rohrbaugh, J. (1983) A spatial model of effectiveness criteria: towards a competing values approach to organizational analysis. *Management Science*, 29, 363–377.

Ramsay, H., Scholarios, D. and Harley, A. (2000) Employees and high-performance work systems: testing inside the black box. *British Journal of Industrial Relations*, 38 (4), 501–531.

Reason, J. (1997) *Managing the Risk of Organizational Accidents*. Aldershot: Ashgate.

Ring, J. (2011) The effect of perceived organizational support and safety climate on voluntary turnover in the transportation industry. *International Journal of Business Research and Management*, 1 (3), 156–168.

Schulte, M., Ostroff, C. and Kinicki, J. (2006) Organizational climate systems and psychological climate perceptions: a cross-level study of climate-satisfaction relationships. *Journal of Occupational and Organizational Psychology*, 79, 645–671.

Scott-Ladd, B., Travaglione, A. and Marshall, V. (2006) Causal inferences between participation in decision making, task attributes, work effort, rewards, job satisfaction and commitment. *Leadership & Organization Development Journal*, 27 (5), 399–414.

Sekiguchi, T. (2004) Person-organization fit and person-job fit in employee selection: a review of the literature. *Osaka Keidai Ronshu*, 54 (6), 179–196.

Simard, M. and Marchand, A. (1995) A multilevel analysis of organisational factors related to the taking of safety initiatives by work groups. *Safety Science*, 21, 113–129.

Simard, M. and Marchand, A. (1997) Workgroups' propensity to comply with safety rules: the influence of micro-macro organizational factors. *Ergonomics*, 40, 172–188.

Sparham, E. and Sung, J. (2007) High performance work practices – work intensification or 'win-win'? Centre for Labour Market Studies, Working Paper.

Tervonen, P., Haapasalo, H. and Niemelä, M. (2009) Evolution of safety management and systems in a steel production organization. *The Open Management Journal*, 2, 17–27.

Tregaskis, O., Daniels, K., Glover, K., Butler, P. and Meyer, M. (2012) High performance work practices and firm performance: a longitudinal case study. *British Journal of Management* (in press).

Tubre, T. and Collins, J. (2000) Jackson and Schuler (1985) revisited: a meta-analysis of the relationships between role ambiguity, role conflict, and job performance. *Journal of Management*, 26 (1), 155–169.

Van De Voorde, K., Paauwe, J. and Van Veldhoven, M. (2011) Employee well-being and the HRM–organizational performance relationship: a review of quantitative studies. *International Journal of Management Reviews* (in press).

Walters, D. (2011) Worker representation and psycho-social risks: a problematic relationship? *Safety Science*, 49, 599–606.

White, M., Hill, S., McGovern, P., Mills, C. and Smeaton, D. (2003) High-performance management practices, working hours and work–life balance. *British Journal of Industrial Relations*, 41 (2), 175–195.

Whitener, E. (2001) Do 'high commitment' human resource practices affect employee commitment? A cross-level analysis using hierarchical linear modelling. *Journal of Management*, 27, 515–535.

Wood, S. (1999) Human resource management and performance. *International Journal of Management Reviews*, 1 (4), 367–413.

Wood, S. and de Menezes, L. (2011) High involvement management, high-performance work systems and well-being. *The International Journal of Human Resource Management*, 22 (7), 1584–1608.

Wu, T., Chen, C. and Li, C. (2008) A correlation among safety leadership, safety climate and safety performance. *Journal of Loss Prevention in the Process Industries*, 6 (3), 261–272.

Wu, T., Chang, S., Shu, C., Chen, C. and Wang, C. (2011) Safety leadership and safety performance in petrochemical industries: the mediating role of safety climate. *Journal of Loss Prevention in the Process Industries,* 24, 716–721.

Zacharatos, A., Barling, J. and Iverson, R. (2005) High-performance work systems and occupational safety. *Journal of Applied Psychology*, 90 (1), 77–93.

Zohar, D. and Luria, G. (2005) A multilevel model of safety climate: cross-level relationships between organization and group-level climates. *Journal of Applied Psychology*, 90 (4), 616–628.

Index